Freelancer's Guide to Corporate Event Design

Advance Praise for *Freelancer's Guide to Corporate Event Design*

"This is the most comprehensive guide to the corporate events industry I've seen in my thirty-five years in the business. Both newcomers and seasoned professionals will find this book invaluable."

—Steve Alford, President, Alford Media Services, Inc.

"Troy Halsey has written a well-researched and comprehensive study of an important part of the entertainment industry—the place where many of us earn our rent! Up until now, even the pros could only learn by making mistakes. Many thanks to Troy for providing a better way."

—Drew Campbell, Author of *Technical Theater for Nontechnical People*

Freelancer's Guide to Corporate Event Design

From Technology Fundamentals to Scenic and Environmental Design

Troy Halsey

AMSTERDAM • BOSTON • HEIDELBERG • LONDON
NEW YORK • OXFORD • PARIS • SAN DIEGO
SAN FRANCISCO • SINGAPORE • SYDNEY • TOKYO

Focal Press is an imprint of Elsevier

Focal Press is an imprint of Elsevier
30 Corporate Drive, Suite 400, Burlington, MA 01803, USA
The Boulevard, Langford Lane, Kidlington, Oxford, OX5 1GB, UK

Notices

Knowledge and best practice in this field are constantly changing. As new research and experience broaden our understanding, changes in research methods, professional practices, or medical treatment may become necessary.

Practitioners and researchers must always rely on their own experience and knowledge in evaluating and using any information, methods, compounds, or experiments described herein. In using such information or methods they should be mindful of their own safety and the safety of others, including parties for whom they have a professional responsibility.

To the fullest extent of the law, neither the Publisher nor the authors, contributors, or editors, assume any liability for any injury and/or damage to persons or property as a matter of products liability, negligence or otherwise, or from any use or operation of any methods, products, instructions, or ideas contained in the material herein.

Library of Congress Cataloging-in-Publication Data
Application submitted

British Library Cataloguing-in-Publication Data
A catalogue record for this book is available from the British Library.

ISBN: 978-0-240-81224-3

For information on all Focal Press publications
visit our Web site at *www.elsevierdirect.com*

10 11 12 13 14   5 4 3 2 1

Printed in China

Typeset by: diacriTech, India

Contents

v

Contents

The industry of *corporate event production* encompasses a vast collection of event types and specialties. Numerous books have been written discussing the strategies and approaches to developing successful corporate meetings and conferences, but acquiring an introduction to the physical design of such events has been left to on-the-job training and mentoring. Although several trade magazines and organizations exist, few offer a fundamental overview of the industry for the layperson. This book fills that introductory void and provides newcomers with the basic knowledge required to jump-start a career in event planning and design. Whether you are a theatrical designer looking for a steady paycheck, a freelance producer transitioning to live events, or a member of a corporate event planning committee, this book will teach you the fundamental technologies and processes needed to design a successful event of any size. Furthermore, with the knowledge you gain from this book, you will be able to comfortably speak to production teams, technicians, and clients on just about any topic related to the field of corporate events.

The idea for writing this book came to me when I was asked to train a new designer by showing him the proverbial ropes. The corporation I worked for was one of the largest and most respected leaders in the event industry. The company's services covered a broad spectrum, including providing trade show decor and booths, staging and environment designs, audio and video equipment, and any number of additional products or services that may be required by a client hosting an event. This service even included a specialized team that could analyze data to show whether or not an event was successful. This company had almost everything and made 10 figures a year doing it. But a crucial piece was missing: a training program for designers new to the industry.

For years, design in the event industry was seen as a second-class citizen. Not much thought was given to how the placement of banners or drape color selections would impact the attendees. Furthermore, design services were usually given away free as a method for selling more "stuff" to clients. This was especially true for general sessions, the main meetings that occur during events, in which stage and scenic designs were used merely to sell more audio and video equipment!

However, in recent years, the traditional handbook for planning events has been rewritten. Clients no longer want big and flashy buckshot productions; instead, they want precision and strategy to guide their event planning. They want to conserve money and time and get the most they can from their corporate events. For this, a different level of design is necessary, and event companies, like the one I worked for, saw an opportunity to expand their services by adding a specialized creative and strategic design department.

As the design department began to grow, so did the demand for faster and more elaborate designs. More designers were needed to fulfill all the requests. Because most designs were visualized with 3D illustrations, a debate was born. Do you hire someone experienced with 3D software and teach that person the business, or hire someone with experience in the business and teach that new hire 3D software?

As a scenic designer by trade, I believe it is more involved to teach someone the nuances of design theory and explain how those theories are applied to the vast assortment of elements contained in the broad industry of corporate events. On the other hand, as a businessperson, I believe that someone who can make pretty 3D pictures from a designer's pencil sketch can quickly become productive and profitable. So, despite my philosophical reservations, I suggested we hire 3D artists and teach them the business – the theory being that over a period of time, taking direction from seasoned designers, they would pick up details of the industry at a natural rate.

In some ways this theory worked. After a few years, savvy 3D artists would eventually pick up enough about the industry to begin designing small events on their own – a form of on-the-job training very similar to an apprenticeship. If, however, the demands put upon the design team grew quicker than anticipated, as was the case in my experience, 3D artists were promoted to designers before they had acquired the necessary knowledge of what makes an event design achievable, safe, and successful.

Here is where the missing piece came into play. How do you quickly train someone in a craft that encompasses so many unique specialties and technologies? The only real resources available were trade magazines that were too technical or specialists who were typically on the road working events. So I decided to track down those specialists and develop a training manual of sorts for new designers, and a few years later this book was the result.

This book is written in the same order you would experience the industry as an intern within a small event design agency or production company. Beginning with an overview of the industry, you will gain an understanding of why companies host corporate events and the different types of events that occur. Next, you will study the fundamentals of each specialty within the industry, such as rigging, lighting, video, and audio. Finally, you will learn how design processes and strategies are applied to the industry to ensure that a client's message is effectively delivered. In the end, you will have the knowledge needed to begin working within an event design team and jump-start your career as an event planner and designer. Best of luck to you in your new career or path, and I hope you enjoy learning about the industry as much as I have enjoyed writing about it.

Troy Halsey
troy@troyhalsey.com

Acknowledgements

I would like to thank and acknowledge a number of people, without whom I would not have been able to complete this book. First, I would like to thank my wife, Brenda, for all her support and patience while I frequently typed away late into the night. Many thanks to Ashley Leies for her editing abilities and literary guidance. Thank you, Cara Anderson, for taking a risk on a new subject matter. And finally, I have many and sincere thanks to my family, friends, and coworkers for all their support and encouraging words.

In addition, in one way or another, the following list of individuals helped make this book a reality, and I would like to sincerely say thank you:

Andrea"Sid"Curtis	Greg Brown	Patrick Moloney
Adelle Mize	Guillermo Becerra	Phillip Collins
Bob Walker	Guy Hollier	Raymond Watkins
Brian Alexander	Jeffrey Cameron	D. Scott Cooper
Carrie Freeman-Parsons	Jerrod Smith	Scott Williams
Cathy Ives	Jim Clark	Stacey Walker
Chris Horne	Joe Krebbs	Terry Price
David Legore	John Kennedy	Tim Platt
David Marks	Kenny Hunt	Tim Wylie
David Sauers	LaManda Minikel	Todd Ethridge
Drew Campbell	Marc Vonderhorst	Wendi Sabo
Dustin Sparks	Marcus Eiland	Willi Clarkson
Fred Gavitt	Mark McGovern	Zhiyong Li

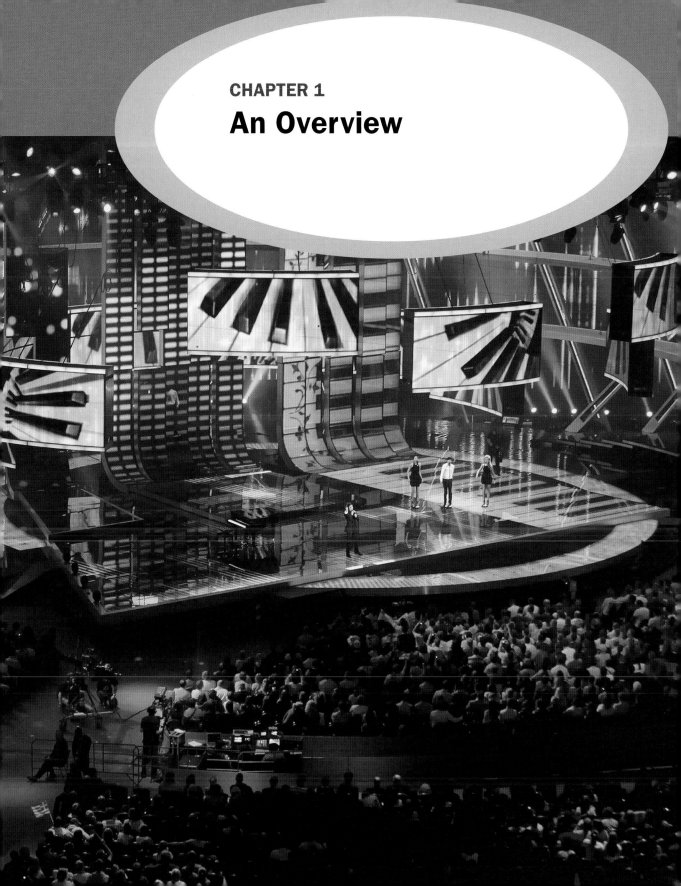

CHAPTER 1
An Overview

WHAT IS A CORPORATE EVENT?

The phrase *corporate events* covers a wide variety of meetings and events, and the use of the word *corporate* can be misleading. The craft is not limited only to corporate meetings; it can also be applied to association gatherings, large nonprofit meetings, speaking engagements, training seminars, and any number of special events. The craft of corporate events has also been referred to as *business theater; corporate theater;* and *conference, seminar,* or *event planning.* Although each name can describe a specific element of the trade, the names are often used interchangeably.

The inclusion of the word *theater,* such as in *business and corporate theater,* may seem odd to traditionally educated thespians, but there are many similarities between corporate and traditional theater. Both traditional and corporate theater have audiences, performers or speakers, scenery or decoration, and typically some form of specialized lighting and sound equipment. In fact, the only real differences between the two would have to be their intentions and their locations. Whereas the intention of traditional theater is to entertain, corporate theater aims to inform or sell. Traditional theater typically occurs in a designated theater building or space; corporate events occur in hotel ballrooms and convention halls and are thereby required to supply their own lights, sound, and production controls. In an effort to alleviate confusion, for the remainder of this book, we will use the phrase *corporate event(s)* to encompass any form of large organization or corporate gathering.

Types of Corporate Events

We will refer to several forms of corporate events throughout this book, but any attempt to classify every possible scenario would be a volume of work in itself. Instead, corporate events are generally classified by either the type of host producing the event or the type of audience attending. Generally speaking, two entities host corporate events: corporations and associations.

CORPORATE EVENTS

Corporate events are primarily internal meetings in which executives present company initiatives, policies, and reports to a targeted sector of their workforce. What separates a corporate event from other events is that audiences are composed primarily of internal employees who are required to attend. Sales conferences, training seminars, and manager meetings are the most common examples of corporate events.

These events host a vast collection of executive presentations, motivational speakers, and entertainment acts all aimed to inform and motivate the audience. As a result, corporate events typically have larger production budgets than association meetings and more elaborate theme development, which in turn dictates the overall design of the event.

To an outside observer, it may seem odd for a company to invest so heavily in a corporate event. Even employees may ask at times if the money spent wouldn't be better served divided among their paychecks. However, addressing employees in person, rather than through an email or video, is still the most effective way to deliver a message. Sales conferences, especially, serve as a form of pep talk before starting a new year, similar to coaches addressing their players before a big game. Training seminars provide a way for employees to receive important education without the distractions of their daily routine. Finally, manager meetings permit peers to exchange advice and tactics regarding effective management styles.

From an executive standpoint, the value of a successful corporate event greatly outweighs the production costs. And as implied previously, these production costs can become quite exorbitant – so much so that it is estimated the business of producing corporate events has evolved into a multibillion dollar industry.

ASSOCIATION EVENTS

Associations consist of members in a similar trade or specialty such as cardiologists, school teachers, or automotive workers, to name a few. The intention of association events is to provide further education and networking opportunities for the association's members.

Most associations are not-for-profit. This does not mean they do not take in revenue; they must generate income to pay their staff and keep the lights on. What is interesting is these types of meetings do not make their money on registration, but rather on selling booth space on the exhibit floor.

Exhibit floors are big business in this industry. They essentially allow vendors to target their message, brand, and/or product to a focused group of potential customers. The association hosting the event makes most of its bankroll by charging these vendors very high rates to set up shop on the exhibit floor. The exhibitors or vendors happily pay the fee because nowhere else would they get such a focused group to listen to their sales pitch. Imagine a company that sells a $5 million MRI machine exhibiting at a medical conference of over a thousand doctors. There would really be no other way for the company to have such one-on-one access to so many potential customers who are out of their office, lacking distractions, and ready to learn or kick the tires of a new MRI machine. This event truly creates a win-win situation for both the association and vendor.

In essence, then, the real dynamic of association meetings is to provide education and networking opportunities for members, while marketing the exhibit floor to potential vendors. And what a sales pitch they have: "We will be bringing together 10,000 doctors that you would never otherwise have an opportunity to meet with face to face; are you interested in renting booth space for our event?"

Associations are easy to identify, as stereotypically their names begin with either *American* or *National* and end with *Association*. In addition, their budgets are typically smaller than corporate events, and motivational meaning is minimal. This is not to say that association meetings are less production intensive. In fact, being membership-based organizations, associations have the added stress of ensuring that their attendees enjoy the event experience and will want to attend the following year and continue their membership with the organization.

Ironically, a common request to production designers from association hosts is that they want an exciting and professional event without it looking as though it cost a lot of money. This request also stems from the fact that associations are membership-based, and their primary income sources are from membership fees. The fear is that association members may feel their financial contributions could have been better spent elsewhere than on elaborate scenery that served as merely eye candy.

HYBRID EVENTS

Though they may not be the most common form of event, *hybrid events* are certainly growing in popularity. Such events are referred to as *hybrids* because they are hosted by a corporation but intended for customers who attend by choice. Such events may also be referred to as *corporate customer events*.

Whereas internal corporate events are usually led by an executive team who speak to employees, the hybrid or corporate customer event minimizes executive exposure to avoid looking like an elaborate commercial for the hosting company. Hybrid events typically have only one or two corporate messages, which are then followed by a series of speakers who focus on industry-wide topics. These industry-wide topics are what attendees are seeking to learn more about and thus are what draw them to attend the event. In turn, attendees provide the hosting corporation with an opportunity to advertise new services and products.

The real meat of hybrid events occurs during breakout sessions, where attendees have the opportunity to explore topics that interest them or try out products they may consider purchasing. This opportunity in turn provides the hosting corporation with an indication of what areas of their businesses are apt to grow and where they should be focusing their resources.

Production budgets for hybrid events vary greatly and are hinged primarily on the size of the industry and hosting corporation, as well as the event's popularity and expected annual attendance. Similar to association events, exhibit floors play a huge role in hybrid events providing both income for hosting corporations and resources for attendees to peruse.

The ingenious element of hybrid or corporate customer events is that often attendees do not realize they are attending what is essentially a multiday sales pitch. They instead believe they are merely attending a training seminar or network opportunity hosted by the leading company of that particular industry. Software and gaming industries, for example, host these types of events several times a year under the guise of training seminars in which attendees have the option to become certified in a particular software package. However, similar to the exhibit floor, hybrid events are truly a win-win for both the hosting company and attendees. Attendees acquire the education and networking opportunities that they seek, and the hosting company strengthens its customer relationships, fortifying its role as an industry leader.

Types of Meetings and Sessions

Without goals and objectives, there would be little point in having corporate events. Furthermore, for goals and objectives to be shared in a meaningful way, they must be organized and presented in a logical manner. To do so, information is distributed among meetings and sessions, with each serving a unique function. Over time several forms of meetings and sessions have evolved as standard in the event industry. Although not every event hosts each type of meeting or session, most contain at least a few of the types described next.

WELCOME OR OPENING SESSIONS

Welcome sessions are generally held either the first evening or morning of a multiday event. During these meetings, the hosting company or organization, as the name implies, welcomes the attendees. Often a video is shown introducing the event's theme, key speakers, and event highlights or reviewing events that occurred since the group's last gathering. Most importantly, the primary function of a welcome session is to excite the audience and prepare them for the days to come.

FIGURE 1.1
Rehearsal of a musical show opening act.
Image courtesy of AMS Pictures (www .amspictures.com)

It is not uncommon in larger events for welcome sessions to be followed by receptions. Welcome receptions can range from conservative cocktail gatherings to full-fledged keg-tapping parties. The style of reception that is held is dependent solely on the culture of the hosting company or organization. Regardless, in its most basic function, a welcome reception provides attendees an opportunity to mingle with their peers and enjoy themselves before an onslaught of meetings.

GENERAL OR PLENARY SESSIONS

At some point during the event, whether it is held on a single day or over the course of several, the entire body of attendees will be asked to gather for a large group meeting. These meetings are known as *general sessions* or *plenary meetings*. Such sessions are often referred to as *main tents*, harkening back to the traveling circus in which the most exciting performances occurred in the main tent. This nickname applies perfectly because these sessions host the most noteworthy speakers and presentations during the event.

It is most often during these sessions that the audience is addressed by organization or company executives and new products or initiatives are revealed. In essence, if specific information must be shared to everyone attending the event, it is done during a general session. Depending on the bulk of information needing to be shared, several general sessions may occur during the course of the event.

General sessions are the primary focus of this book because they require intense planning and thoughtful design. However, the fundamental knowledge you need to plan and execute a successful general session will carry over easily to other forms of corporate meetings and events you might plan.

BREAKOUT SESSIONS

Breakout sessions are specialized meetings that focus on specific topics, such as corporate procedures or software packages. With several breakout sessions occurring simultaneously, audiences consist of a mere fraction of the entire attendee body. When events are held at large hotels or resorts, smaller meeting rooms throughout the property are typically used to house breakout sessions. Although breakout sessions for corporate events tend to be more evenly distributed due to required attendance,

FIGURE 1.2
Keynote speakers are the stars of general session meetings.

association breakout sessions can vary greatly with audience size depending on the topic's popularity.

Depending on the size of the event, the number of breakout sessions that occur can range from a mere handful to several hundred over the course of the event. For each breakout session occurring simultaneously, there must be a dedicated speaker or presenter, audio/video equipment, if necessary, and some form of support staff. As you can imagine, organizing and managing the hundreds of presentations and support materials associated with breakout sessions can be quite a daunting task. In response, specialized services called *speaker support* or *presentation management* are now offered by most large audio/video providers. These services will be covered in more detail in Chapter 9, "Speaker Support."

FIGURE 1.3
Breakout sessions allow attendees to delve deeply into specific topics.

From a production design standpoint, breakout sessions typically are little more than an empty room full of chairs with a video projector connected to a laptop computer. Larger breakout rooms may require an audio system of some kind, to ensure that the speaker can be heard by all attendees. Generally speaking, very little is done creatively to transform bleak meeting spaces into environments that tie into the hosting company's or organization's branding or the event's theme. If anything, a banner might be added for a hint of branding. Often, this lack of branding is due to the sheer number of rooms being used, as designing each space would be cost prohibitive. However, more often than not, designing breakout sessions, creatively or thematically, is not seen as a priority by the hosting company or organization. This is unfortunate to say the least, because attendees will spend most of their time during the event in one of these spaces. As a production designer or event planner, you should keep breakout sessions in mind for extending event or theme branding beyond the general session.

LEGISLATIVE OR PARLIAMENTARY SESSIONS

Legislative or parliamentary sessions are unique to association events. It is during these sessions that the association elects new officers or votes to install new policies or bylaws. Such meetings often take place in the same room as the general session, but may require additional audio/video equipment to accommodate a large panel of executive officers on stage.

These sessions are typically less creative or thematic, focusing purely on operational tasks within the association. Microphones may be needed in the audience to allow members of the association to address the panel of executive officers during legislative discussions. Some associations may discuss sensitive topics

FIGURE 1.4
Legislative meet-
ings are unique to
association events and
allow members to vote
on new officers and
legislative issues.

that require security to be posted at the room's entrances to prevent uninvited guests from overhearing privileged information.

EXHIBIT FLOORS

The exhibit business has been and continues to be a very profitable industry for production companies. The amount of money companies spend on the design and fabrication of their exhibits can be staggering. These exhibits are investments that can be showcased at several events over the course of many years. Furthermore, an exhibit is not only a portable booth displaying a company's line of products and services, but also an extension of the company's brand itself. Larger exhibits can truly become experiences in themselves. Exhibit designs can range from small, off-the-shelf 10' × 10' booths to elaborate multi-story labyrinths of technology.

As mentioned previously, the reason these investments are made is that there is no other place, aside from the exhibit floor, that a vendor can meet face to face with so many customers eager to try their product. In addition, exhibit floors are a source of income for the hosting association because exhibit floor space is rented by the square foot at exorbitant prices. The amount of money generated by this industry on a yearly basis is in itself a testament to how successful the exhibit floor model has become in recent years.

The design and science behind successful exhibits are a craft of their own and will not be discussed in great detail in this book. However, the fundamentals of event design, as laid out by this book, can be easily translated into exhibit design.

FIGURE 1.5
The exhibit floor is big business and provides a unique face-to-face marketing environment.

AWARD BANQUETS/SHOWS

Award banquets and shows are perhaps the most glamorous of meetings held at both corporate and association events. It is during these sessions that employees and members are recognized for their contributions and work from the previous year. Award winners are welcomed to the stage to receive their prize, be photographed with other award winners, and on occasion address the audience with an acceptance speech.

From a production standpoint, award shows can be the most demanding. With the proliferation of televised award shows such as the Academy Awards, the Emmys, and the Grammys, most Americans are familiar with what high-end award shows look like. Unfortunately, the average observer does not realize the amount of money and time that is invested into producing such extravaganzas.

Clients requesting a production designer to simulate the look and feel of a televised award show should be handled with care. Such requests make clear the clients' lack of experience in planning award shows in the corporate event industry, where budgets and install times are a mere fraction of similar televised events. This is not to say, however, that event production designs are creatively subpar to those on television, but merely that they must be functionally and technically appropriate for the selected venue, budget, and time frame allotted for the session.

In addition, lighting and audio designs, as well as video production, play huge roles in producing successful awards shows. Even the best scenic designs will fall flat with poorly designed lighting plots, and neither will be noticed if audiences are distracted by badly produced video sequences. All production elements must come together seamlessly for award shows to be as magical and memorable as event planning committee members intend.

CLOSING SESSIONS

With there being an opening or welcome session, it would seem only natural to have a closing session. Closing sessions provide a clear conclusion to an event, after which attendees depart and begin their journey home. Closing sessions also permit the host to recap highlights that occurred during the event, reiterate the most important messages of the event, and leave attendees with a final thought.

It is not uncommon for a highlights video to be shown during this session, consisting of footage shot during the event and showcasing the many smiling faces of attendees. Such video sequences say in essence to the audience, "See how much fun everyone had; aren't you glad you were a part of it all?" *Smiling faces videos*, as they are often referred to as, are especially important for both association and hybrid events in which attendance is optional. Reminding attendees how great the event they just attended was encourages them to attend the following year.

Closing sessions for corporate events tend to have a motivational flare, intending to leave attendees on an inspired note. Such sessions may include a musical performance, a motivational speaker, or a touching message from a high-level executive. One could read between the lines of a message from a closing session of a sales conference, for example, as "Now, get out there and sell, sell, sell!" For an association meeting, a similar subliminal message may be "Thanks for coming; we'll see you and your membership fees next year!"

FIGURE 1.6
Music performances are a common feature of closing sessions for large events.
Image Courtesy of Atomic Design, Inc. (www.atomicdesign.tv)

CORPORATE THEMES

Most corporate events have a theme of some form that heavily influences their branding, scenic, and environment designs, as well as guest speaker and entertainment selections. However, themes are less common in association and hybrid events. The reason is that most themes are intended to inspire and motivate rather than educate and inform, the primary functions of association and hybrid events.

The theme selection process typically begins several months, if not a year, before production design gets underway. This investment of time spawns from a common belief in the industry that a successful event begins with a solid theme. Indeed, every subsequent design element of an event ties directly back to the selected theme. Despite the amount of time and thought that is put into theme selection, themes tend to be generic motivational or inspirational catchphrases pulled from pop culture. Examples of such themes include "Take It to the Limit," "Mission Possible," and "Pump Up the Volume," to name a few.

Although having a catchy theme is important, it is meaningless if is not backed by well-thought-out goals and objectives. It is not uncommon for inexperienced meeting planners to begin with a clever tagline and then force the event's content into that selected theme. As a result, attendees are left with a confusing and disjointed message.

A preferred method of theme selection begins by laying out meeting objectives, reviewing the state of the organization, and determining what goals should

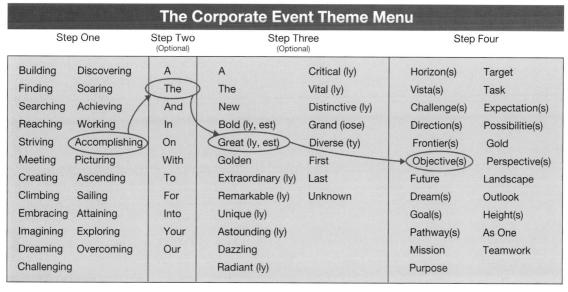

		Step One	Step Two (Optional)		Step Three (Optional)		Step Four	

The Corporate Event Theme Menu

Step One		Step Two (Optional)	Step Three (Optional)		Step Four	
Building	Discovering	A	A	Critical (ly)	Horizon(s)	Target
Finding	Soaring	The	The	Vital (ly)	Vista(s)	Task
Searching	Achieving	And	New	Distinctive (ly)	Challenge(s)	Expectation(s)
Reaching	Working	In	Bold (ly, est)	Grand (iose)	Direction(s)	Possibilitie(s)
Striving	Accomplishing	On	Great (ly, est)	Diverse (ty)	Frontier(s)	Gold
Meeting	Picturing	With	Golden	First	Objective(s)	Perspective(s)
Creating	Ascending	To	Extraordinary (ly)	Last	Future	Landscape
Climbing	Sailing	For	Remarkable (ly)	Unknown	Dream(s)	Outlook
Embracing	Attaining	Into	Unique (ly)		Goal(s)	Height(s)
Imagining	Exploring	Your	Astounding (ly)		Pathway(s)	As One
Dreaming	Overcoming	Our	Dazzling		Mission	Teamwork
Challenging			Radiant (ly)		Purpose	

FIGURE 1.7
Though created for humor, the theme chart might actually help during brainstorming sessions.

be achieved during the event. From the information gathered, it can then be determined if an upbeat theme is the way to go or if a rallying motivational message is more appropriate for the event. Generic themes may be tempting and easier to get the ball rolling in the beginning, but a truly unique theme built on solid goals and objectives will help deliver a meaningful and longer-lasting message. If clear objectives and goals have been established but an event theme isn't developing, try using the theme chart in Figure 1.7 to get the creative juices flowing.

WHO ATTENDS A CORPORATE EVENT?

Returning to using the phrase *corporate events* to cover the gamut of event types, we can turn our attention to the most common audience types. From the most basic view, audiences can be divided between those who choose to attend and those who are required. Most often audiences who are required to attend consist of internal corporate employees. In contrast, audiences composed of customers, association members, or members of the media are classified as external audiences, and attendance is generally optional. There is a third type of audience, however, that comprises a good portion of the event industry known as the *hybrid* or *franchise audience*. Each type of audience has its own unique characteristics that must be factored into production design and event planning.

Internal Audiences

Most internal corporate events are geared toward a specific mission or theme as described previously. The audience is composed primarily of employees who are required to attend. This required attendance gives internal corporate events a different feel when compared to association meetings. Meetings held during an internal corporate event typically deal with relationships between executives and sales teams or executives and general employees. The focus of events with internal audiences is typically message driven as opposed to one that creates a memorable experience, as may be the case with association events.

External Audiences

Corporate events composed of external audiences or customers usually focus on new product rollouts or user forums. These meetings generally consist of passive sales pitches, but the goal is not to let the audience realize they are being given a sales pitch. That is accomplished by interweaving sales with education. That education can come in the form of user forums or breakout sessions, where individuals of similar professions can get together and discuss the specific products. Another form of education that is laced with sales is to provide the audience with *sneak peeks* of what is to come such as by revealing new products at the event or showing what is in the pipeline of development. The intention of these meetings is to resell the brand or reaffirm customer loyalty and entice attendees into purchasing the latest products. The hybrid or corporate customer event is generally composed of an external audience.

Hybrid Audiences

The best example of a hybrid audience consists of franchise owners. Franchise owners are both employees and customers to their parent companies. As entrepreneurs, these audience members paid the parent company a sum of money to purchase their license to franchise a store or product. In return, the parent company supplies the store or product, brand recognition, advertising, and standards that apply to all stores. These services continue to cost money during the operation of the franchise, and franchise owners continue to pay the parent company a percentage of their earnings for as long as they own their franchise. This relationship can become strained when franchise owners feel the parent company is not keeping its end of the bargain. Therefore, another crucial element of these meetings is to butter up the franchise owners and reassure them that they are appreciated and fully supported. By revealing new advertising campaigns and company-wide sales growth projections, among educational classes, the parent company is able to reaffirm the franchise owners' loyalty to the parent company and improve their morale.

WHERE DO CORPORATE EVENTS HAPPEN?

Corporate events can happen anywhere – in a traditional theater, the middle of a field, a large parking lot, or even a remote tropical beach. This versatility is possible due to the systems and resources that have been developed for the modern event industry. Any location in which a semi truck can travel is a potential event locale. Choosing an event destination begins with the broad selection of a location, followed by the booking, or reserving, of a specific venue.

It must be noted, however, that venues are typically booked a year or more in advance of the actual event date. A corporation's or organization's projected growth in attendance must be anticipated when selecting an appropriate venue. The question is not how many people have attended the event previously, but how many people will be attending this event in three years when this particular location or venue is available.

Event Locations

Event planning committees, a team of people chosen by a company or organization to plan an event, vary in the types of locations they select to host their meeting or event. Most often, hotels, resorts, or convention centers in large metropolitan cities are selected as event locations. Popular cities selected to host events in the United States include New York, Las Vegas, Chicago, San Diego, San Francisco, Dallas/Fort Worth, New Orleans, and Miami.

FIGURE 1.8
Venues such as the Boston Convention Center are among popular event destinations.

FIGURE 1.9
A hotel ballroom is by far the most common venue type utilized for corporate events.

The selection of an event location depends on several factors, including an event's budget, the location of the organization's home office, and the amount of travel that will be required of attendees. Many cities offer great incentives, most notably discounts of various forms, to play host to large events. These incentives stem from the amount of economic influx a large event can generate for a city through hotel fees, taxicab fares, and tourism, to state the most obvious sources.

Types of Venues

The most common venues selected for large events are hotel ballrooms and convention or exhibit halls. Ballrooms and convention halls can be referred to as *controlled environments*, meaning all key elements (air flow, lighting, sound, etc.) are controlled rather than left to nature. In contrast, an uncontrolled environment, like an open field, can quickly become an insurance liability with the first unexpected gust of wind or rain cloud.

Selecting the best available venue for an event is a pivotal step toward producing a successful event. Even the best designers are subject to the limitations of a poorly selected venue. The topic of venue selection is broad and includes several pitfalls for the inexperienced. The following chapter will delve into this process in much greater detail.

WHAT EXACTLY IS CORPORATE EVENT DESIGN?

Event design covers a wide gamut of specialties, and it is safe to say that one designer cannot be an expert in every aspect of the trade. Even when narrowing the scope to only corporate event design, there remain dozens of unique applications and requirements of design. This book will focus on three predominant areas of corporate event design: stage and scenic, environment, and experience design.

Stage and Scenic Design

Stage and scenic designs are probably the most recognized forms of corporate event design. They are, however, only a small portion of the many forms of design that make their way into the event industry. The reason scenic designs receive so much recognition is merely that they are the most obvious form of design present during an event, let alone the fact that audiences are forced to stare at them for the entire duration of a meeting.

FIGURE 1.10
Scenic design serves to enhance and support the client's message.
Designer: Lynn Leuck

The purpose of a good scenic design is not only to provide a pleasant but neutral backdrop for action that occurs on stage, but also to support the message and theme of the overall event. Note the key word *support*. It is not the function of a set design to deliver an event message on its own, but instead to create an environment suitable for that message to be delivered. Although the difference may seem subtle, it is an important one.

Above all, a scenic design must be safe, functional, and practical for use by not only trained professionals, but amateur speakers and award recipients as well. Scenic designs for general sessions or main tent meetings will be the primary focus of design references throughout this book. Furthermore, the design approaches and techniques used for general session scenic design can be applied to virtually every element of event design as a whole.

Environment Design

Environment design strives to bring a finished and thematic feel to the spaces beyond the general session stage. Techniques such as draping the walls of an entire room and uplighting or tying lobby decorations in visually with the

FIGURE 1.11
A very dramatic entrance design using rental tension fabric shapes and lighting.
Image courtesy of Transformit (www.transformitdesign.com). Project: USS Monitor Center, Newport News, VA. Client: Mariner's Museum. Designer: Batwin + Robin. Builder: Transform-It

general session stage design fall into the category of environment design. By impressing audience members the moment they step into the room, the production team members have taken one large step toward producing a successful show. Although the primary objective of environment design is to break the proverbial fourth wall of the presentation and performance space, it is important that such elements do not compete with the functionality of the meeting space. Thus, the true art of environment design is to create a memorable ambience without eating up real estate for seating, catering, and staging.

Experience Design

Some elements of design, though not always visible to the casual observer, are equally important if not more important to the success of an event than the obvious design elements. These elements, when combined, create an experience. Experience design touches on all elements of event design and combines them into one cohesive experience, as the name implies. Determining the best placement for branded materials such as banners and other printed goods is one possible role of an experience designer. Yet another is directing the creation of video content used throughout the event space to add ambience to the event. There are truly few aspects of an event that a skilled experience designer does not influence or improve upon.

A great analogy for the effect experience design can have on an event is to think of an event as a coffee shop. There are plain and ordinary coffee shops, and then there are Starbucks coffee shops. They both offer similar products, but it is the experience that Starbucks offers, such as the relaxing decor and aromas, ambient music, and hip branding, that draws devoted customers in every morning. It is the visceral elements of Starbucks, in this analogy, that provide customers with more than just a hot cup of coffee; these elements provide an *experience*.

At its core, the objective of experience design is not only to aid event planners in delivering their messages creatively, but also to place attendees in a mindset suitable for receiving those messages. Thus, experience designers must play the role of artistic director as well as social psychologist.

WHAT MAKES A GOOD CORPORATE EVENT DESIGN?

As with most forms of design, the success of corporate event design can be subjective. There is one question, however, to which the answer determines whether or not an event design was successful: did the design support the client's message?

Learning that this is not an industry for artistic expression can be a difficult lesson for beginning event planners and designers. While a gifted imagination and creative mind are paramount for success, such tools are only a portion of the skill set needed to create successful events. While many event designs are very forward thinking artistically, art is not the focus of such events. Clients hire designers to create an environment and ultimately an experience that supports the delivery of a corporate or association message.

In addition, good designers must learn how to interpret what clients are asking for and return what is needed and suitable for their event. Designers have a responsibility to steer toward designs that not only support the event's message, but account for and overcome any number of limitations that may be present in the clients' requests. After all, a full-scale reproduction of the Academy Awards will not fit every client's message or budget.

There is an adage that states, "You can either have it cheap, fast, or good … pick two." Sadly, there is a lot of truth to this saying, which justifies its longevity and why it applies to so many aspects of this industry. For example, if the production is last minute and has to be top notch, then it will be expensive. If there is plenty of preproduction time, then more affordable solutions can be found.

Budgets and time, however, are not the only limitations involved in an event's planning. Less-than-ideal venue selections, labor union regulations, and availability of technology resources are also potential hurdles during event preproduction. Every limitation, however, has a solution and, by requiring creative problem solving, will often lead to a better event experience in the end.

Ultimately, a good corporate event design is one that leaves attendees with a complete understanding of the client's message and is executed creatively, efficiently, and most of all, safely. However, achieving such results not only requires an immense amount of planning and design, but also demands experience. Although nothing can replace the experience earned over time, this book will provide a solid foundation in fundamentals in each key area of event design, better preparing new designers and event planners for the challenges to come.

A BRIEF HISTORY OF CORPORATE EVENTS

The concept of corporate events, as we know it today, is actually relatively new in the big scheme of things. During the middle of the twentieth century, a shift occurred in corporate thinking. During the 1950s the American economy was the strongest on the world. Furthermore, the Depression-era mentality of every person for himself was replaced by a sense of unity and understanding that the state of the economy affected, and was also influenced by, each employee through salary ranges, interest rates, and the price of goods purchased. Employees were no longer viewed as merely cogs in the corporate wheel but were valuable assets of the corporate team – and America for that matter – who required nurturing and motivation.

Technology and media of the time were also evolving, and television, with the addition of color, had officially become the center of entertainment for the American public. Television could now be broadcast to and from anywhere in the world, making "the tube" the premier source of world news. Around the same time, Hollywood introduced 3D movies, stunning audiences with an entirely new dimension of visual entertainment. While still in its infancy, the concept of a computer was also making its way into common lexicons. Post-war technologies were making their way into every home at an increasing speed, and the American appetite for new technologies began to grow rapidly.

As a result of this shift in thinking and advancement of technologies, a new trend arose in the event industry. Corporate meetings, which had previously existed in the most basic of forms, were beginning to transform from dull assemblies into *events*. Simple signs were hung behind the speaking platform to add branding and decor. Comedians and musicians were hired to keep audiences entertained between presentations. Speaking platforms grew into large stages, and over-sized banners were hung around the room announcing the company's new slogan. Awards were given to the most successful employees. Year after year, more and more bells and whistles were added. Soon corporate events more closely resembled televised variety shows rather than business or association meetings.

FIGURE 1.12
Before the 1970s, corporate events greatly resembled vaudeville or televised variety shows.
Image Courtesy of Felix Man/Hulton Getty Images

Within a few years, most corporate events had developed a similar formula: put the event's message to the tune of a Broadway musical, hire some performers, and put on a show. In between performances, a presentation or address was given. Audiences were captivated by the entertaining shows and listened patiently to speakers and presentations. At the end of each day, attendees enjoyed an after-party where peers mingled.

As the mid-1970s approached, 35 mm slide projectors became commonplace, and audiences became accustomed to seeing customized graphics that illustrated key points during presentations. Then came a breakthrough: multi-image slide projection.

FIGURE 1.13
Before video projection, 35 mm slide projectors were aligned to create one seamless image.
Image courtesy of Alford Media (alfordmedia.com)

Multi-image projection consisted of two to three projectors that fed into a dissolve box allowing for smooth transitions between slides as opposed to the half-second black screen that occurred between slides with a typical system. When these dissolve boxes were daisy-chained together, large widescreen presentations began to evolve. With time, the technique became so streamlined that audiences could almost be convinced they were watching a motion picture. There was a great advantage that multi-image slide projection had over modern video equipment. Today, video projection can simulate large widescreen images by using several video projectors aligned to create one image. However, the resolution of video, even HD video, cannot compare to the crispness of actual 35 mm film. Audiences of yesteryear were able to gaze upon amazing panoramic images of oceans and forests wrapping around them in stunning detail, an effect that has been momentarily lost with video projection.

When video cameras made their way to the industry, I-Mag (Image Magnification) was born as well as recording events for archiving. For smaller- to mid-size events, several 25-inch or larger television monitors were rolled into the meeting space and placed down the aisles of seating. These television monitors allowed the audience to see the eyes of the speaker and view moving graphics. But the mixture of slide projection and television monitors was not used for long because the advent of video projection was nearing.

The early 1980s gave birth to video projection, and the technology quickly made its way into the event business. The images videos projected were dull and dim. When slide projectors were mixed with early video projection, the slide projectors had to be turned down in brightness to match the lacking video equipment. Video projectors were large and expensive, but for the first time audiences were able to watch video created just for them, and they could see the person on stage being magnified onto giant projection screens. Within a few years, the audience could receive their very own copy of the event they attended on videocassette.

As the years advanced, so did the technology. Video projection became brighter and more affordable. With the addition of surround sound, audio systems simulated cinema-quality sound to support high-end video productions. Computers were used to design presentations with dynamic graphics. Robotic lighting was introduced, transforming stage lighting from the mundane into a true art form.

Today, those same corporate meetings, at times, more closely resemble an episode of *American Idol* or a top-dollar rock concert than actual business functions. Celebrity performers and speakers are commonplace, and the technology utilized could rival any Hollywood studio. The event industry as a whole has grown into a multibillion dollar business spawning a vast assortment of specialized services and resources.

THE FUTURE OF CORPORATE EVENTS

The distant future of corporate events is anyone's guess, but there are a few indications of where the industry may be heading. As PDAs and smartphones, wireless hotspots, and social networking sites continue to grow in popularity, ways of adapting these technologies into events will increase accordingly. Already, Web sites such as Twitter.com and Facebook.com are making their way into hotel lobbies, displaying live updates posted by event attendees. Custom micro Web sites are also becoming frequent add-ons to events, creating a virtual meeting point for attendees before, during, and after an event. With the ease of access to these Web-based sources through PDAs and smartphones, their roles in future events may quickly become commonplace.

Video technology is also rapidly evolving. One technology in particular that holds a lot of potential for the event industry is Organic Light Emitting Diodes, or OLED. LED technology is already a dominant lighting and video source, but

FIGURE 1.14
Concept artwork of future event.
Artists: Marcus Eiland and Troy Halsey

OLED can turn a sheet of plastic into a video display surface. Imagine unrolling and handling a 20' × 40' sheet of OLED film and hooking up a laptop to it through a USB connection for an instant video system. No longer will projectors and their power-consuming disposable bulbs be needed.

Infrared technology will have a large impact on the future of lighting scenery and presenters or performers on stage. Through the use of a body-heat map, robotic lighting will be able to follow specific individuals on stage, lighting them perfectly, without spilling excess light on the scenery behind them. This same technology can be applied for projection, if still in use, allowing presenters to walk in front of a front-projection video screen without being hit with the projection itself. The infrared map will instantly map their body shape and mask the projection accordingly, a handy feature for small venues.

The most exciting technology of the future in the event industry, however, will undoubtedly be one that is not foreseen. Imagine trying to explain LED lighting or the World Wide Web to someone 50 years ago; it would be nearly impossible. An interesting tidbit to keep in mind is the impact you, as a designer or event planner, will have on future technologies. Products that do not sell do not evolve. Thus, as an event planner or production designer, you are responsible for staying informed of new technology and test-driving these innovations during future events.

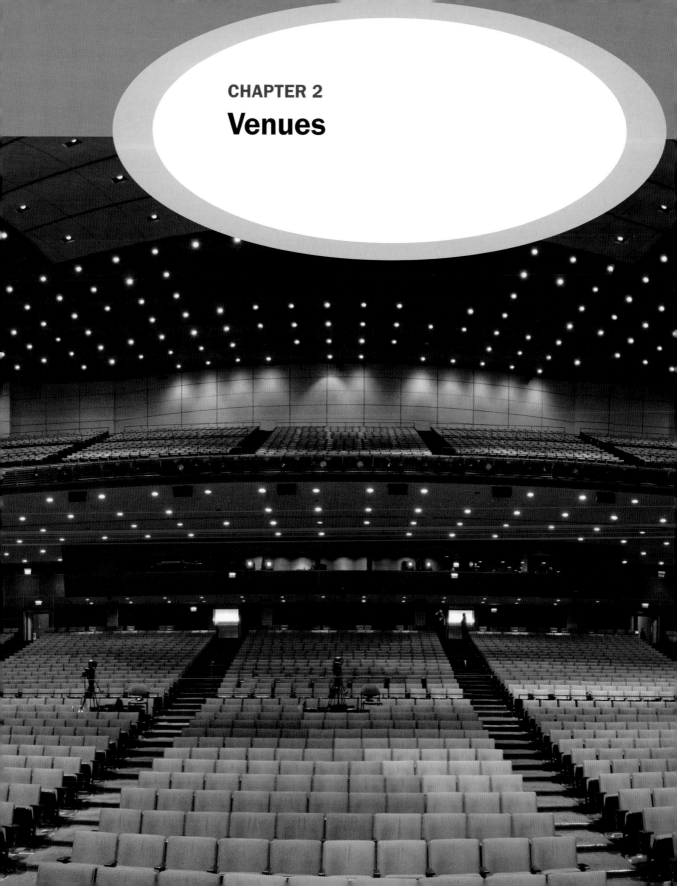

CHAPTER 2
Venues

INTRODUCTION TO VENUES

Event venues come in many shapes and sizes, and no two venues are identical. Venues vary structurally for several reasons, including architectural design, expected use of the venue, climate, and geography. All these factors impact what designs will be successful and which will be less than memorable within the space. Before any event production work can begin, a venue must be booked, and its unique challenges and advantages must be understood and deemed acceptable. Thus, venue selection is a critical step in planning a successful event.

Hotels and convention centers are by far the most frequently selected venues for corporate events because they provide a total solution for event planners. Hotels and resorts provide lodging for attendees, catering, various meeting spaces, support staff, transportation, and often recreation and entertainment options. Although convention centers do not offer lodging, several hotels are typically available within walking distance. It is no wonder meeting planners gravitate toward these locations; they are truly an all-in-one solution.

As an event designer, you will not always have an influence over what venue is selected and thus will be required to work with what has been booked in advance. Therefore, it is important that you are versed in each type of venue and its unique features. Whether the event is to be held in an elegant ballroom of a large resort or even on a remote Mexican beach, it is your job to know what questions to ask at the beginning of the design process. This chapter will give you an overview of common types of venues, their advantages or disadvantages, and ways to avoid common planning mistakes through site surveys.

TYPES OF VENUES

Although hotels and convention centers are the most common venues booked, they are not the only locales selected to host corporate events. Furthermore, within each of these venues, rooms and spaces are designated for specific functions and meetings. Following are the common characteristics of each space and the associated challenges.

Lobbies and Foyers

Lobbies are by far the most designed spaces within a large hotel or resort property. Their intention is to project grandeur to guests and event attendees. Lobbies are the venue's public center of operation, containing check-in and registration counters, concierge desks, and management offices. In addition, lobbies and foyers may showcase any number of statues, pieces of artwork, and botanical arrangements.

For smaller events, this space is not typically addressed other than perhaps a few banners, directional signage, or iconic scenic elements declaring the event's presence. For larger events, however, these spaces are ideal for environment designs, which will be discussed in Chapter 14, "Environment Design." Be aware that the amount of promotional materials and design elements allowed in these spaces

FIGURE 2.1
Hotel lobbies are
focal points of interior
design.

varies from venue to venue, so you should address this issue with the venue's representative early in the design process.

Foyers, on the other hand, are the areas outside ballrooms and convention halls. These spaces are less decorative and more functional; they usually contain large windows, restrooms, and lounge furniture. These locations are often used for event registration counters, promotional materials, and branded attendee lounges. Again, such elements fall under environment design and often require an additional designer to address. Undoubtedly, the venue will have restrictions for these areas as well, but they are typically less stringent.

Ballrooms

Ballrooms are just one of several types of meeting spaces found on hotel and resort properties. These spaces are typically reserved for large events such as weddings, corporate meetings, and seminars. Generally speaking, ballrooms are highly designed spaces and can be ornately decorated, serving, along with lobbies, as tokens of the venue's quality of interior design.

The primary advantage to designing an event within a ballroom is that it has been engineered and designed for just such a purpose – or should have been at least. Additionally, by hosting an event in a hotel ballroom, you typically have access to the hotel's labor force for installing seating, cleaning, and catering. Later in this chapter, we will look into a few of the technical and engineered features that make ballrooms ideal spaces for corporate events.

As with all venues, however, there are disadvantages to working within a ballroom. Due to the ornate decorations of the space, it is very common for a ballroom to have large low-hanging chandeliers that can cause rigging and projection

FIGURE 2.2
A hotel ballroom is by far the most common venue type utilized for corporate events.

dilemmas. In addition, ballrooms are often designed to be broken down into several smaller rooms through the use of *air walls*. Air walls are temporary walls that hang from and slide along tracks in the ceiling. When the air walls are not in use, they collapse and are stored in closets along the perimeter of the ballroom. These systems allow for several events to take place at once but do not provide good sound absorption. Therefore, if your event does not require the use of the entire space and air walls separate your event from another, try to coordinate with the other event to ensure a music performance is not occurring on one side while an inspirational speech takes place on the other.

Convention Halls

Convention halls are very similar to ballrooms and can often be used interchangeably for certain types of events, namely corporate meeting events. The primary differences between the two venues are the size of the spaces and the interior finishing detail. In convention halls, it is extremely common for the structural steel in the ceiling to be exposed, which also reveals air conditioning ducts, sprinkler systems, and electrical conduits. All these exposed elements are typically painted black and do not draw attention, nor do they distract from your design. In fact, convention halls are often preferable for large corporate events because they provide ample ceiling height and easy rigging access, and generally have a loading dock or bay that allows for direct access from the street.

There are, however, a few downsides to designing an event within a convention hall. Because of the size of the space, there may be columns throughout the space that can cause sight-line issues. The flooring is generally polished concrete as opposed to carpeting, thus creating a nightmare for the audio team. And finally, as mentioned previously, the interior finishings, meaning the walls and ceiling,

FIGURE 2.3
Convention halls, while less finished aesthetically, are ideal locations for exhibit floors.

FIGURE 2.4
Traditional proscenium theaters are also common hosts to corporate events.

are typically less aesthetically pleasing and more industrial than ballrooms, thus sometimes requiring additional masking drapes.

Proscenium and Traditional Theaters

A *proscenium theater* is any venue space that contains a built-in stage with a structural arch separating the playing space from the audience. This arch typically masks fly-rigging systems from the audience's view and frames the stage, allowing for a definitive edge of scenic space. This is not to say scenery cannot bleed out beyond the proscenium arch, as it often does in both traditional theater and corporate events.

The advantages to such a space are numerous. Namely, raised staging is already provided within the architecture of the space. The fly-rigging system, a series of battens or pipes hanging from an adjustable wire system, reduces the amount of additional truss rigging needed for lighting and scenery. Masking drapes are usually pre-attached to downstage battens and can be adjusted per event. And finally, as mentioned previously, the proscenium arch provides a tidy frame for your scenic design if you should decide to keep your design at or behind the proscenium line.

The benefits to proscenium theaters can also be disadvantages, depending on the event needs. Hotels that have proscenium stages built into ballrooms often do not have a functioning fly-rigging system and drapery may be less adjustable than in traditional theater spaces. Furthermore, if rear projection is intended, you might need to add an additional stage in front of the existing stage to allow for proper projection distance, depending, of course, on the depth of the built-in stage.

Arenas and Stadiums

Arenas and stadiums are also frequent hosts to large corporate events. Technically, they are similar to working in convention halls with the exception of higher ceilings and potentially more costly rigging. If only the arena floor is to be used for staging and seating, projection and staging are fairly standard. However, if the built-in stadium seating is to be utilized, projection and audio systems must be adapted for this unique venue type. A common practice is to place staging at one end of the arena floor and mask all seating behind and perpendicular to the stage with drapes, narrowing the wraparound seating to three-fourths of the venue. With this approach, projection is needed in only three directions. However, if the stage is placed in the center of the arena with all stadium sections open, then the event must be treated as theater in the round, which will be discussed in more detail in the next chapter.

FIGURE 2.5
Arenas and stadiums pose unique challenges for designing corporate events but offer plenty of ceiling height and design real estate.

Breakout Rooms

Breakout rooms are any smaller meeting rooms used during a conference or event. The name comes from the action of breaking out of the general session, where everyone attends an event-wide address or presentation, to rejoin in smaller topic-specific sessions. Audience sizes in breakout rooms vary from 10 or fewer attendees to thousands.

Technically, breakout sessions usually require one projection screen and a small sound system. Scenically, a common request is to incorporate an iconic element from the general session design so that both the general session and breakouts are thematically similar. This request is commonly added as an afterthought. As a designer, you would be smart to ask early in the process if the breakout sessions require scenery.

If constructing additional scenic elements proves cost prohibitive, as is often the case, consider printing a themed banner to hang behind the presenter or adding a few uplights around the room while dimming the overhead lighting to give the room a sense of thematic ambience.

Outdoor Venues

Outdoor venues have a number of challenges and few advantages, and due to this fact, they are rarely selected for corporate events. Far more likely uses of an outdoor venue in the corporate arena are galas, banquets, and entertainment performances.

If an outdoor venue is a permanent structure intended for events, it often is equipped with similar features to a ballroom or convention hall. However, if the venue is a temporary structure built for a specific event, arrangements need to be

FIGURE 2.6
Breakout rooms are typically partitioned using air walls within a larger ballroom.

FIGURE 2.7
Creating an outdoor venue from scratch can be quite an undertaking. Fortunately, outdoor venues are not common in the corporate event industry.

made to acquire power, staging, some form of audio system, and at minimum, a basic lighting package with a ground-supported truss-rigging system.

Planning a large outdoor event is quite an undertaking, and the topic could fill a book on its own, so this short summary will not give the subject its due respect. However, many of the basics found in this book can be applied as a foundation of knowledge for outdoor event planning.

ANATOMY OF A VENUE

Although each event location has its own unique advantages and challenges, common features can be found throughout the assortment of venue types. The hypothetical venue described next serves to illustrate generic venue features and summarize their functions.

The *main entrance* is the primary entry point for attendees. Large ballrooms are often designed to be broken into two to six smaller rooms through the use of air walls, and as a result, there may be a number of main entry points running along one or two walls. When the entire ballroom is being used, it must be determined which doors will be declared the official main entrance of the event because this will determine what attendees first see as they enter the room. Keep in mind all entrances, whether deemed the event's main entrances or not, must not be blocked or obstructed to stay in accordance with most fire codes.

Service entrances are the venue staff's access to the space. Catering, maintenance, security, and installation crews will use these entrances throughout your event, so it is crucial not to block these doorways. Some designers and planners prefer to cover the walls of an event space with black drapes, which are often hung

Anatomy of a Ballroom

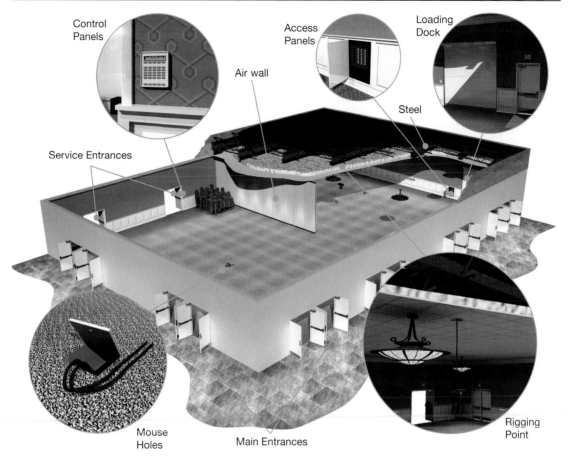

FIGURE 2.8
The anatomy of a hotel ballroom.

from floor-supported pipes. When these drapes are used, extra care needs to be taken to ensure that the pipes supporting the drapes will not be knocked over during the flurry of catering. Sandbagging the bases of pipe supports may not always be sufficient. Consider additional safety lines attached to ceiling rigging points for extra safety.

The *loading dock* is the place where equipment and scenery are loaded and unloaded from transport trucks. Docks are generally attached to either the convention or exhibit hall or primary ballroom if these spaces are on the ground floor, allowing equipment to be unloaded directly into these spaces. However, for various reasons, it is not always possible to have direct access to a loading dock – for example, when the room is not on the ground floor or the layout of the building prevents such a feature.

If the event space is on a second floor and does not have a loading dock, a *service elevator* should be available. Service elevators do not usually connect directly to a room, but instead open access to service corridors running behind the hall or ballroom. Service elevators are considerably larger than standard passenger elevators. In fact, some are large enough to transport fully loaded trucks. The lift mechanisms designed to support immense amounts of weight, however, are very slow and can dramatically increase load-in time.

Access and control panels can be found throughout event spaces. These locations allow audio/video engineers to connect their equipment to the house's power supply, sound system, and lighting controls. The term *house* applies to the venue itself. This term is theatrical in origin but can be used to refer to venue-provided elements, such as house lights, house sound, house risers, etc. In addition, the expression *front of house* refers to the wall facing the staging, where the show director and lighting and audio operators reside during the show.

Conduit access points or *mouse holes* provide access to conduits built into the architecture of the space that are used to temporarily conceal cables and wiring during the production, and allow cabling to run between rooms and under carpeted floors. However, conveniently accessible mouse holes are rare and shouldn't be relied on.

Venue *ceilings* vary greatly in shape and dimension. Various elements can be found in venue ceilings, such as lighting fixtures, chandeliers, air wall tracking, air conditioning vents, and speakers for the house sound system. It is important to take note of these elements because they can affect the placement of staging and drapery. Similar to placing pipes and drapes in front of service entrances, placing the same under a large air conditioning vent can have disastrous effects if the drape line is not sufficiently secured.

Ballroom ceilings with architectural elements such as domes and coves can also create challenges for rigging and create less-than-ideal audio acoustics, so solutions must be determined well in advance of load-in. When requesting floor plans from a venue, ask if one is available that has a *reflected ceiling*, meaning it shows important ceiling details such as soffits, chandeliers, and rigging points.

Chandeliers are often the bane of production and lighting designers because they can create several potential problems. Most professional productions will want to hang large rigging systems for lighting, video projection, and sound. Chandeliers can prevent ideal placement of these rigging systems and limit production capabilities. Some venues allow temporary removal of chandeliers, but at a significant cost. Look into such options and costs when considering a venue.

Keep in mind venue documentation may show ceiling heights as 24 feet high but fail to mention eight large chandeliers throughout the room that reduce the actual working height to 18 feet. This height difference reduces how close to the ceiling rigging systems can be hung and results in less-than-ideal angles for various instruments. However, if accurate measurements are taken early in the planning process, solutions can be found to most projection and lighting challenges.

During site surveys, a laser measuring device will prove invaluable in determining the venue's true working ceiling height, meaning how high rigging can be hung without dealing with projection obstructions. In addition, when possible, have your lighting designer and audio engineer accompany you during a site survey to aid in determining rigging dilemmas as early as possible.

Rigging points are secure points in and above the ceiling that have been designed to allow heavyweight loads to be fastened from them. In finished ceilings, such as found in a hotel ballroom, the rigging points are often hidden above canned lighting fixtures or above ceiling tiles. By removing the canned light fixtures or tiles, rigging professionals can anchor chain motors to secure steel above the ceiling. After striking the production, the rigging professionals can remove the anchors and replace the canned lights or tiles.

With an open beam ceiling, as found in most convention halls, specific beams are designated as safe for rigging within a given distance from each point used. Open beam ceilings allow for more flexibility in rigging capabilities but are not as aesthetically pleasing as finished ceilings.

Rigging points have a limit to how much weight they can support. As a result, it is most common for several rigging points to be utilized in a full production installation. Chapter 5, "Rigging," will cover this topic in much more depth.

SITE SURVEYS

Surveys are the event planner's or event designer's opportunity to ensure that the venue has all the elements desired, such as plenty of square footage and ceiling height, rigging options, ample power supply, and of course, rent within budget. It must be pointed out that there will never be a perfect venue, so you must weigh which venue contains the most manageable flaws.

Site surveys are one of the most important pieces of successful event planning. A site survey should be performed at any location that is being considered to host a large event. While reviewing the location online through the venue's Web site is helpful for building a list of possible locations, nothing replaces physically walking the space. Even if you have worked in the space before, schedule a quick visit to ensure that the venue has not remodeled and made your previous measurements and drawings inaccurate.

During an arranged site visit, as opposed to an unannounced visit, which isn't advised, a hotel representative should provide a tour of the entire venue and introduce support staff, including the Head of Catering, Convention Manager, and Head of Engineering. From the venue's standpoint, this tour is not about helping you analyze the space, but rather it is an opportunity to sell you its services. After the tour, ask if you can have a few moments to review the spaces in more detail and take a few measurements and photographs for your notes. Because no two ballrooms or convention halls are identical, each will come with unique challenges that must be carefully studied and overcome with detailed planning.

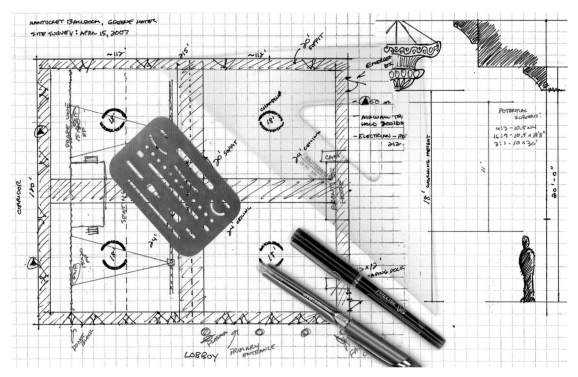

FIGURE 2.9
Although having to do so is less than ideal, taking detailed measurements of a venue is often necessary.

It is helpful to have a site-survey toolkit prepared for these visits. This toolkit should include a standard measuring tape, laser measuring device, digital camera, and plenty of grid-lined notepads. Laser measuring devices are extremely handy for site surveys. As mentioned previously, venue documentation rarely notes the true working ceiling height of event spaces, so taking your own measurements is critical. Laser measuring devices have difficulty giving accurate measurements when bouncing back data from mirrors and highly reflective surfaces, so keep your standard measuring tape nearby as well.

Take plenty of photos of the venue, specifically of the meeting spaces but also of the exits, loading docks, access panels, ceilings, and lobby areas. You may be surprised which photos will be needed during your production planning, including close-ups of wallpaper and carpet patterns if you plan on creating 3D illustrations of your scenic design within the space. Use the grid-lined notepaper to map out the perimeter of each space and paths to the loading dock or service elevators. Get as much information as possible and take your time; the more thorough your survey is, the less likely you will be blindsided when loading in the show months later.

Project: _____

Site Survey Overview

Survey Date: _____

Location Information

Venue: _____	Telephone: _____
Room: _____	Fax: _____
Address: _____	Email: _____
_____	
_____	

Contacts Information

	Name	Number/Ext.	Email
Event Coordinator			
House Engineer			
House Electrician			
In-House AV			
In-House Rigging			
Local Labor Rep (If Req)			
Fire Marshal (If Req)			
Stagehands (If Req)			

General Facility Info

	Available	Unavailable	Size	Quantity
Facility Floorplans	☐	☐		
Reflected Ceiling	☐	☐		
Rigging Diagrams	☐	☐		
Stage Risers	☐	☐		
Motorized Lifts	☐	☐		
Power Supply	☐	☐		
Sound System	☐	☐		
Lighting System	☐	☐		
Catering Services	☐	☐		
Security Services	☐	☐		

Room Information

Ceiling Height: _____

Width: _____

Length: _____

Largest door size: _____

Is loading dock connected? _____

Smallest door size to dock: _____

Columns? _____

Chandeliers? _____

Cost to remove chandeliers? _____

Do windows need to be covered? _____

Can you rig in the room? _____

What is the best wall for stage? _____

How loud is the A/C unit? Air flow? _____

Where will crew park? _____

Use Back of Form for General Notes and Sketching

Venue Specifications

Among the first questions that arise when selecting a venue should be how early you can enter the space to load in and set up, and how much time you will have to strike and load out the set and equipment after the event. Load-in and strike times can range from a few hours for smaller events to several days for larger productions, and some venues offer discounted rates or no charge at all for those load-in and strike dates. Make sure you are fully aware of the space availability before and after the event and the costs associated with those dates before booking the venue.

Next, you should tour all available meeting spaces on the property. Ensure there is ample room in hallways and foyers for flow of traffic between events, plenty of restrooms, and space for registration tables and attendee lounges. Ensure that the rooms used have enough ceiling height, rigging points, and a lack of low-hanging obstructions to accomplish your intended design. Ask what is typically provided by the facility for meeting spaces, such as seating, tables, staging, trash-cans, concession stations, etc.

Inspect the loading dock and take note of its size and how many bays are available. How are load-ins scheduled and do dock bays need to be reserved? Are they large enough for an eighteen-wheeler to back into safely? Walk the path from the loading dock to primary meeting spaces and take measurements of the smallest corridors and doorways that equipment and scenery will need to pass through. If there is not a loading dock available on the event floor, inspect the service elevator for its size, speed, and load capacity.

Where will empty equipment cases, known as *dead cases*, be stored during the production? New event planners often neglect to consider case storage; the amount of space required can be immense. Loading empty cases back onto delivery trucks is an option if space is tight, but you will need to add time for this on both your load-in and strike schedules.

Finally, take note of the service and catering entrances because you will not want to block them with your stage placement. Catering and maintenance crews will not be pleased if they have to traverse your crowded backstage to deliver dinner plates or install seating.

Labor Resources

Without labor resources, a production cannot move from the planning stage. The number of people involved in producing a large corporate event can be staggering. Following are a few key areas of labor that should be investigated early in the planning phase.

One of the first questions in regards to labor is whether or not the venue has a contract with specific vendors for audio/video services. Vendor contracts prevent event producers from bringing in outside vendors of their own choosing. This arrangement can be less than ideal if the contracted vendor provides subpar equipment or labor. If the venue requires a specific vendor to be used, ask for references that can vouch for the vendor's quality and reliability. If the results are not positive, avoid booking the venue or ask for an exception to be made. Cheap equipment or poorly trained operators can condemn the most carefully designed event to failure.

Many locations around the country require *union labor*. Union labor can refer to any industry craft whose specialists have unionized to enforce regulations such as pay scale, working hours, and benefits. IATSE, or International Alliance of Theatrical Stage Employees, is one union frequently involved in event productions. Although unions are very beneficial for their members, they can at times complicate productions due to the numerous policies and standards to which members must adhere. Ask the venue for the local union representative's contact information so that you can obtain a list of production standards before scheduling labor for your production. If your production travels and you wish to use the same crew for each production, many unions permit *labor shadowing*. Labor shadowing describes the practice of allowing nonunion crews to work in a union venue provided a union member supervises each position. Labor shadowing is expensive but sometimes necessary if the show is complicated technically and requires the same crew for all shows.

Another area of labor that is sometimes thought of as a last-minute addition is security. The venue will undoubtedly have some form of security, but whether or not the security staff can be dedicated to your event is questionable. Millions of dollars' worth of equipment is brought in for large productions and must be secured both during load-in and after hours when the space is not in use. Sadly, many laptop computers and other valuable pieces of equipment have mysteriously vanished from productions over the years, sometimes bringing shows to a complete halt. To avoid having to make character judgments of hotel staff, make it a policy to bring in 24-hour security from an outside source that provides insurance and background checks on its employees. In addition, set clear instructions for who should and should not be allowed into the event space. Attendee and crew badges can be very helpful in aiding security, even to the degree of color coding badges to signify clearance levels.

Lastly, you should meet with the venue's head of convention services to understand the venue's standard practices for setting up rooms, loading in seating and stage risers, and dealing with cleaning and maintenance. Ideally, stage risers provided by the venue will be set up before load-in begins or right after all equipment has been moved into the room. Load-in schedules are very fragile and hinge on all parties delivering on time. When a venue is selected and booked, you should acquire a detailed contact list of venue department heads for quick reference during setup and production of the event.

Fire Safety and Special Effects

Fire safety is not a topic that should be taken lightly. With events that are composed of thousands of attendees packed into one room, clear and organized evacuation routes should be planned, taking into consideration seating arrangements and staging placement. Most venues require fire marshal approval of production and seating layouts. This topic will be covered later in the book, but during your initial site visit, ask for the local fire marshal's contact information and research any unique regulations.

Special effects and *atmospherics* create the largest risks in event environments. Atmospherics, such as haze and fog, if permitted by the venue, often require smoke detection systems to be disengaged during use, which in turn requires a fire marshal to be present as long as the detection system is not functioning. This is not said to detour the use of haze or fog, because it can add a lot to the event experience, but rather to prepare event planners and designers for what is needed to safely use such effects.

Pyrotechnics – the controlled use of fire such as fireworks, flame torches, or combustion-activated effects – requires a licensed operator in addition to the presence of a fire marshal. The risk associated with pyrotechnics, regardless of the caution used in planning, makes acquiring permission from venues for such effects at times difficult. If your environment or scenic design requires the use of atmospherics or pyrotechnics, discuss these elements with the venue before booking.

Also ask if there will be carpet cleaning charges for effects such as streamers, confetti, balloon drops, or bubble machines. Large ballrooms and carpeted convention halls contain a lot of carpet, and the cleaning charge can be shocking if not budgeted for in advance.

Sound Systems

House sound systems are rarely sufficient for large events but can be used for general announcements and ambient pre-show music. This being said, venue representatives tend to exaggerate the quality of their in-house sound system, so ask for a demonstration. For smaller meetings such as breakout sessions, however, house sound systems may be sufficient and will be more cost effective than bringing in an outside system. Higher-end facilities may have the capability to allow rooms to be patched in for recording in a central location; this is especially useful for recording training sessions that may need to be distributed after the event. If an outside vendor is hired for providing sound equipment, capturing audio from general sessions or breakout meetings is a common service available by request.

Lighting Equipment and Capabilities

When checking for house lighting capabilities, you should first locate the facility lighting controls and determine their flexibility. Determine if they can be dimmed or only turned on and off. Can they be remotely controlled? Can the house lighting be controlled by sections, such as dimming the lights only over the stage? Does the facility provide locations for follow spotlights to be operated, such as on catwalks or lighting booths? Can the venue provide spotlights and at what costs?

Locate rigging points and fully understand all rigging restrictions from the venue. Ask if the venue allows outside vendors to install lighting systems or if venue or union labor is required. Are man, scissor, or basket lifts available from the facility, and if so, at what cost? Often there will be regulations for bringing in outside lift equipment such as using only battery-operated machinery or protecting flooring with plastic or plywood.

Electrical Services

In regards to electrical services, you should speak with the head facility electrician to determine how much power is available and how it can be distributed. Pricing structures for electrical services vary greatly from venue to venue and will impact your budget. In addition, ask how power hook-up times are scheduled and who the electrician on duty will be during your event and especially during load-in. Waiting hours for a venue electrician to hook up your power distribution will affect your install schedule and inflate your budget due to labor overtime because several tasks during load-in require power be supplied within the first hour.

Communications and Computers

Communication services are very necessary during events in today's high-speed age and should be a priority when selecting a venue. Determine if land-line telephones are available, although the prevalence of cell phones makes this less of a requirement. However, Wi-Fi Internet or T1 lines are a necessity. Furthermore, if venue Internet services are to be used, ensure there is plenty of network security to prevent guests not associated with the event from accessing sensitive information. If the facility does not offer these services, plan on bringing in an outside vendor because attendees will expect them.

Two-way radios are invaluable for production staff and crews to stay informed and quickly respond to unexpected issues, and many venues offer radio packages either for rent or as part of the venue rental package. But they are useful only if they are functioning properly, so you need to be aware that the thick concrete walls of hotels and convention centers can create radio dead spots. Map out these dead spots and remind crews that communication will be poor in such areas.

Computers are also a necessity for successful events, ranging in use from registration, email, and printing stations to PowerPoint presentations used in breakout sessions. While many attendees and presenters will bring their own laptops, it is a general practice for large events to provide computer stations for those who do not have personal laptops to check email, print schedules, or find directions to nearby entertainment or restaurants. If an outside audio/video vendor is used, this vendor can assist with managing computer and printing needs.

Finally, determine if the venue has a business center of adequate size and capability for last-minute photocopies, conference calls, or any number of business-related activities. If no such facility is available on the property, locate the nearest office supply and copy center to the venue.

COMMON VENUE OVERSIGHTS

The ability to anticipate problems and find solutions before they occur is a necessity for successful event planners and designers. Following are a few topics that are often overlooked or underestimated in regards to how they might impact your event experience.

As mentioned several times, ceiling heights are usually not listed accurately within venue documentation. Typically, only the highest point is listed, with no mention of obstructions such as chandeliers, soffits, or irregular architecture. During your site survey, take careful note of anything that may reduce rigging heights or obscure projection of video or audio.

Be on the lookout for highly reflective surfaces such as glass or mirrors that may reflect lighting or projection back into the audience. From an attendee's standpoint, it is very difficult to enjoy a presentation with numerous 1000-watt lights shining in their eyes. In addition, natural sunlight can greatly reduce the clarity of video projection. Ensure that all windows are properly masked to prevent sunlight from bleeding into the space.

Check for venue commodities that can interrupt an event such as house phones or loud air conditioning systems. And while we're on the topic of air conditioning systems, it's a good idea to keep the room a few degrees cooler than preferred the night before the event because thousands of human bodies, stage lights, and projectors can increase the room temperature significantly. And furthermore, be careful of free-hanging decorations or scenic elements that are in the path of air flow from air conditioning vents because nothing is more annoying than a scenic element in the audience's line of sight slowly swaying throughout a session.

Ensure while designing your event that you are aware of all exits and entrances within the space and avoid blocking them with seating, scenic elements, or AV equipment unless approved by the facility and local fire marshal. As a general rule, no exit should ever be blocked to ensure fire safety.

Check for squeaky or heavy doors and keep a can of WD-40 handy because attendees will be frequently entering and exiting the space, and loud squeaks or door slams can be distracting. A strip of cardboard and tape are great for cushioning heavy doors that close loudly. Make sure that main and backstage entrances do not lock automatically, leaving stage managers or attendees stranded or driving them to desperately bang on doors during performances.

Finally, when selecting a meeting or event space, determine the true meeting space. On occasion, the architecture of a space will prevent clear lines of sight for audience members in the extremes of the room. Walk the space during your site survey and ensure that all areas intended for seating will allow attendees to see the stage and projection screens. Also, keep in mind that the show audio/video equipment will need to be set up in the room, generally backstage, and ample space will be needed. In addition, the show director and lighting and audio engineers will also need a clear view of the stage and will typically be stationed in the back of the room behind the audience on risers. Although it is feasible for operators of PowerPoint, video playback, camera control, and prompters to be situated outside the meeting space, such as in a connecting hallway or service corridor, the show director, lighting operator, and audio engineer will have to be in the room to effectively produce the show, so plan accordingly.

SELECTING A VENUE

When selecting a venue, consider known factors for the event including the show budget, number of attendees, number of meeting spaces needed, and whether or not lodging and catering will be required. It is also important to remember that ultimately the attendees will determine whether or not the event was successful with their feedback to your client. With these points in mind, as you stand in potential meeting spaces, ask yourself, "Can I see from every angle, will I be able to hear the speaker, and am I comfortable in this environment?"

After you have narrowed your list of potential venues to those that meet the event's basic requirements, consider if the space will support your creative vision and technical needs. Will a stage large enough to support an orchestra or a photo shoot with a hundred award winners fit in the space and still leave enough room for the required seating?

Reflect on how attendees will be entertained between events? Are there ample entertainment options of varying price ranges near the venue or an assortment of restaurants if meals are not provided? If lodging is required, will everyone fit in one hotel? If not, will transportation be provided for attendees staying elsewhere?

When you are equipped with the knowledge of what is needed and know what questions to ask, selecting a venue that will support your event becomes relatively easy. This is not to say it is a quick process, as surveying multiple properties can be very time consuming in the beginning. With time, however, you will begin to build your own catalog of venues that work well for certain types and sizes of events and will be able to book venues yourself or advise your clients to do so with confidence.

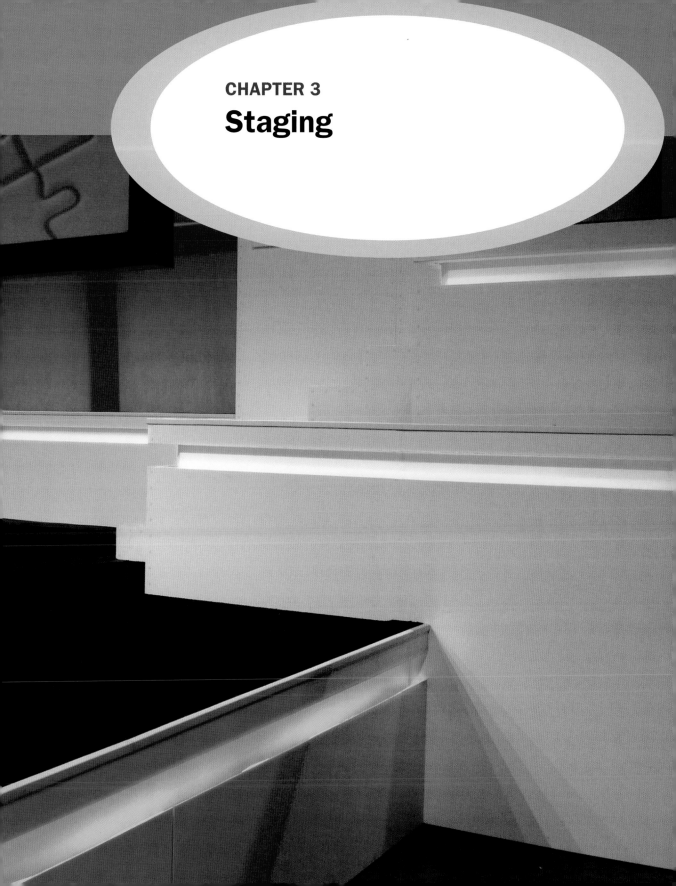

CHAPTER 3
Staging

WHY IS STAGING NEEDED?

Staging, also known as decking, risers, or platforms, is the literal foundation of scenic design for corporate events. In its most basic function, staging serves to elevate presenters and performers, thus allowing a clear line of sight for audience members. In addition, staging creates boundaries for the performance area, separating the audience from the performers. Staging also plays a psychological role, because it gives those standing on the stage the illusion of authority and aids in commanding the audience's attention. In a curious way, the higher the stage, the more important the event will feel in the audience's subconscious.

The quality of staging can also sway an attendee's opinion of the event as a whole. If old, banged-up house decking is used, the event will feel like a typical meeting held in a typical venue. In contrast, if the staging is composed of internally lit acrylic and changes color throughout the show, the audience's perception will be they are attending a very special event.

Determining the best staging for an event is important, but it's easy when you know your options and needs. Many factors play into this decision, including budget, venue and audience size, direction of video projection, how the stage will be used, and requirements contained in entertainment riders. The more of these factors that can be determined early in the design process, the more likely you are to pick the best stage for your event.

TYPES OF STAGING

Staging can be custom made, supplied by the venue, or rented from outside vendors. Each choice comes with advantages and disadvantages. Following are the most common staging solutions available for corporate events.

House Decking

Typically, venues that regularly host events have staging available for rent or include staging in their venue rental packages. Staging provided by the venue is commonly referred to as *house decking*. House decking is generally composed of prefabricated staging units that can be folded and rolled away for storage. Staging units of this nature come in either 4' × 8' or 6' × 8' modules and are adjustable in 12-, 24-, 32-, 36-, and 48-inch increments. These units are constructed with locking mechanisms that allow several modules to be safely joined to create one large performance area.

Although using house decking for your event is convenient and reduces freight costs, it is important to inspect the quality of the provided staging before relying on it for your design. As portable staging ages, its carpeted surface will become stained, worn, and generally unattractive. Furthermore, the metal framing and legging systems of prefabricated staging may contort and become misshapen with time, resulting in an uneven, noisy, and potentially unsafe stage.

FIGURE 3.1
A basic 6' × 8' prefabricated staging unit commonly found in large hotels and convention centers.

FIGURE 3.2
Collapsible parallel wood platforms can be stored flat for transport. Their assembly on show site, however, can be time consuming.

If the house decking does not pass your quality inspection, consider renting staging from an outside vendor or constructing your own. Although the additional cost will certainly affect your budget, it is your responsibility as an event producer or designer to ensure the stage you provide is safe.

Wood Staging

When house decking is not used, *wood staging* is a possible alternative. Similar to manufactured portable staging, cleverly constructed wood staging can be quickly dismantled and stored for repeated use.

One construction method for wood staging consists of four perimeter frames that are screwed or hinged together to create an open box while an additional fifth frame is added across the center to keep the structure square and add additional support. A sheet of 3/4-inch plywood is then screwed atop the box frame.

An alternate wood staging design consists of wood platforms supported by 2" × 4" legs with cross bracing. These platforms are constructed with a 2" × 4" frame and plywood surface. The legs, which have been cut to the desired stage height minus 3/4 inch to account for the plywood stage surface, are then bolted to the inside of the platform frame. Additional boards are then used to cross-brace the structure.

Benefits wood staging has over house or rented decking include how it will impact your budget. Wood staging is typically more affordable than prefabricated portable decking and custom shapes, and nonstandard heights are easier to achieve with wood stages because they can be quickly built for individual productions. And finally, wood staging allows scenic elements to be screwed directly into the stage floor, an option not usually available with rented staging without paying additional repair fees.

Metal Scaffold Stages

Metal scaffold staging is very similar to wood staging in its structural design, but has the obvious added strength of metal piping, rather than wood, as a

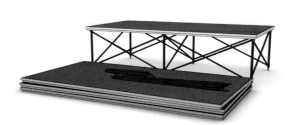

FIGURE 3.3
A basic scaffold staging system.

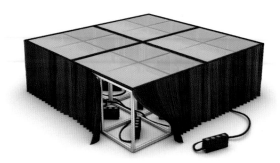

FIGURE 3.4
Acrylic staging and dance floor systems are ideal for high-tech or flashy designs, especially when combined with LED lighting instruments.

construction material. This added strength permits taller structures that can support heavier loads.

Although metal scaffolding also must be assembled on location, it is typically erected more quickly than wood staging. In addition to staging, metal scaffolding is ideal for projection, spot light, and camera platforms.

Acrylic and Specialty Staging

Acrylic staging is actually more of a stage covering than a staging solution of its own because it generally requires a supporting structure to rest upon. Acrylic can be used in several ways to enhance staging because it is available in a variety of colors, finishes, and thicknesses. Clear and translucent white sheets, commonly referred to as *milk-plex*, are by far the most commonly used acrylic materials.

A do-it-yourself method of acrylic staging is to apply sheets of black acrylic directly to the stage surface to create a highly reflective floor for a sleek and modern look. Prefabricated acrylic light boxes are also available and can be used to construct stage surfaces that can then be internally lit with LED lighting and synchronized with stage and environment lighting designs.

Video displays can also be incorporated into staging, potentially turning the entire stage into a video surface. Known as video LED floor panels (LED technology will be discussed in more detail in Chapter 6, "Lighting"), these units are ideal for low-detail video such as abstract graphic animations. Video floor panels are very expensive and can be time consuming to install; hence, they are primarily used for high-end music concerts and television talent or game show staging.

Specialty staging solutions are impressive but really beneficial only when audiences are looking down onto the stage, such as in an arena with raked seating, or if the event is being filmed with a jib camera system capable of getting aerial shots of the environment.

PARTS OF THE STAGE

The parts of the stage originate from traditional theater and are named from the performers' point of view facing the audience. Therefore, *stage right* is to the performers' right and to the audience's left. To prevent confusion, stage directions are always given a point of origin or viewpoint, such as *stage right* and *left* or *house right* and *left*.

Similarly, to describe movement and positions toward the front and back of the stage, the terms *upstage* and *downstage* are used. Downstage is closest to the audience, while upstage describes the region furthest from the audience. These terms originate from English theaters built during the Middle Ages that had raked stages and flat audience seating. Raked stages sloped slightly toward the audience, permitting a better view of action that occurred upstage. This meant a performer further upstage was physically higher than a performer downstage. When a performer moved toward the audience, he literally walked down the stage. This incline spawned the term *upstaging*, meaning to steal the focus of the audience because a performer downstage was forced to turn his back to the audience to interact with those performers upstage and behind him.

Today, theaters and performance venues that have permanent seating are designed with flat stages and inclined seating for the audience. However, the parts of the stage have remained. The diagram below (Figure 3.5) shows the parts of the stage in more detail.

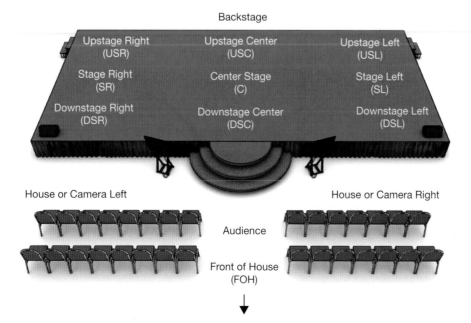

FIGURE 3.5
The basic parts of the stage are labeled from the performers' perspective.

STAGE CONFIGURATIONS

Stages vary in design, but their configurations can be organized into six basic categories, as detailed next. Whereas proscenium and apron stages are the most commonly used configurations in corporate events, they are not the only option available to you as a designer. In addition, as a designer, you are not limited to literal interpretations of the six basic configurations; indeed, varying and combining configurations can yield very interesting results in staging. As mentioned previously, staging provides a foundation for event designs, and

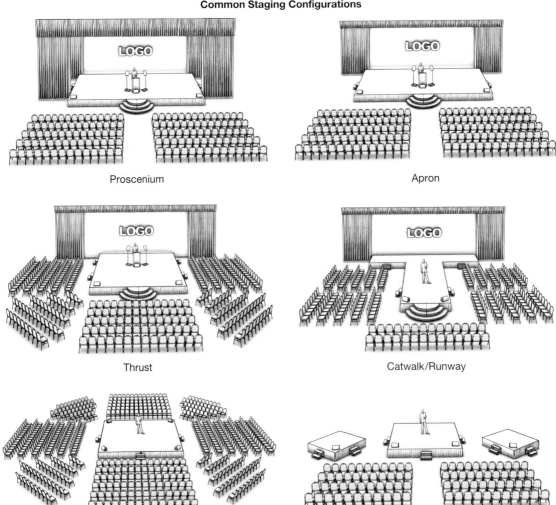

Common Staging Configurations

Proscenium   Apron

Thrust   Catwalk/Runway

In the Round/Arena   Vignette

FIGURE 3.6
Six common variations of staging.

selecting the right staging configuration is just as important as the scenic elements placed on it.

Proscenium Staging

The *proscenium stage* is named for its proscenium arch, which separates the audience from the performers via a structural frame around the stage. Proscenium stages are common in corporate events because many large venues have some form of proscenium stage available in their larger event spaces. In addition, many designers opt to create their own proscenium arch by way of black drapes or scenery. Proscenium stages provide a nice, clean look with defined visual edges and allow for grand show openings when a *traveler curtain* is used downstage. A traveler curtain spans the width of the stage and opens from either side or the middle to reveal the performance area. A downside to a proscenium stage is all the action occurs behind the proscenium arch, potentially preventing the audience from feeling as though they are a part of the show.

Apron Staging

By far the most common form of staging for corporate events is the apron stage. The name *apron stage* originates from the small section of stage located just in front of the proscenium arch in traditional theaters. Today, this configuration brings the performer closer to the audience because the proscenium arch or frame has been removed. Typically, in this configuration scenic elements provide a visual backdrop and are located on the upstage extremities of the stage and behind the action. This approach makes sense for corporate events because performers do not typically interact with scenic elements other than to occasionally enter through them.

Thrust Staging

The *thrust stage* configuration is an extreme form of the apron stage because it literally thrusts into the audience with seating on three sides. This approach is great when the design objective is to bring the audience into the action for a more intimate experience. However, inexperienced speakers and presenters may find it difficult to focus their performance in three directions and present only to the center audience, giving the house right and left sections a profile view for the entirety of the presentation.

Catwalk/Runway Staging

Much as the thrust is an extreme of the apron, the *catwalk* or *runway stage* is an extreme of the thrust configuration and is popular for fashion shows. Catwalks are composed of a narrow strip of staging that slices through the audience with house right and left sections of seating facing each other. This configuration can make video projection tricky because screens need to be placed behind each section of seating, and presenters addressing the audience will have their back to one side or the other. Alternately, catwalks can be configured in a T shape, with the audience facing the cross section, allowing for screens to be placed on either side of the stage and allowing presenters to face the audience as a whole. With this configuration, however, the audience will have to look sharply to their right or left when the runway is in use.

In the Round/Arena Staging

For a very dynamic stage configuration, consider an arena stage commonly referred to as *staging in the round* or *arena staging*. This stage is located in the center of the audience with all seating facing center. Keep in mind that many presenters find this configuration very uncomfortable because they can face only a quarter of the audience at a time and will be required to rotate their focus throughout their presentation. This being said, when presenters are familiar with how to successfully address an audience in the round, the experience will be very intimate and the audience will feel they are part of a discussion rather than watching a presentation. Scenery is typically very limited for arena stages because elements of any height will present sight-line issues. As a result, designers are most often limited to scenery that is hung overhead or replaced altogether by video projection screens.

Vignette Staging

When one large stage does not resonate with your design vision, *vignette staging* may be your solution. Vignette staging is composed of several small stages placed throughout a meeting space. This configuration is great for award show events because presenter locations can be rotated randomly among the stages, keeping the audience on their toes, so to speak. Separate stages could also be designated for specific uses, such as placing a band on one stage, while leaving one or two other stages for presentations and performances. Vignette staging works best when all staging sections favor one side of the space, relieving audience members from having to sharply turn their heads throughout the event. Vignette stages provide one approach for transforming a boring meeting space into an exciting environment. Such a configuration allows for not only the performance areas to be scenically designed, but also the space between stages. In addition, vignette staging brings with it the intimacy of staging in the round without neglecting portions of the audience during presentations because seating is oriented in the general direction of the combined performance areas.

ALWAYS INSPECT STAGING

When a stage has been constructed, it must be thoroughly inspected. During events and performances, decking will be abused and pushed to its limits. Stages are intended to support not only speakers and performers, but also an array of scenery and equipment.

Prefabricated stages come with weight limitations that must be strictly adhered to in order to prevent injury. In addition, prefabricated staging units generally have locking mechanisms for connecting several pieces to create a larger performance space, but these locks can bend and loosen over repeated use, rendering them

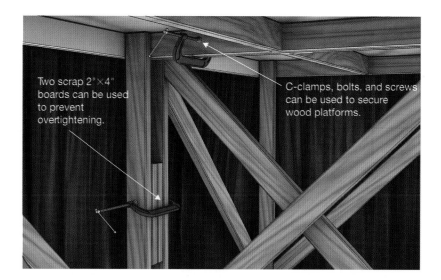

Two scrap 2"×4" boards can be used to prevent overtightening.

C-clamps, bolts, and screws can be used to secure wood platforms.

FIGURE 3.7
C-clamps, screws, and Velcro can be used to secure platforms together and reduce squeaking.

ineffective. Inspect the stage by walking, running, and jumping on every inch of it. If it wavers, buckles, or squeaks, it is not safely secured or interlocked.

If the stage is securely interlocked but still feels loose or squeaks, consider using zip ties, duct tape, hook-and-loop tape (Velcro), or additional C-clamps between legs for added support. When adding additional locking support, however, do not overtighten because this can result in misshaping the stage units and weakening their structural integrity.

Wood staging is a bit easier to secure because individual units can be bolted or screwed together. Similar to prefabricated units, however, overtightening legging can split the wood supports, weakening or collapsing the stage as a whole. Use a block of wood to fill the space between parallel legs to prevent bending the supports as C-clamps are tightened.

Finally, building foundations are not level in all spots. Dips and divots are abundant in all concrete floors and can result in slightly uneven staging. Ensure that all deck and stage leggings and the framework rest evenly on the floor. If you find spots that do not, use wooden shims, metal plates, or even cardboard to fill in the gap.

STAGE CARPETING

Carpeting a stage serves a number of purposes, including the obvious aesthetic improvement. Both prefabricated stage units and wood decking, regardless of how tightly they are locked together, have noticeable seams along their edges, creating a grid of deep grooves throughout the staging area. Stage carpeting covers these grooves and gaps between decking units, thus reducing tripping hazards and allowing for technology cabling to be hidden beneath the carpet. Carpeting also reduces the sound of footsteps that would otherwise be amplified by stage decking.

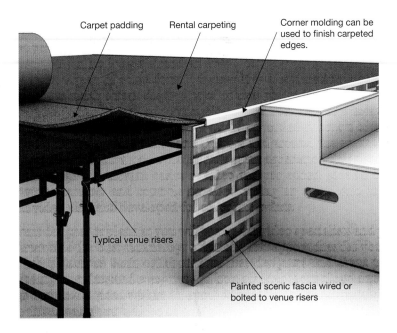

Carpet padding   Rental carpeting   Corner molding can be used to finish carpeted edges.

Typical venue risers

Painted scenic fascia wired or bolted to venue risers

FIGURE 3.8
House decking can truly be transformed using carpeting, fascia, and corner molding.

If outside decorators are hired for the event, for an additional charge, they can provide you with carpeting for both the venue, especially if the event space has concrete flooring, and staging. Professional event decorators have access to vast collections of carpet colors, thicknesses, and finishes. Carpeting from decorators is typically available for rent because even custom cut carpeting can be cleaned and resewn to be recycled into future events. In 2010, carpet pricing ranged from a few dollars to just under $10 a square foot, depending on quality, color, and availability. If the staging area is abundant with dips, gaps, or massive amounts of cabling, consider adding carpet padding before applying carpet to further aid in creating a smooth performance surface.

To finish the carpet around the edge of a wood stage and prevent it from fraying, apply prepainted corner molding and tack or nail into place. For all other types of staging, including prefabricated metal decking, 4-inch-wide black gaffer's tape works very nicely. And if custom step units are to be used, consider carpeting these steps as well to tie them into the staging visually.

STAGE FASCIA AND SKIRTING

When not covered in some way, the sides of the stage reveal to the audience all the support structures and scaffolding of the stage, audio and video cabling, and possibly an assortment of stored equipment cases. This mess of *stuff* gives stages of any significant height an unfinished appearance.

The height of the stage is referenced here because stages with heights of 24 inches or less will be visible only to the first few rows of seating during an event, with the exception of what is visible from the aisles between seating. However, if the

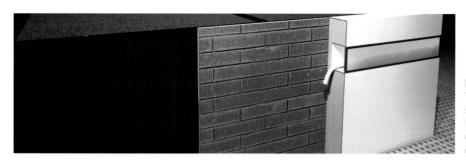

FIGURE 3.9
Three examples of stage fascia, drapes being the default option, but not the only one!

event is to be documented with handheld cameras or jib cameras, it is best to assume the entire stage will be visible.

It is a standard practice to aesthetically finish the perimeter of the stage. A basic treatment is to adhere black skirting or drapes to the edge of the stage with Velcro. Stage skirting is very affordable; in fact, it is usually included when renting staging from a venue or outside vendor, and allows for quick installations and breakdowns.

If the design calls for something more than skirting, however, an alternate but potentially expensive option is to build custom stage fascia. Stage fascia is in essence theatrical flats built to the height of the stage and attached with U-bolts, clamps, or screws. Fascia can be painted to complement scenery or engineered for built-in lighting fixtures or audio equipment, as in Figure 3.9. Well-designed fascia can add a lot of ornamentation to a stage design and bring the design detail closer to the audience.

MULTILEVEL DECKING

For the majority of corporate events, staging consists of one level. If, however, multiple discussion panels or organization officers need to be seated onstage for the majority of the event, it is not a bad idea to create two or more levels of staging. Multiple stage levels allow for better visibility of those onstage and can give the design, even if it is a straightforward business meeting, more visual interest. *Entertainment riders*, documents listing a performer's or ensemble's production requirements, occasionally require specific stage levels for their performances. These staging requirements can range in complexity, so it is extremely helpful when such riders are available early in the planning phase.

Step units between levels must also be factored into your design when using multilevel decking. Although steps will be mentioned in more detail later in this chapter, when considering multiple levels of staging, keep in mind that many amateur speakers and presenters find navigating steps stressful. This stress comes from a common fear of tripping or falling onto the stage, a fear that is only enhanced when in front of hundreds or even thousands of coworkers and peers. With this fact in mind, it may be preferred to keep a path in the performance space spanning from backstage to downstage on one level, leaving raised platforms for those presenters and performers who are comfortable using them.

Experienced clients are aware of the risks associated with multilevel staging, and it is not uncommon for a completely flat stage to be requested. When considering a multilevel stage in your design, ensure the client is aware of your intention and has no reservations.

TURNTABLES/WAGONS

Turntables and wagons (also referred to as *opera wagons*) are types of platforms that allow movement within the stage structure. Modern turntables and wagons can be either manually operated or motorized. Manual systems are more affordable but require *stage hands*, dedicated crew members who assist with elements related to the stage during performances, to physically move the platforms.

Motorized systems, on the other hand, although they may be more expensive and heavier, can be controlled remotely and preprogrammed for exact movements. If the wagon or turntable being used in your design will be supporting any significant amount of weight while being moved, it would be wise to invest in the more expensive motorized system.

For both manual and motorized systems, it is sometimes necessary to build into the stage surface some form of tracking to ensure that wagon platforms move as they are intended. This is especially true when the wagon will be used repeatedly during the event. These tracks add to the risk of presenters tripping on the stage and should be clearly marked for safety.

A turntable is simply a round platform with fixed casters or wheels that allow the platform to spin on a center axis. When a theatrical flat is placed in the center of

Turntable

Wagon

FIGURE 3.10
Turntables and wagons have been used onstage since the beginning of theater and performance arts.

the turntable, it creates a reveal mechanism, a form of stagecraft trickery used to reveal a person or object.

Wagons, on the other hand, typically move only forward and backward or side to side. In addition, due to the weight of wagons, a hard stage surface, such as plywood or laminate, is needed to reduce friction during movement. Complex paths are possible but require more advanced equipment and tracking. Wagons are ideal for bringing in large elements that would otherwise require too much time or space to set during a performance. Live orchestras, for example, can be positioned and ready to perform on a wagon backstage and quickly moved as one unit to center stage upon queue, a task that would otherwise take several minutes to accomplish.

Both wagons and turntables are great tools for adding excitement to live performances, but require detailed planning and experience to be used effectively and safely. When incorporating either of these systems into your design, consult seasoned professionals for their execution.

RAMPS AND STEP UNITS

When designing ramps and step units, you need to keep one principle in mind: function over form. If a performer or presenter cannot safely navigate the step unit or ramp you designed, then you designed it poorly. As a corporate scenic designer, you must remember that your performers are not typically trained actors used to working on tricky sets; rather, they are business executives and award recipients who are familiar with stairs found in homes and office buildings.

Ramps and steps can do more than simply provide a way onto the stage. Both structures are also excellent tools for creating dramatic lines and visual movement within a design. Wraparound steps not only provide access to the stage from any direction, but provide a three-dimensional fascia as well. Elegantly curved ramps leading to a second level of staging will draw a viewer's eyes smoothly up the design, giving focus to anyone entering down the ramp, a design trick used frequently for award shows.

Step Units

For steps, similar to stage decking, you have the option of renting or purchasing prefabricated products or designing custom step units. If you are not concerned with how the step unit will blend with your design, consider using prefabricated rental step units. Such units are usually available from the venue, if it is providing staging, or an outside staging vendor. Rental steps serve their function and are typically designed to match prefabricated decking with a black powder coat finish and gray carpeted treading. These units, however, are generally not attractive and just like well-used manufactured staging can contort and stain with time.

When constructing custom step units, you need to understand the phrase *rise over run*. Rise over run describes the height and depth of a step, and it

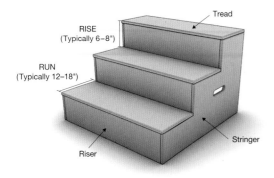

FIGURE 3.11
Rise and run of a
step unit.

is assumed each step is identical in dimension unless otherwise noted in your design. *Run* refers to the tread or the top of each step, while *rise* is the step's height. A custom step unit in event staging is typically built with an 8-inch rise and a 12- to 18-inch run. Eight inches is a hair higher than most stairs found in homes, which range from 7 to 7 1/2 inches, but this difference is due to most prefabricated staging systems being divisible in height by 8; the most common stage heights being 24, 32, and 48 inches tall.

Your design and budget determine the style of steps you will use, and nothing says you are limited to the standard rise over run. Perhaps for a more glamorous design, you want a shorter rise with a deeper tread. Avoid treads, however, that are too deep because such steps can cause *stutter steps*, meaning the user is not sure if he is supposed to take one or two paces per step. While varying tread depths is not typical or ideal, you can do so if your design should require it, but you will need to ensure that each step has the same rising height because even a half inch difference in step height can throw off a nervous award recipient.

Tapered and curved step units are especially tricky in maintaining comfortable rise over run. Nothing is wrong with tapered or curved steps; in fact, they can greatly enhance the customization of a stage design. However, you should make sure that at least 24 inches of each tread's width are no less than 12 inches deep.

Ramps

When bulky step units do not fit into your design vision, ramps may be an alternate solution. Ramps allow for smooth transitions between levels and can be seamlessly incorporated into scenic elements. Ramps do, however, have a larger footprint than steps and can quickly consume valuable stage real estate. Curving ramps can add style to your design but will also require creative engineering during construction and transportation.

Ramps are also handy when large groups of award recipients will need to be gathered on the stage at one time for photo opportunities. When recipients are positioned along the span of the ramp at various elevations, similar to a class photo, larger groups can be photographed at a time.

Although ramps can reduce fears of tripping, they can be difficult to navigate confidently when too steeply inclined. This is due to the need to shift your center of gravity by leaning slightly forward when walking up a ramp or leaning backward when going down.

Ramps may also be used when wheelchair access is required for an event, and such ramps should adhere to Americans with Disabilities Act (ADA) guidelines.

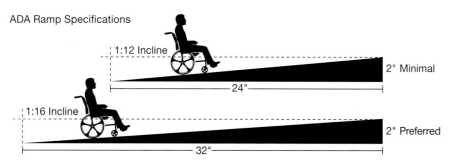

ADA Ramp Specifications

FIGURE 3.12
Ramps intended for wheelchair access must be built to ADA specifications.

ADA-Approved Ramps

As a designer, you should be sensitive to making your stage design accessible to everyone needing to utilize the stage during the event. This is especially true if the client specifies that an award recipient or presenter will need wheelchair access. The Americans with Disabilities Act (ADA) specifies that ramps intended for wheelchair access should not have a slope greater than 1:12, with a 1:16 incline being preferred. This means for every 1 inch of rise, there should be 16 inches of run or at a minimum 12 inches.

Therefore, a 24-inch high stage would require a 32-foot long ramp for a 1:16 incline or 24 feet for a 1:12 incline. In addition, a stage requiring wheelchair access via ramps should be no higher than 30 inches. ADA-approved ramps should be at least 36 inches wide with minimal turns. If the event space is not large enough to accommodate ADA-approved ramps, consider renting a hydraulic wheelchair lift to allow for backstage entrances.

MAKING STAGES SAFE

As mentioned previously, safety is the first priority when you are an event or scenic designer. This is especially true in regards to staging systems. While there is not a true governing body responsible for issuing safety regulations for the event industry, many standards can be borrowed from related topics covered by the Occupational Safety and Health Administration (OSHA). The following three excerpts can be found on OSHA's Web site (www.OSHA.gov) and filed under Regulations: Scaffolds or Staging:

> 1915.71(j)(1)
> Scaffolding, staging, runways, or working platforms which are supported or suspended more than 5 feet above a solid surface, or at any distance above the water, shall be provided with a railing which has a top rail whose upper surface is from 42 to 45 inches above the upper surface of the staging, platform, or runway and a midrail located halfway between the upper rail and the staging, platform, or runway.

1915.71(k)(1)
Access from below to staging more than 5 feet above a floor, deck or the ground shall consist of well secured stairways, cleated ramps, fixed or portable ladders meeting the applicable requirements of 1915.72 (Ladders) or rigid type non-collapsible trestles with parallel and level rungs.

1915.71(k)(2)
Ramps and stairways shall be provided with 36-inch handrails with midrails.

The legal lingo in these regulations can be difficult to follow and isn't very exciting to read, so we will summarize the topics covered in simpler terms. And keep in mind, these regulations are slightly flexible because their original intention was for construction and work sites rather than entertainment and event staging.

According to the first excerpt, when a stage surface is higher than 5 feet, hand or guard rails should be placed on the sides and back of the stage. Experienced designers and fabricators will suggest that even a 48-inch stage should have railing because falling unexpectedly from such a height is likely to cause injury in an environment full of audio/video equipment. Furthermore, the railing used should be 42 to 45 inches high, with midrails. A midrail is the cross piece of the rail found one-half or two-thirds the way from the top rail. Its function is not only to give the structure additional support, but also to prevent someone from crawling or falling under the top rail.

The second excerpt simply states that platforms with a height of 5 feet require sturdy steps or stair units. Again, it is safe to assume that your client would like a step for any platform over 12 inches, and even then a 6-inch step is usually provided.

Finally, ramps and step units should have a handrail 36 inches high. Typically, this is translated to mean that steps or ramps leading to platforms higher than 48 inches require handrails. However, manufacturers of staging and step

FIGURE 3.13
Platforms, stages, and step units of any height must be made safe using handrails.

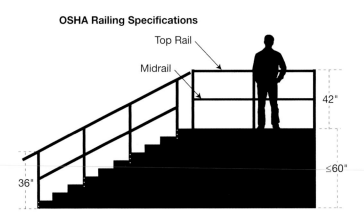

OSHA Railing Specifications

Top Rail

Midrail

42"

36"

≤60"

units tend to add handrails to any system over 32 inches in height. In addition, a venue may require handrails and guardrails to be used at a height it specifies, so ask about the venue's regulations before finalizing your design. Should your step unit span the width of a long stage, it is a good idea to place a handrail every 8 feet.

In addition to handrails, keep in mind black step units are difficult to see in low-light situations, and glow tape should be placed on the edges of each tread. Glow tape is a great product and can be found plastered sporadically all over traditional theater stages. Like most glow-in-the-dark products, glow tape is charged when lit and emits

FIGURE 3.14
Glow tape is a must for stage edges and step units used in dark areas within the performance space.

a slight greenish hue when placed in a darkened environment. And step treads are not the only locations glow tape should be applied. Stage edges, protruding scenic elements, and backstage obstructions should also be clearly marked with glow-in-the-dark paint or tape. If the stage design is composed of several sharp edges that could be dangerous when navigated in the dark, it is a good idea to tape out a safety path from backstage to center stage to allow presenters and performers to enter when the stage is dark.

CHOOSING THE BEST STAGE FOR YOUR EVENT

The process for choosing the best staging solution and configuration for your event is similar to that of selecting a venue. Determine how the stage will be used, the size of the space, the amount of audience space required, and of course, your budget. Ensure your stage meets the requirements found in the entertainment riders of booked talent for the event, and that the staging system selected can be loaded and struck from the space within the allotted time frame.

When your physical requirements for staging are known and met, consider what impact the staging should have on the design or vibe of the event. Does the client want the audience to feel as though they are part of the performances and presentations? Then you may want to provide a short stage in the round. Does the client want the experience to seem larger than life and spectacular? Then perhaps combining a tall thrust stage with an ornate proscenium arch would provide the framework for such an environment.

Understanding both the physical and psychological impact staging can have on the audience and the event as a whole will help guide you to the best selection. Whatever your vision and budget, just keep in mind the stage supports the rest of the design and should never be taken for granted.

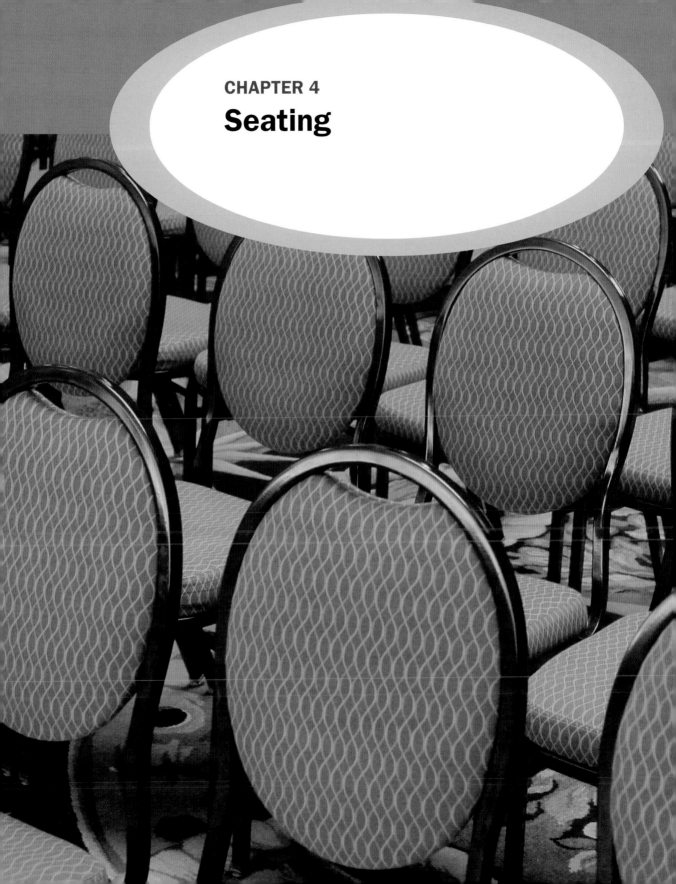

CHAPTER 4
Seating

THE PROBLEM WITH SEATING

Venue seating capacity charts are often deceiving and at face value are not good measures of how many people an event space can actually hold comfortably. The reason is that capacity charts do not take into account the amount of space required for staging, audio and video equipment and controls, related storage, and projection distance. They instead list the maximum number of seats permitted as determined by the building code inspector when the venue was first constructed or during the most recent renovation.

To more accurately estimate the seating capacity for your event, you must take into account the amount of space needed for all production elements. A few production elements that should be factored include the stage size you intend to use, whether you will be front- or rear-projecting video, and how large you need the backstage. A good rule of thumb is to reduce the maximum seating capacity by one-third because, on average, production elements fill one-third of the space before chairs are even rolled into the room.

Another item of consideration is chair width. Most event chairs have a width of 18 to 20 inches, while the average human shoulder width ranges from 20 to 24 inches. Because of this, event seating can be very uncomfortable for long durations. Having attended a number of conferences myself, I know firsthand how miserable standard event seating can be with a packed audience. Be kind to your attendees and provide more seating than is necessary to allow for an occasional empty seat and breathing room.

To ensure that you are selecting the best seating solution for your event, you must ask yourself two questions: what is needed and what is available? What you need will be determined by the size of the audience and the itinerary of sessions held during the event. Whether you're planning an award show or a training seminar, specific furniture and configurations will be more functional

FIGURE 4.1
Although common dimensions exist, it is important to confirm the dimensions of chairs used in a specific venue.

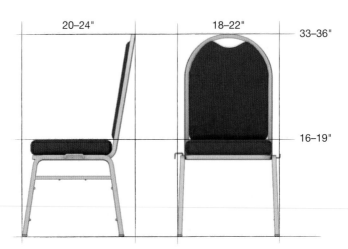

than others. This chapter will review standard chair and table options, common seating configurations, and a few pitfalls that you should avoid to answer the question of what is available.

TYPES OF CHAIRS AND TABLES

Seating is obviously a necessary evil in the event business. There seems to be an ongoing battle between designers and planners in regards to seating. Scenic designers will use every inch of square footage allotted to them for staging and technology, while in contrast event planners will pack in as many attendees or audience members as the venue will allow. In the end, a compromise is found, and seating layouts and scenic floor plans are finalized. Before the official seating layout can be handed over to the catering manager, however, it must be determined what type of seating should be used and in what configuration.

Banquet Chairs

Venues that regularly host events, especially hotels and convention halls, maintain a large inventory of chairs commonly referred to as *banquet chairs*. However, the term is rather general and doesn't properly describe the various kinds of chairs that venues may provide. To reduce the generality of the term, we will break the description of banquet chairs into two categories, which are detailed next.

EVENT CHAIRS

Event chairs come in a variety of styles and shapes. They are typically stackable, can be interlocked, and have solid supportive backs. They do not usually have armrests, and their seat base could be considered narrow, ranging from 18 to 20 inches wide.

The chair finish is usually selected by the original interior designer hired during the venue's construction and is updated only during a major remodeling of the space. The most common frame finishes for event seating are chrome, brass, and gold, while the upholstery ranges from solid colors to subtle pinstripes or floral patterns.

The locking mechanisms for event chairs are in place not only to keep rows of seating nice and straight, but also to adhere to fire codes requiring that seating be locked or clamped together to prevent a mess of chairs from becoming an obstruction during an emergency exit.

The benefits to using standard event seating are limited to availability and affordability because this form of seating is generally ordinary and uncomfortable. This being said, audience seating for most events merely serves a function

FIGURE 4.2
A standard stackable event chair.

and is not intended to enhance an experience or visual design. So needless to say, if your event has more than a few hundred attendees, you would be wise to settle for the provided house banquet chairs.

CATERING CHAIRS

While event chairs are used to create massive sections of fixed seating and are a bit more utilitarian, catering chairs tend to be more ornate in their design and are not designed to be interlocked to create neat rows, but rather to surround banquet tables. Catering chairs also make a few sacrifices for their good looks because they provide less support and padding for the back, which makes them less than ideal for long meetings. In addition, they often cannot be stacked like event chairs and require greater care and space for storage. And finally, whereas event chairs are generally available from the venue, catering chairs may need to be rented from an outside vendor.

Specialty Seating

Specialty seating typically must be rented from an outside vendor and is not provided by most venues. Catering and special event companies offer a variety of seating and table options in their rental catalogs. This being said, remember that corporate meetings can be several hours long per session, and seating must be functional and comfortable. Consider how attendees will feel after sitting all day in a piece of furniture before including that piece into your design.

FIGURE 4.3
Catering chairs tend to be more ornate than event chairs and are not always stackable.

FIGURE 4.4
Specialty seating ranges in design and practicality.

Stools and High-Backs

Stools and high-back stools (a.k.a. bar stools or drafting stools) are great for creating a more casual environment. If a sea of fixed seating isn't what you envision, a room full of cocktail tables and stools may fit the bill.

Stools are also handy onstage, especially when you want to give a panel of high-level executives a down-to-earth appearance. Keep in mind, however, women wearing skirts will find such a seating arrangement unacceptable in front of thousands of their peers. Also, if stools are indeed used for panel discussions of great length, be kind to those onstage and provide high-back stools that offer some form of back support; otherwise, your panel will quickly evolve into slouching and uncomfortable cavemen.

Bleachers

For very large audiences and even larger venues, you may want to consider bringing in bleachers. Although the word *bleacher* harkens back to uncomfortable metal high school and college stadium seating, event bleachers are actually just risers for event seating. Each brand of riser varies in dimension, but typically each platform is composed of several 3- or 4-feet deep sections. For a rental provider, visit SGA Production Services (www.sga.net). This provider has a solution for any situation. But be forewarned: bringing in outside stadium or bleacher seating can be expensive and time consuming during load-in.

FIGURE 4.5
High-boy tables, also known as *tall-boys*, are common in lounge and party settings.

FIGURE 4.6
Event risers and bleachers elevate the audience, providing a better view of the stage and presenters.

Lounge Seating

Lounge seating can range the most in style and dimension. Usually, however, some forms of couches or plush chairs are used for creating comfortable lounge areas. For a more modern and stylized environment, acrylic and plastic chairs are available but are truly more for appearance than actual use.

Companies such as Cort Event Furnishings (www.cortevents.com) and AFR Event Furnishings (www.afrevents.com) have vast collections of lounge furniture for rental and delivery. Keep in mind that although these elements are stylish, they are still rental and will wear with time. When renting from any furniture source, be sure you request new products when available and inspect each piece when delivered before the truck drives away!

Tables

Tables are a bit more straightforward. The majority of events use tables provided by the venue and generally stick with the basic round or classroom table. There will, however, be occasions when something a bit more specialized or unique is needed, so it is important to be aware of all options.

ROUNDS

The term *round* primarily describes circular banquet tables of any size. But for ease of communication, any table in which there is seating on all sides is referred to as

FIGURE 4.7
Rental furniture for lounges can transform a generic hotel environment to one that more closely aligns with your design vision.
Image courtesy of Cort Event Furnishings (www .cortevents.com)

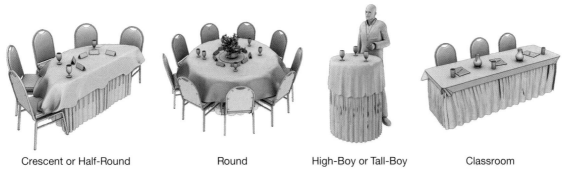

Crescent or Half-Round   Round   High-Boy or Tall-Boy   Classroom

FIGURE 4.8
Four common table configurations used during events.

a round, despite there being rectangular and square shapes available from many vendors. The most common sizes for circular rounds are 48 inches (6–8 people), 60 inches (8–10 people), and 72 inches (10–12 people) in diameter. When you are describing seating in rounds, it is the practice to refer to the diameter of the table and the number of seats per table; for example, a 60-inch round of 8 describes a 5-foot diameter table with 8 seats surrounding it. If you want a specific number of seats per table, be sure to make this need clear to the catering manager and on your seating layout; otherwise, the venue will default to its preferred configurations.

Rounds are ideal for banquets and awards shows and, when properly dressed with tablecloths and centerpieces, can add an elegant touch to an event. However, if the audience will need to observe videos or take notes from slides, rounds are less than ideal because half of the audience will be required to turn their chairs around to be able to see the screens and stage. For these situations, consider using half-rounds.

HALF-ROUNDS AND CRESCENT ROUNDS

A *half-round* or *crescent round* can refer to either a banquet table that has seating on only one side facing the stage or a specific table pattern cut to the shape of a capital *D*. The term *crescent round* is typically reserved for the latter but is occasionally used to describe either approach. Both approaches serve the same purpose: to prevent attendees from having to turn their seats around during a presentation or performance. When crescent rounds are used, less square footage is wasted. While in contrast, using only half of a full-size table wastes a tremendous amount of space and distances attendees from the stage.

CLASSROOM

Classroom tables are rectangular and come in either 18- or 30-inch widths and 6- or 8-foot lengths. As the name implies, this configuration is ideal when the audience will need to take copious amounts of notes during a meeting, or if they will use laptop computers as part of the presentation.

HIGH-BOY/COCKTAIL TABLES

Cocktail tables have lots of names, but in the event and hospitality industry are typically referred to as *high-boys*. High-boys are most frequently used in lounge and party settings, but can work inside the event space as well if a more casual free-flowing atmosphere is intended. Occasionally, stools are placed around these tables, but usually the intent is for attendees to stand around them and to serve as a place to set drinks and exchange business cards.

CONFERENCE

Conference tables are not found in main event spaces unless onstage for dramatic effect. They are very useful, however, in much more intimate settings with groups of 2 to 20. Seating is placed on all sides of a conference table, with the primary focus being those attending the meeting or a video screen at one end. Conference tables generally are not used in a corporate event unless located in a breakout room. Most tables of this nature are found in office buildings and venue business centers.

SPECIALTY

Tables that fit outside the norm can be referred to as *specialty* tables and range in shape and construction materials. Such tables typically are available only through an outside vendor.

One example of a specialty table includes the internally lit acrylic table, a product with growing popularity. Many furniture rental sources have vast collections of internally lit products composed of glass, acrylic, or fabric. A visually interesting arrangement for stylish banquet configurations is to rent a mixture of rectangular, square, and round acrylic tables internally lit with color-changing LED fixtures and randomly mix them into the seating layout. If nothing else, you will provide an environment attendees are not used to seeing, a welcome surprise.

Other specialty products include brushed metal; ornately painted, stained, and varnished wood; or mirrored table tops. Even inflatable tables and chairs are available. With a quick search online, you can find a vendor to accommodate any design vision provided the budget is right.

SEATING CONFIGURATIONS

As you will quickly notice, the name for seating configurations often correlates with a specific chair or table type. It cannot be assumed, though, that the two always go hand in hand. For example, it is feasible to have classroom tables in a chevron configuration or use cocktail tables in a banquet configuration. It is for these rare seating options that we separate the specific chair or table from the configuration of the same name.

Basic Theater

When event chairs are aligned in rows and aisles, the arrangement is referred to as *basic theater seating*. Chairs should be locked together to both keep

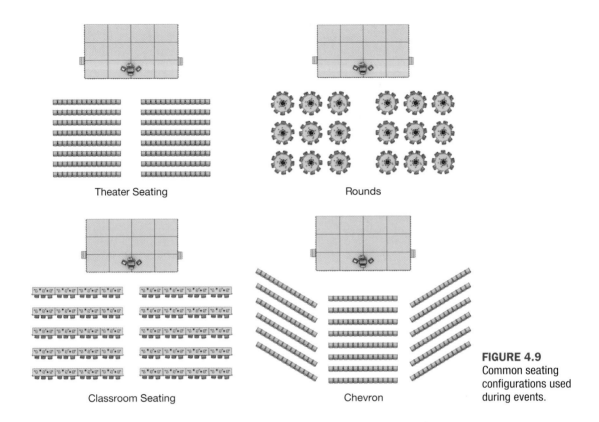

Theater Seating

Rounds

Classroom Seating

Chevron

FIGURE 4.9
Common seating configurations used during events.

the rows straight and adhere to most fire codes. Although codes vary from city to city, most require a 6- to 8-foot aisle between every 14 chairs and an 8- to 10-foot aisle between every 20 rows. Rows should be spaced no less than 36 inches apart.

Chevron/Clamshell/Crescent

Curved and angled seating can be tricky and takes a little extra care in the planning phase. Truly curved seating is generally not possible when chairs must be locked together, allowing instead for only the row as a whole to be angled.

One common configuration resembles a chevron and is so named. In *chevron seating,* the audience is divided in three with rows angling toward the center. Another is the *crescent* or *clamshell* arrangement in which each row is angled so as to form a half circle facing the stage. Such arrangements can aid in focusing the audience to a center point but can provide a few challenges with screen placements.

Finally, be aware that your carefully designed arrangement is at the mercy of the hotel or venue crew that installs your event seating. On more than one occasion a meeting planner's seating layout has been ignored entirely due to its complexity. If you feel very strongly that your seating layout be followed precisely, be prepared to tape out guidelines on the floor and oversee the installation yourself.

Classroom

Classroom describes any seating arrangement that provides a writing surface for each chair. In breakout rooms and depending on the venue, this may include actual classroom desks in which the writing surface and chair are connected. In general sessions, however, classroom tables are typically used. Classroom tables are arranged in rows and have seating on one side of the table facing the stage with aisles breaking the rows every four to six tables. In addition, classroom seating can be arranged in either of the previous two configurations, theater or chevron, with rows of tables replacing rows of interlocked chairs.

Banquet Seating/Reception

When rounds are used, the seating configuration is referred to as *banquet* or *reception seating*. When rounds are laid out, there are generally only two methods for table placement: a grid or diamond pattern. A grid layout allows for clear aisles between rows of tables, while a diamond pattern allows for better sight-lines and utilizes the space more efficiently.

Reception seating is often more spacious and reserved for special events such as weddings or anniversary dinners where attendees spend more time mingling than sitting. The terms, however, are often used interchangeably.

When circular banquet tables and seating are laid out, there should be a minimum of 54 inches between table edges. This space not only allows attendees to be seated comfortably, but also allows catering staff to maneuver the space for delivering dishes and refilling glasses.

ESTIMATING SEATING CAPACITY

As mentioned at the beginning of this chapter, most venues that frequently host events provide seating capacity charts that have been developed based on square footage. These estimates are further broken down into various configurations such as theater, banquet, and classroom. These numbers do not, however, take into account staging and projection. Remember, to get a more realistic maximum seating number, subtract a third from the venue's seating estimates.

The remaining two-thirds of the room are for seating, camera stations, and front of house (FOH) control. Now get out your calculator and start determining a few numbers. Remeasure the width and length of the remaining two-thirds of the room and multiply these numbers together to get your remaining square footage. For example, if two-thirds of the room measures 100 feet by 50 feet, then the square footage is 5000.

SEATING PER SQUARE FOOT

For banquet seating, the size of the table does not dramatically affect seating capacity as long as the maximum number of seats that will fit around that specific table is used. This being said, the shape does change things. For example, when

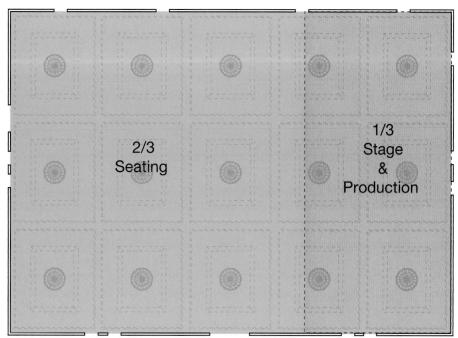

2/3
Seating

1/3
Stage
&
Production

FIGURE 4.10
It should be assumed at least a third of the room will be used for production and projection.

using rectangular tables, divide the audience square footage by 8 to determine how many seats can fit in the space. For circular tables, divide by 10. Again, this calculation is used to *estimate* the maximum seating. If you can afford the space, bump up these numbers by a few for breathing room. For classroom seating, divide the audience square footage by 8, and for theater seating, divide by 6.

To recap, when estimating seating capacity divide the audience square footage using the following guidelines:

Rectangular tables: divide by 8
Round tables: divide by 10
Classroom tables: divide by 8
Theater seating: divide by 6

Keep in mind that these numbers factor only for chairs and standard aisles. They do not take into account larger aisles or additional obstructions such as columns, service entrances, or dead space due to the room's architecture. They also do not account for camera placements and production platforms, but these topics will be covered in Chapter 11, "Designing from the Ground Up." The results from these formulas should be used only for estimations, and detailed, scaled floor plans will need to be created after the production is in full swing.

CLEVER SEATING IDEAS THAT DON'T WORK IN REALITY

During your time as an event or scenic designer, you will likely have a client who wants to step away from the norm when it comes to seating. Such opportunities are great as creative exercises and at times can lead to a very clever seating solution that adds to the event experience. More often than not, however, the result is seating that more closely resembles a mild form of torture than functional pieces of furniture intended to bring comfort. Keep in mind that the entire event truly revolves around the attendees, so keeping them comfortable should always be a top concern. Following are a few examples of clever seating ideas that were less than successful in practice.

A Packed Audience Isn't Fun for the Audience

Requiring your audience members to move closer together just to fill empty seats is not recommended – although this may just be one of my personal pet peeves. Doing so only serves those hosting the event and allows presenters to feel as though they are speaking before a packed audience. In reality, being seated in the middle of a packed audience can be very claustrophobic and can lead to panic attacks for some people. In addition, not everyone is physically able to be seated in one place for long periods of time due to a variety of medical reasons, and packing in the audience makes getting to the aisles tricky and distracting. Be kind to your attendees and allow them to sit where they prefer, and furthermore, when space permits, add a few additional seats to provide buffer seating.

Ultra-Stylish Seating

Many catering and special event vendors have large collections of chair styles, ranging from traditional event and catering seating to unique objects of art barely resembling something a person would want to sit upon. The latter is what we are referring to as *ultra stylish*. Whether it is the shape of chair or the material used, such as a hard plastic, always think of your audience's comfort. Sitting in any chair for more than a few hours at a time will begin to cause some discomfort, but this will be even more pronounced when a chair is designed for its looks rather than ergonomics.

Bleachers

There are several kinds of bleacher seat options, most of which only provide decking, with event chairs used for the actual seats. But some vendors specialize in temporary outdoor seating and offer traditional bleachers, the kind you might find on the sidelines of a little league football game. One client hosting a sports-focused event thought it would be fun to have the audience sit on such bleachers to tie into the theme. The complaints were so intense that, after the opening session, the show crew had to work through the night removing the bleachers and replacing them with standard event chairs. Seating that provides back support should never be taken for granted and should always be provided for any event lasting more than 15 minutes.

Swivel Chairs

A cool concept does not always translate to a cool result. One example of this was a client who wanted everyone in the audience to be seated in comfortable executive chairs that could swivel and recline. Although using such chairs was a very generous consideration for the audience's comfort, the reality was a room full of 500 constantly moving and very distracting chairs. The client greatly regretted the idea post production. So needless to say, swivel chairs should be avoided within the event space and should be reserved for small meetings surrounding a traditional conference table.

Bean Bags

Bean bags seem like a really innovative and creative seating solution, but in use they are painful for anyone over the age of 10. An event that forces a room of attendees, who may be in skirts or who spent hours primping to impress their coworkers and superiors, to sit in bean bags will not be well received. And many people find having to roll back and forth to get out of a bean bag a bit embarrassing. If you are convinced, despite this warning, that using bean bags for seating is the only way your event will be successful, then leave them in lounge areas outside the main meeting space where attendees have the choice of using them when checking email or relaxing between sessions.

CHOOSING THE BEST SEATING CONFIGURATION

When selecting seating configurations, begin with broad questions. Will food be served? Will attendees be taking notes or using laptops during sessions? Is there an award ceremony requiring audience members to walk up to the stage? From these questions, you can derive whether rounds, classroom, or theater seating is required.

After you have determined what is needed, consider the shape of the stage and the size of the audience. Is a chevron shape appropriate for this design or should a basic theater configuration be used? Do you have time to install a complex seating configuration like chevron or crescent arrangements? If banquet rounds are used, is there a screen that needs to be visible throughout the session or are large aisles for mingling more important?

No one knows an event space better than a venue's catering manager. Work with this person to determine whether or not your preferred seating configuration is appropriate for the space. What seating options are available from the venue? Will certain layouts cause sight-line issues or make catering more difficult? Is there dead space in the venue that should not include seating? Those who regularly operate within the space must be called upon to help answer these questions.

An event space may host several sessions over the course of multiple days, requiring a different seating configuration for each event. When this is the situation, not only must each layout be carefully planned, but schedules must be drafted detailing when each configuration is to be used and when it will be installed. Work with the venue or seating vendor to determine how long each installation will take before finalizing schedules.

In the end, the most simple and affordable seating is usually selected. The reason is that seating is generally considered as merely serving a function and has minimal impact on the event as a whole. Meeting planners and designers just beginning their careers often forget to consider seating options altogether. We hope this chapter has shown that although seating may not be the most interesting of topics, poor seating decisions can indeed affect the success of an event on many levels.

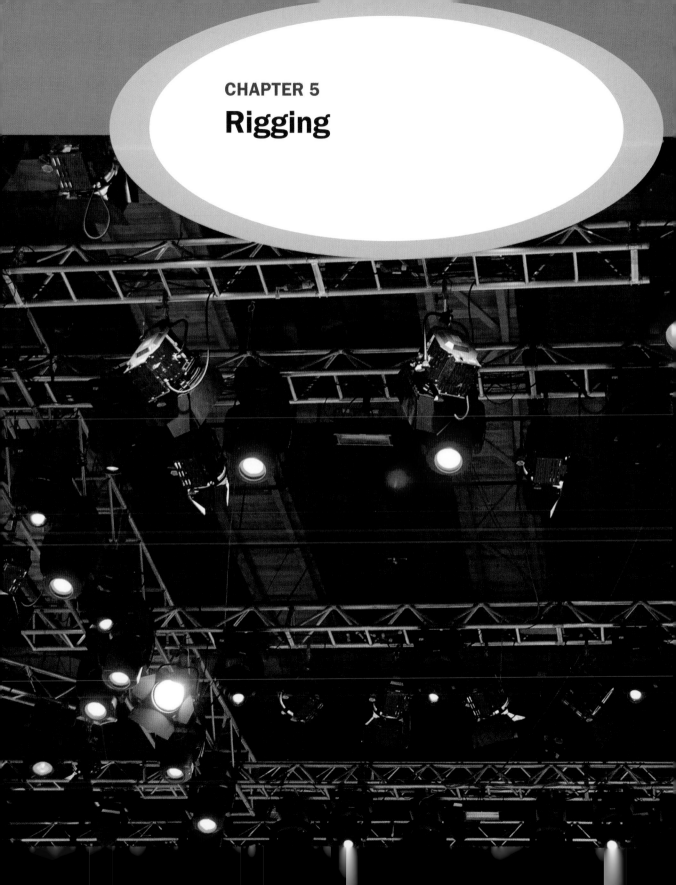

CHAPTER 5

Rigging

INTRODUCTION TO RIGGING

The process of safely hanging weight overhead is known as *rigging*. The concept may seem simple, but it is truly a feat of engineering and science. Improper rigging can not only result in the destruction of expensive equipment, but more importantly can seriously injure or kill those below. At no time, regardless of the situation, should rigging be performed by anyone other than trained and professional rigging specialists.

After venue selection, researching rigging capabilities within the meeting space is one of the first steps in event planning. Specifically for general sessions, the location of the stage, audience seating, and screen placements cannot be determined until the first rigging point has been identified. If an event planner or designer is unfamiliar with the space, documentation and rigging diagrams should be available from the venue. Even with these documents, however, a site visit should be scheduled with a rigging specialist to ensure that the provided drawings are accurate and current.

This chapter will focus on rigging systems used in general session environments. General sessions typically involve the most complex rigging during an event, but are not the only locations where rigging may be necessary. Exhibit hall and lobby designs may require rigging as well, and lobbies in particular can pose unique challenges due to venue architecture such as vaulted ceilings and limited access to rigging points. For such scenarios, rely on a rigging specialist to determine the best solutions available before moving forward with a design.

The field of rigging has developed a collection of specialized equipment and standard practices. This chapter will give an overview of the most common elements and procedures of rigging that may be encountered during an event. This chapter should not be used as instruction for rigging, but as an overview of the rigging process and how it supports event design.

THE BASICS OF RIGGING

When a structure or building is designed, a structural engineer determines how much reserve capacity is available within the building's superstructure or steel framework, meaning how much weight can be added to the steel structure holding up the building before it collapses. All buildings are constructed with an amount of reserve capacity to account for unforeseen stresses on the structure, such as snow buildup, ice, or strong winds. When the reserve capacity is known, specific load capacities can then be assigned to steel beams available for rigging. To ensure structural stability, loads must be distributed along a beam rather than concentrated. For example, an engineer may determine a 300-foot beam's reserve capacity is 18,000 pounds, but its load capacity is 1,500 pounds every 25 feet.

This information is collected by the venue into diagrams available to rigging specialists. The rigging specialists then work with the audio and lighting designers to determine where and how much equipment needs to be hung. After the rigging layout is determined, the stage design can be added to the floor plan, moving it from the conceptual to the practical.

During an event installation, rigging is the first task that must be completed. Using mechanical lifts, riggers use wire rope slings to attach chain hoists to the structural steel. Attachment locations are known as rigging points and are determined and calculated during preproduction planning. The chain hoists are then connected to either structures designed to raise audio speakers or in most cases aluminum trussing. When all items are connected, the collective rig is raised and leveled. After the rig is in place and secured, instruments can be focused and the installation of rigging is completed.

Admittedly, this is a simplified explanation of rigging, but at its core it really is a simple concept. In the event industry, however, nothing is that simple. When thousands of pounds of equipment are hung over attendees, things get a bit more complicated. The science and engineering of rigging are what allows such a simple concept to be repeated and applied to any venue safely and efficiently.

RIGGING EQUIPMENT

Only industrial-designed materials and equipment should be used for rigging, and this does not include climbing equipment. If a working load limit is not printed directly on a piece of equipment, it should be avoided, as well as items labeled "not for overhead lifting." In simpler terms, avoid using anything not specifically designed for the purpose of rigging. Following are the most common pieces of equipment used by rigging specialists.

Chain Motors/Hoists

Chain motors or electric chain hoists are a staple of professional rigging. These precision instruments allow for safe and controlled lifting of loads up to three tons. Without chain hoists, many modern event production capabilities would not be possible.

Chain hoists are mechanisms that raise and lower pieces of equipment using chain that is connected to a wire sling anchored to structural steel. This movement is achieved by turning a primary gear within the hoist that grabs several links of the chain at a time and pulls them through the unit and into a chain bag attached beneath the hoist encasement. The chain bag collects the excess chain as the hoist is raised.

Beneath the hoist is a chain hook used to attach various loads. A chain hoist's load capacity defines how much weight the hoist can safely lift. Chain hoists are often referred to by their load capacity, such as quarter-ton, half-ton, and one-ton hoists. Finally, a spring-loaded hoist brake within the unit prevents the chain from slipping. Hoist brakes are engineered to handle weights up to two times the weight rated for the unit, ensuring the unit will not fail during a production.

FIGURE 5.1
Chain motors allow incredibly heavy rigs to be safely hung overhead.

Basic chain hoists are designed to climb at a constant rate of 16 feet per minute regardless of their load. However, as with all hoists, when pushed to the limit, this climb rate will not be consistent. High-speed and variable-speed hoists are also available and can allow for dramatic scenic and rigging movements during productions. These types of effects are more common during music concerts but do make their way into the event industry on occasion in larger productions.

When several hoists are used in conjunction, as is the case when raising and lowering trusses, a distribution, or *distro*, remote control is used to ensure all hoists are activated at the same time. Distro remote controls can raise all the hoists connected at one time or isolate each hoist for slight adjustments. This flexibility in control plays an important part in safely raising complex truss rigs. When the rig is in place, the distro control is disconnected and stored until the production is struck.

Motorized Lifts

Motorized lifts are a necessity on production sites and enable riggers and technicians to access any number of hung items, such as lighting instruments, speakers, projectors, and decorations. Although ladders are still used on occasion, they do not offer the speed of movement or height range of mechanical lifts. Also, it is not uncommon for a piece of equipment, such as a video projector, to be hung after the rig has been raised, a task not possible using a ladder alone.

The three most common lifts used in the event industry are the single-person, scissor, and boom lifts. Although each model serves essentially the same function, the size differences allow for different applications. For example, the

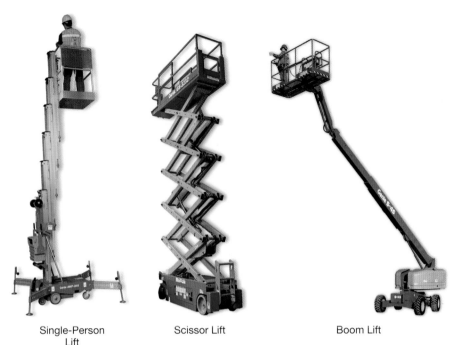

Single-Person
Lift

Scissor Lift

Boom Lift

FIGURE 5.2
Three common models
of lifts used in the
event industry.
*Images courtesy of
Genie Industries, Inc.
(www.genielift.com)*

massive gas-powered boom lift has a very versatile range but requires large open venues for maneuvering. Single-person lifts are great for adjusting instruments in tight spots, but not ideal for lifting bulky equipment like projectors or speakers. Scissor lifts offer the perks of both booms and single-person lifts. They do not require much room for navigation and provide enough space for two engineers with equipment. These traits make scissor lifts very popular for events of all sizes.

Lifts can be either gas powered or electric. Although gas-powered units like boom lifts may offer more horsepower and lifting capabilities, they do emit exhaust and as a result are not permitted in all venues. Electric units require charging after use and can be slower moving, but are allowed in most event spaces. Most venues require that flooring be covered by plywood or plastic prior to the use of mechanical lifts. Before renting lifts, check with a venue representative to ensure compliance.

When not properly operated, lifts can be dangerous vehicles. Not only should operating procedures be followed, but extra care should be taken for those below. Dropped tools and equipment can cause great harm to unsuspecting bystanders, which does happen on occasion. Wrenches and other hand tools should be tied to the lift railing in case of slippage. Being aware at all times of surroundings both above and below is crucial during lift operation, especially during the hectic buzz of tightly scheduled installations.

Trusses

Miles and miles of trussing are used in the event industry, and trusses are an iconic element in the trade. Trussing supports a variety of items including lighting instruments, projectors, scenery, projection screens, and drapery. Like rigging as a whole, trussing supports many common event features that would not be possible otherwise.

FIGURE 5.3
Box trussing is a staple in the event industry.

Lightweight and durable aluminum is the material of choice for event trussing and comes in a variety of sizes and shapes. Individual pieces of truss are commonly referred to as *sticks* and come in 10-, 8-, 5-, 4-, and 2-foot lengths. Although most trussing is polished, powder-coated black trussing is also available from most vendors. Trussing used for overhead rigging, however, is typically general-purpose box trussing.

Box trussing is essentially an oversized *Erector Set* for industrial applications. When connected securely using bolts, several pieces can quickly span massive lengths. However, the longer the line of trussing, the weaker it becomes structurally, requiring additional rigging points. The documentation provided by the manufacturer states load limits of various lengths.

Not all trussing has to be straight. Corner blocks allow for 90-degree turns, whereas circular trusses offer variety in possible rig shapes. In addition, many vendors offer hinge plates, which allow for

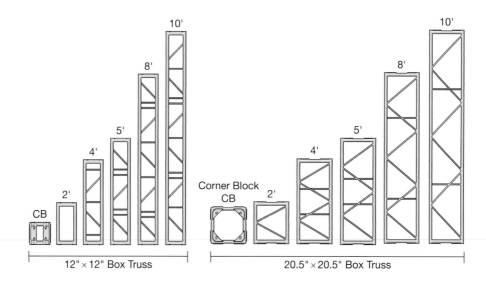

FIGURE 5.4
Common sizes and lengths of box trussing.

any angle to be accommodated. Even custom corner blocks are an option if your budget allows. This flexibility in configuration makes aluminum trussing ideal not only for rigging, but scenic designs as well.

Hardware

All the hardware used for rigging is extremely strong and most often constructed from drop-forged steel. For a designer to know each piece of hardware involved in rigging is not necessary. Just in case you find yourself killing time with the installation crew – perhaps waiting for the venue electrician to arrive – here are a few notes on rigging hardware as conversation starters.

Only heat-treated steel chain, typically 1/4-inch or 5/16-inch thick, is used for professional overhead rigging. This is not the kind of chain you can find in a hardware store, nor can it be cut with standard bolt cutters. Grab hooks are pretty straightforward and can be used in many scenarios. Chain hoists are typically equipped with two chain grab hooks: one on the top to connect the chain to slings or shackles, and the other attached to the hoist itself to connect the load.

FIGURE 5.5
Trusses are not limited to 90-degree angles; various diameters of circle trusses are available from many vendors.

Slings or wire assembles are used in attaching chain to structural steel and come in many materials. Slings are easy to remember because they are *slung* over steel beams to begin the rigging process. Shackles are U-shaped apparatuses used to connect a rope, cable, or chain to another device or a hanging point. Eye bolts are occasionally welded to a venue's structural steel, providing quick and designated rigging points.

RIGGING POINTS

Rigging points are merely access locations to the building's structural steel. The act of connecting rigging equipment to this steel deems that location as a rigging point. Although many venues, especially those with aesthetically finished ceilings, specify exact points of access, in theory a rigging point can be anywhere engineers have access to structural steel. When a rigging point is described or classified, the method of rigging is what is being noted. Following are the four basic types of rigging points.

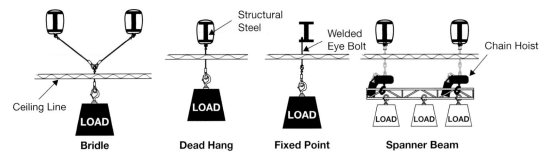

FIGURE 5.6
The four basic rigging points.

Dead Hanging

A *dead hang* is the simplest of rigging points. Cabling is looped around a structural beam, chain is connected to the cabling, and the load is attached to the chain hoist and raised. Dead hangs are used most often for rigging speaker clusters or single-item loads.

Spanner Beams

When trussing is used to span a distance, these rigging points are collectively known as *spanner beams*. When trusses are used, additional weight can be added to a more specific area than is possible using a single point. In addition, spanner beams allow instruments to be hung between rigging points. For example, two rigging points, each with a load capacity of 2,000 pounds, are available 15 feet apart. When a line of truss 30 feet long is hung, with each end being supported by one of these points, a collective weight of 4,000 pounds (minus the weight of the truss itself) can now be hung between the two points. Furthermore, if the ideal placement of a projector is between two rigging points, trussing can be hung from the two points, allowing the projector to then be hung from the truss in the ideal location. Spanner beams are by far the most common form of rigging for large productions.

Bridles

Similar to spanner beams, *bridles* turn two or more rigging points into one. However, they do not necessarily combine the load limits for the two points used. Because the force being exerted on the two points introduces horizontal force rather than straight vertical force, their load capacities are diminished. The venue documentation should notate whether bridle points are permitted and what their collective capacities are.

Fixed Points

Occasionally, a venue provides fixed rigging points within its event spaces. *Fixed points* are typically eye bolts or shackles that have been permanently secured to structural steel. If the eye bolts are not visible below the ceiling line, they can be accessed by moving ceiling tiles or light fixtures. No diagonal force should be applied to fixed points to prevent damage to the ceiling or failure of the point.

WHEN RIGGING POINTS ARE NOT AVAILABLE?

It is not uncommon for events to occur in venues that do not provide access to structural steel. When this is the case, the venue is said to have no rigging points. Lights and projectors are still needed for professional productions, so a solution must be found. The simplest solution is to work from the ground up.

Box trussing is not limited to being hung; it can also construct ground-supported structures that create metal canopies over staging. When the load that is hung overhead is limited, ground-supported trussing can span as much as 40 feet before needing an additional upright support. For smaller events that still require rock concert lighting, this may be a solid solution.

For larger events, however, 40 feet of span may be too limiting. In these scenarios two additional techniques are available. One is the use of hand-cranked lifts. The manually operated lifts are small enough to roll through a standard doorway, but when secured in place can support immense amounts of weight. These lifts can act as reverse rigging points for upstage truss lines used to hang front-projected screens or drapery.

The second solution uses lighting trees. Lighting trees are ground-supported vertical truss sticks or specialized T-shaped poles on which lighting instruments can be attached. Lighting trees are less-than-ideal solutions for live events because

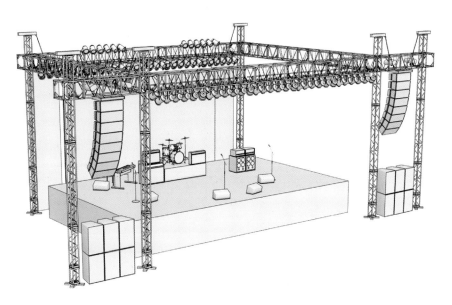

FIGURE 5.7
A ground-supported truss system, as used for an outdoor concert stage.
Designer: Todd Ethridge

FIGURE 5.8
Manually operated lifts can provide a rigging solution when hanging points are not available.
Image courtesy of Genie Industries, Inc. (www.genielift.com)

they can obstruct sight lines if not placed behind the audience. This distance from the stage requires brighter lighting instruments to be used with more concentrated and harder-to-focus lenses. In addition, lighting trees cannot safely reach the same heights as rigged trusses and result in sharp lighting angles that are not flattering to those onstage. Despite these drawbacks, when there is no other option within a given space, these solutions are adequate. They also show the importance of rigging when selecting a venue.

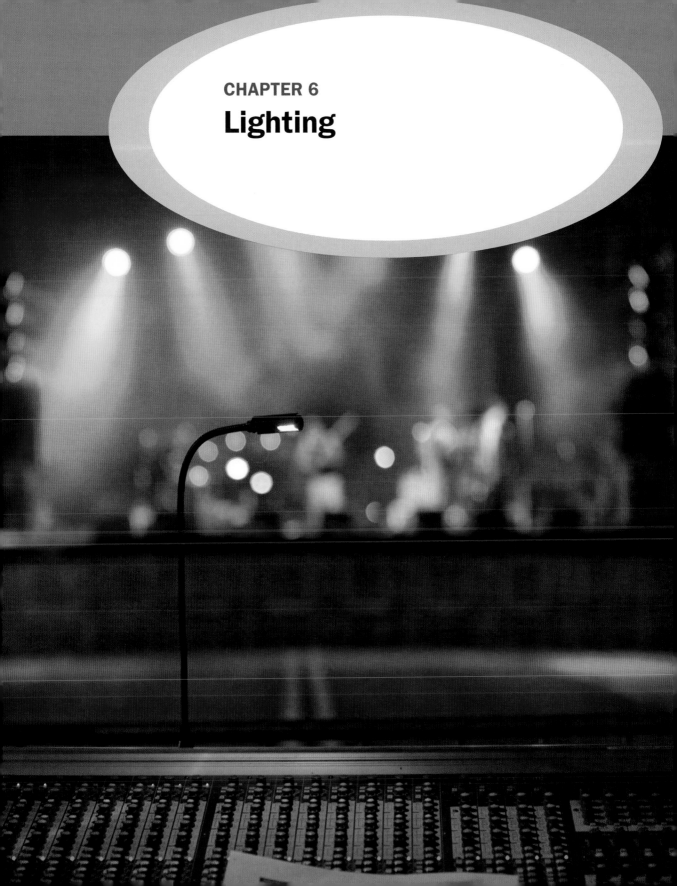

CHAPTER 6
Lighting

INTRODUCTION TO LIGHTING

Without a doubt, lighting is one of the most important aspects of a successful stage or environment design. Not to discredit the physical design side of things, but some of the best stage and environment designs are merely neutral canvases for lighting designers to perform their magic upon. It is important for designers and event planners to have a good understanding of how light can enhance a design and know the limitations of lighting technology.

A good lighting design can make a set made of cardboard and masking tape look like a palace. Conversely, bad lighting can transform the most beautiful of scenic creations into a depthless structure void of any visual interest. Lighting can either enhance a stage design by highlighting scenic elements with good lighting angles and complementary colors or remove all depth and texture by using flat lighting angles and combative colors. Lighting also has the capacity to direct the audience's view toward what is most important and can subtly effect emotions through the timing of lighting cues, color palettes, and instrument focus. Finally, a solid lighting design that is well programmed can enhance the flow or tempo of a production and amplify the attendee experience.

This chapter will address the fundamentals of lighting as used for general sessions or keynote meetings within the corporate event industry. The instruments and techniques discussed, however, can easily be translated for use throughout the event space, including lounges, entrance ways, and environment designs. It must be acknowledged, however, that lighting is a complex science, and many volumes have been written on the topics of lighting techniques for the stage, color mixing theory, and the technical aspects of light equipment. In no way can one chapter in this book explain all the mysteries of lighting.

Therefore, the explanations used in this chapter are simplified in an effort to teach the basics without delving too deeply into the sciences and theories of light. As an event designer, you would be wise to consult a professional lighting designer for determining the best way to achieve your desired look. Understanding these fundamentals, however, and their associated terminology will allow designers and event planners to communicate their vision more clearly with lighting designers and technicians and ultimately lead to an accurate realization of the intended design.

ELEMENTS OF LIGHT: AN EVENT DESIGNER'S VIEW

The function of lighting used in an environment or stage design goes far beyond simply illuminating objects and persons. It is meant to enhance physical designs, set tone and mood, as well as direct visual focus. As with all forms of design, however, to successfully use lighting as a design tool requires an understanding of its fundamental elements – or at least, an event designer's modified version of those fundamentals.

Intensity

Simply put, the *intensity* of light is its appearance of brightness and can be affected by several factors. Most obvious is the lamp, or bulb, used within the fixture and how much current is provided to the lamp. In addition, the filter color, distance between the fixture and surface, and the focus of the lighting instrument affect the apparent brightness of a light source. Intensity comes into play when determining how a light is to be used and the surface it is intended to illuminate. For example, an overly intense key light, the primary source used to light a person, will wash out a subject by removing all shadows. Scenic elements that are underlit may reduce the intended effect of texturing, producing an unimpressive and muted finish. The intensity of a light also affects the color of light emitted from the light instrument. As less current is supplied to the instrument, the tungsten filament in the lamp glows more orange instead of white, or a color close to white. This is known as *amber drift* or *amber shift*. This phenomenon becomes a nonissue, however, when using LED fixtures, which will be addressed later in the chapter.

Texture

Texture is created with lighting through the use of shapes and shadows and gives an environment depth. The *shape* of a light refers to how a light beam appears when it hits a surface creating a pool of light, whereas *shadow* describes the void of light behind an object or mass. There are several ways the shape of a light and the resulting shadow can be controlled – namely, lens focus, gobos, and source angle.

LENS FOCUS

Adjustments made within the light fixture itself, such as how close the lamp and reflector are to the lens, can affect the shape of the light beam produced. These adjustments are known as *lamp* or *lens focus,* as opposed to *instrument focus,* which describes where a light is pointed. A tight lens focus, for example, produces a light shape that has a clear and definitive edge, whereas a soft lens focus results in a diluted light shape that fades or dissipates from the center. Diffusion gels are also used to dissipate light more evenly and reduce the hotspot produced at the center of a light pool.

GOBOS

A second method of light shape control employs the use of gobos or breakup patterns. *Gobos* are thin discs, made of glass or metal, that when placed in front of a lamp in a lighting fixture, force the light through specific patterns. In essence, they are stencils for light and, when combined with other light patterns, create immense texture upon a staging environment. Gobos play a big role within lighting design for the event industry and will therefore be discussed in greater detail later in the chapter.

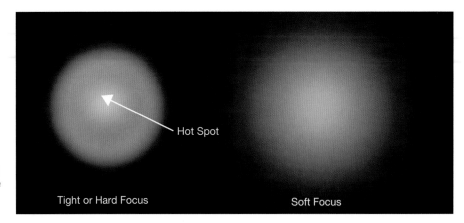

FIGURE 6.1
Many stage lights can be focused to produce a hard or soft light edge.

Hot Spot

Tight or Hard Focus

Soft Focus

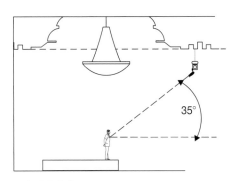

35°

FIGURE 6.2
Lighting instruments should be hung 35 degrees from their intended focus.

SOURCE ANGLE

Source angle refers to the relationship of the lighting fixture to the object being lit. The steeper the angle – meaning the light source is close to the object and hung high above – the more dramatic the effect as it creates angular shadows. A flat angle means the fixture is farther away and hung lower and focuses directly onto the surface or object being lit; this produces few shadows. Scenery benefits from steep lighting angles, and the resulting shadows add depth to the staging environment. People and performers, however, should be more evenly lit with flatter source angles to prevent unflattering shadows.

Color

Color can affect a design in so many ways it can be mind boggling. Color influences the mood of attendees, such as blues creating a calming effect, whereas bright reds and oranges induce excitement and adrenaline. It can enhance or diminish textures and depth. It can draw attention to one element or blend an entire design into one big blur. Color is a very powerful tool and made even more powerful when added to a design through lighting. In a discussion of light color, there are two primary topics: how to describe light color and how to mix or filter light color.

DESCRIBING COLOR

Describing color can be tricky because it is perceived differently by each observer. So to prevent a philosophical discussion, we will focus on *colorimetry*. Colorimetry is one of several systems developed to define color but works very well for describing the color of light. Before we delve into it, let's cover the basics. White light, as discovered by Isaac Newton and his prism, is the combination of all visible light colors. Black, on the other hand, is the absence of color and thus the absence of light altogether – because all light has some form of color, whether visible to the human eye or not. So white is all colors combined; black is the absence of colors. Dominant wavelength (DWL) or hue, brightness, and purity are the main descriptors of light color.

Dominant Wavelength or Hue

A beam or ray of light contains every wavelength contained in the color spectrum of light. The human eye can register wavelengths between 380 and 750 nanometers (nm), known as the visible or optic spectrum of light. True white light would be the combination of every light wave in equal amounts. However, such an exact distribution of energy – and light waves are energy – does not occur in nature. Thus, there are always dominant waves within a beam that determine a light's apparent color. This apparent color is often described as a *hue,* such as red, violet, blue, cyan, or green.

Brightness

The brightness of light, or intensity, in regards to color measures only the dominant wavelengths. The higher the amount of energy present in the DWL, the brighter a light will appear. Again, a hypothetical true white would appear the brightest of light beams because it combines the full energy of every light wave.

Purity

Purity of light color describes how dominant a specific wave is within a beam of light. If a light beam consists of only one DWL, say red, then the light is said to be 100 percent pure red. Consider red paint as being 100 percent pure. The more white paint that is added, representing the other waves of light color, the less pure the red becomes. A mixture of half white and half red would result in a 50 percent purity of red.

COLOR MIXING

What gets really interesting, and potentially confusing, is how color is filtered and mixed. There are two methods of affecting color, which are known as *subtractive* and *additive color mixing*. Both methods are discussed here, but again, these are simplified explanations intended to illustrate the basic concepts. If you find yourself scratching your head, don't worry; you are not alone. Just focus on the basics for now, and if you find the topic interesting, pick up a few volumes on color theory for a more in-depth study.

Subtractive

Mixing paint colors is an additive color process, one that is focused on pigments, not light. How our eyes perceive paint color is actually a subtractive process. It is subtractive because specific light waves are removed from the beam that is reflected back to our eyes. For example, when a blue object is hit with a beam of white light, all the color light waves contained in the beam pass through the surface except for the blue light waves, which are bounced back and received by the cones and rods in our eyes telling our brains the object is blue. This process is described as *reflective light color*.

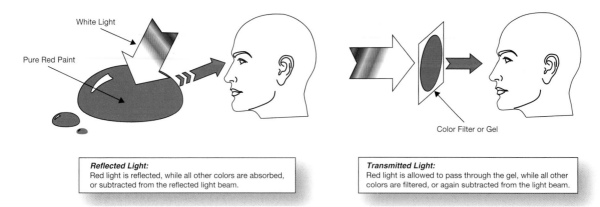

White Light

Pure Red Paint

Color Filter or Gel

Reflected Light:
Red light is reflected, while all other colors are absorbed, or subtracted from the reflected light beam.

Transmitted Light:
Red light is allowed to pass through the gel, while all other colors are filtered, or again subtracted from the light beam.

FIGURE 6.3
Subtractive color mixing removes light waves from the light beam, resulting in a perceived color.

When a colored gel or filter is placed in front of a lighting instrument, this is also a subtractive mixing process, but this time the process is known as *emitted light filtering*. A blue color filter blocks or filters all the light waves coming from a lamp except for those in the blue range. In addition, like the way our eyes perceive mixed paint, the more color filters that are added to a light instrument, the fewer light waves can pass, leading ultimately to black, or the absence of light. So subtractive color mixing removes light waves from being emitted or reflected and ends with black, or the absence of light.

Additive

Additive color mixing is what occurs when different color beams converge. What is tricky with lighting, however, is the more color you mix in, the whiter the light appears. When the primary colors of light – red, green, and blue (RGB) – are mixed in varying amounts, any color in the visible spectrum of light can be produced.

Mixing blue and red leads to magenta, while blue and green make cyan, and finally red and green produce yellow. These mixes are known as secondary colors (CMY). If you mix a secondary color with its opposite primary, like yellow and blue, you return to white light. This is where the concept of complementary colors originates. Yellow is the complementary color of blue because, when combined, they complete the light spectrum and produce white.

WHY DO I NEED TO KNOW THIS?

Aside from simply understanding the basics of color, there are two practical reasons a designer needs to understand this rhetoric. First, when a client asks for a corporate color scheme to be replicated with lighting, trouble is on the horizon. Some print colors can be replicated very closely using light, but other print colors (most notably shades of color that are produced by adding black) cannot be reproduced with light because adding black to light merely diminishes its intensity.

Second, the color palette chosen to paint scenery will be affected by light colors. In a perfectly dark room, a solid red object will appear black when hit with a solid blue beam of light. With no red waves contained in the blue beam, there is nothing to reflect back from the red object to the human eye; thus, it appears black. When a secondary color like magenta is shown onto an object, only the primary colors that make up that secondary color, red and blue, will be reflected back. For this reason, a scenic flat painted with various patterns of red, blue, and green will have an entirely different feel under various light colors. Therefore, for a truly neutral stage design, shades of gray are typically used for painting scenic elements. Although a grayscale set may not look like much under house lighting, it is the most flexible when painting an environment with light.

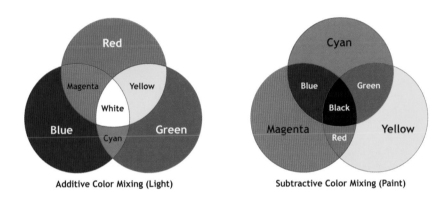

Additive Color Mixing (Light)   **Subtractive Color Mixing (Paint)**

FIGURE 6.4
A comparison of additive and subtractive color mixing.

The Effect of Filtered Light on Painted Scenic Elements

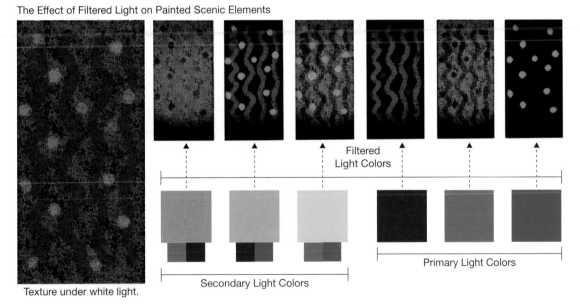

Texture under white light.

Filtered Light Colors

Secondary Light Colors

Primary Light Colors

FIGURE 6.5
A study of the way paint treatments appear under various lighting; this scenario requires ideal conditions.

Atmospherics

Atmospherics are a great way to add depth and visual interest to an environment. For a basic definition, consider *atmospherics* to be dense groups of particles floating in the air that, when illuminated, define the edges of light beams. Beating an old pillow in front a window will produce such an effect, with dust particles providing atmosphere for beams of sunlight to become visible. Perhaps a more poignant example is to shine a powerful flashlight above a campfire in which the smoke produced by the fire provides atmosphere for the beam from the flashlight to become visible. This latter example is very similar to what occurs within a stage design utilizing atmospherics, only the smoke or haze is controlled and the flashlight is replaced by a number of stage lighting fixtures.

There are two major types of atmospherics used during live events: fog and haze. Fog can be further divided into heated and chilled fogs. Heated fog produces thick billowing smoke, an ideal option for simulating fire, steam, or clouds. In addition, a dramatic stage entrance might be enhanced by the use of heated fog spilling in from backstage. Chilled or cold fog, on the other hand, which is typically chilled with dry ice or liquid nitrogen, lies close to the ground and dissipates quickly as it begins to rise. Cold fog is great for grand entrances or for creating spooky or dramatic performance spaces.

When the desire is only to amplify lighting effects, the visibility of fog is not important; haze is the way to go. Haze creates just enough density in the air so as not to be visible to the naked eye except when pierced by a strong beam of light. Haze has become the preferred choice for highlighting lighting or laser effects. Due

FIGURE 6.6
Haze and fog can be used to enhance the effects of a dramatic lighting design.
Image courtesy of Brian Alexander (www.brianalexanderphotography.com)

to its low density, it is less obtrusive on performers and audience members and, depending on the venue's ventilation, hangs in the air much longer than fog.

All atmospherics require that fire detection systems be turned off to prevent false alarms. As a result, a fire marshal must be present when atmospherics are in use. Arrange this well in advance of the event and budget for fire marshal observation. Not doing so could cost several thousands of dollars' worth of fines and potential damages produced by activated fire prevention systems.

LIGHTING EQUIPMENT

Lighting fixtures and equipment have come a long way since their early theatrical origins. Candles and bottles of colored liquid were the dominant lighting tools in theaters until the late 1700s, when kerosene lamps were introduced. In the early 1800s, lime and gas lights became commonplace and stuck around until as late as the 1920s, when they were replaced by the electric bulb. Today, the bulbs, with *lamps* being the preferred term, used in lighting fixtures are extremely advanced pieces of engineering. Conventional stage lights typically use tungsten-halogen (or quartz-halogen) lamps, and more powerful spot and robotic lights use short-arc discharge lamps. LED lamps are also a big player in the industry and quickly growing in popularity due to their low power consumption and cool temperatures. Lamps, however, are only one piece of a lighting fixture. Lamps, lenses, reflectors, and a number of moving parts work together within a lighting fixture to produce shapes and movements of light that would have been unimaginable by the forefathers of theater. Modern stage lighting fixtures can be placed in four categories: conventional, intelligent or robotic, LED, and follow spot fixtures.

FIGURE 6.7
PAR cans, Fresnels, and ellipsoidal lights are still among the most commonly used lighting instruments.

Conventional Fixtures

Conventional fixtures are nonmoving lights. They are hung and focused toward a fixed location. They generally receive one color filter, though color-changing systems can be mounted on them, and are typically used for stage washes and to light stationary scenic elements. Although on the surface they are more cost effective than robotic fixtures, they are less versatile and can be more labor intensive to install and maintain during a production. Conventional fixtures can be further divided into wash and spot fixtures.

Wash fixtures are intended to illuminate large areas of a performance space but have a limited ability to control what surfaces or objects are affected by the light beam produced. A parabolic aluminized reflector, or PAR, and Fresnel, so named for its Fresnel step lens, are among the most common wash instruments used in modern lighting designs.

Spot fixtures are much more controllable light instruments, allowing for sharp or soft edges of light. In addition, they contain shutters that allow the light beam to be cut or blocked to prevent the light emitted from spilling onto scenery not intended to be lit by the fixture. The ellipsoidal reflector spotlight, commonly referred to as an ERS or leko, is the most popular conventional spotlight instrument. It derives its name from an ellipsoidal or half-domed reflector contained within the instrument's body that, when combined with a lens, focuses and intensifies the light produced. Various lenses are available for lekos that affect width of the light beam produced. Gobos can be used with leko lights, and due to their focusable lens, the gobo pattern projected can have sharp or soft edges.

Intelligent and Robotic Fixtures

Intelligent lights, also known as robotic fixtures or movers, can alter many aspects of their output with little more than the touch of a button. They are more expensive than conventional fixtures but can reduce the number of lighting instruments needed for a production and require less time to install and focus, as focusing can be done from the lighting operator's board rather than manually.

FIGURE 6.8
Moving lights or robotic fixtures allow for more freedom and dynamics in lighting design.
Image courtesy of Brian Alexander
(www.brianalexanderphotography.com)

There are two major types of intelligent lights: moving mirror fixtures and moving yoke fixtures. Both have their merits; however, the moving yoke variety is much more prevalent in modern events. The main benefit of the moving mirror fixture is that the light beams can get from point A to point B much faster because all that needs to move is a little lightweight mirror.

Moving yoke fixtures, on the other hand, consist of a rotating head supported by a yoke that, in turn, rotates on a fixed base. This configuration allows moving yoke fixtures to hit nearly any spot within an event space. The Martin Mac 2000 Performance II and VARI*LITE VL3500 Spot are among the more popular moving yoke instruments available.

Both moving mirror and moving yoke fixtures offer color mixing capabilities as well as rotating gobo wheels, shutters, and even zoom lenses, allowing for a diverse selection of light shapes and textures. The capabilities offered by these lights, especially moving yoke fixtures, have made them very popular for use in music concerts and award shows, both live and televised. Although moving mirror fixtures have fewer moving parts than moving yoke fixtures, it is a best practice not to rig either robotic or moving fixtures from the same truss used for hanging projectors because the vibrations produced by fixture movements can cause a projected video image to shake.

LED Fixtures

The future of stage lighting, and even video displays, is in LED technology. LEDs, or light emitting diodes, are solid state lamps that deliver a bluish white light and generally have color-changing capabilities. Remember additive color mixing? Color-changing LED lamps consist of three groups of smaller diodes, with either an RGB or CMY configuration, that are mixed in various intensities to produce a desired color, which is an additive color mixing process. This color-changing capability put together with their narrow light beams make LED fixtures ideal for uplighting drapery, scenic flats, and cycloramas.

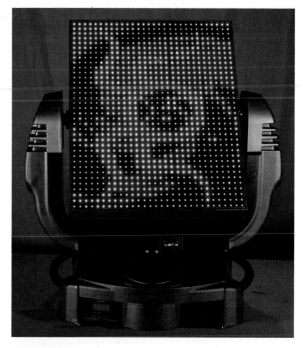

LED lamps also require less power than conventional stage lights and emit significantly less heat. This low heat output makes LED fixtures the preferred choice for any situation where the audience or attendees have to be in close proximity to the lights, such as in entryways, lounges, exhibit booths, or along the perimeter of a meeting space. In addition, LED light sources can be used safely to internally light tension fabric shapes or translucent podiums and scenic elements without the fear of igniting the materials due to extreme heat as would be produced by conventional stage lights.

LED fixtures come in a wide variety of shapes and sizes. Among the more popular products available are the 72-inch and 48-inch Philips Colorblaze, ideal for uplighting soft goods, and the Chroma-Q Color Block 2, perfect for internally lighting smaller scenic elements, columns, and trussing.

FIGURE 6.9
An advanced moving LED light instrument.
Image courtesy of Mainlight (www.mainlight.com)

Follow Spots

Follow spots are manually controlled moving lights that swivel and tilt on a base and are typically positioned in the back of the house on platforms or above the audience in a catwalk. Of all modern stage lights, follow spots seem to have been left in the dark ages. The few features they offer, such as built-in color gels, gobo slots, lens focus, and iris control are all adjusted manually by the operator. As a presenter or performer moves across the stage, the operator pans and tilts the light accordingly. These simple fixtures are handy for giving an event a nostalgic or elegant awards feel or can be used as dramatic lighting sources for a dark stage.

Although manual follow spots are still used in live events today, they are quickly being replaced by robotic lighting fixtures that can be controlled with a remote joystick or lighting console touchpad. In the near future, they may become entirely obsolete as infrared tracking systems become commonplace in robotic lighting fixtures. For now, however, be prepared to have a few extra crew members on-site when follow spots are needed.

GOBOS

Gobos, also known as *templates* or *break-up patterns*, are cost-effective lighting accessories and great for adding texture, depth, and branding to an environment design. Gobos come in specific sizes correlating with the type of light fixture to be used, and range from 1.5 to nearly 4 inches in diameter. In some cases the size of a gobo determines the level of detail possible for a specific pattern or shape, especially when dealing with metal gobos. The fundamental difference between metal and glass gobos, other than price because glass gobos are considerably more expensive, is metal gobos are created by cutting the image

FIGURE 6.10
Follow spots, although simple, still have their uses in modern events.

FIGURE 6.11
Glass gobos can attain much greater detail than metal gobos, which are essentially stencils.

into metal, whereas glass gobos are created by printing the image onto glass. If you have an intricate image or several words or lines of text, it can be difficult for gobo manufacturers to cut such detail into a tiny metal disk. Glass gobos, on the other hand, can include significantly more detail and color options.

Metal Gobos

The sole advantage of a metal gobo is price. Custom metal gobos are significantly cheaper than glass gobos and can typically be ordered for under $75. Beyond price, the appeal of metal gobos quickly diminishes. Due to the high heat they endure, metal gobos have a tendency to warp, which distorts the pattern they produce. Patterns with fine details or discs that have more cutouts than metal are frequently ruined when removed from fixtures due to warping and a weakening of the metal due to heat. Thus, metal gobos are not ideal for repeated use, so it is a good idea to purchase duplicates of custom patterns.

Furthermore, the artwork and patterns used for metal gobos must be interconnecting like a stencil. This is especially important when dealing with text. Letters and numbers with closed characters like *D*, *e*, and 8 have to be altered so the negative space remains connected to the pattern. Images also need to be altered to address the same issue. These alterations may become an issue when dealing with branded artwork and corporate logos. If your design budget is limited and you are required to use metal gobos, ensure that the client or executive producer is aware of the alterations before ordering your custom gobos. Otherwise, plan on investing in glass gobos.

Glass Gobos

Glass gobos range in cost from $150 to $500, but with the added cost comes a number of benefits. For one, because glass gobos are printed rather than cut, there is no need to alter letters and images. The artwork you create or that is provided by the client can be printed in its original state. Second, because there is no metal to be warped or small cutouts to be bent or broken, glass gobos have a much longer lifespan. Finally, multiple colors can be included in a glass gobo, allowing for a variety of possibilities in design.

When ordering glass gobos, you need to determine if the image or pattern printed will be black-and-white, two-color, or multicolor because these options determine pricing. In addition, you must decide which direction the projected image will come from, meaning front or rear projection. Just like video projection, rear-projected gobos must be mirrored to appear correct when seen on the reverse side of translucent materials. This is important because glass gobos have a protective heat shield coating on one side, dictating how the gobo will be inserted into the fixture and preventing the gobo from being flipped; doing so would shatter the glass when heated by the fixture's lamp.

THREE-POINT LIGHTING: A BASIC LIGHTING TECHNIQUE

There are several schools of thinking in regards to lighting design for events. Furthermore, every lighting designer has his own spin on standard techniques. The reason for this lack of uniform approach is due in part to event lighting designs having to accommodate for both live audiences and video cameras. While designers and specialists may debate the best color filters, fixtures, and equipment for addressing both mediums, common ground can be found in how the light fixtures are positioned. Lighting configurations for both stage and video utilize a three-point lighting system.

FIGURE 6.12
A version of the three-point lighting technique.

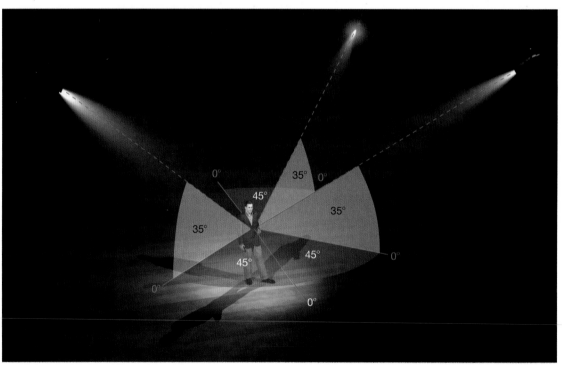

In a three-point lighting system, objects and people are illuminated with three primary light sources: a key light, fill or soft light, and back light. The key light provides the most intense lighting and is meant to simply make an object visible to the audience or camera. When placed at a 45-degree angle to one side (and 45 degrees above the subject), a key light will define the edges and surface features of an object or person by creating highlights and shadows. To soften these shadows, a less intense fill light is added from the opposite side, also at a 45-degree angle. Lastly, to separate the object from the background, a back light is added behind the object, again at a 45-degree angle. Hanging these lights at eye level, however, would produce unflattering shadows and strong reflections, let alone blind the performers and presenters. Instead, lighting fixtures are hung from above at an ideal angle of 35 degrees from the object or person being lit. So now you have one element lit, what's next?

First, we need to back up a bit and determine what parts of the stage need to be addressed with lighting. More often than not, there will be one or two podiums, a head table, a general performance space, and scenic elements that must be included in a stage lighting design. To begin a design, each podium and head table, and really each seat behind the head table, should be lit individually using the three-point system described previously.

Next, the general performance space needs to be divided into areas, such as downstage right and upstage left, with each area being lit using the same three-point system. When the general performance space is broken into areas, lighting can be applied to only the parts of the stage that are being utilized. If a speaker walks to the right side of the stage, the rest of the stage can be dimmed,

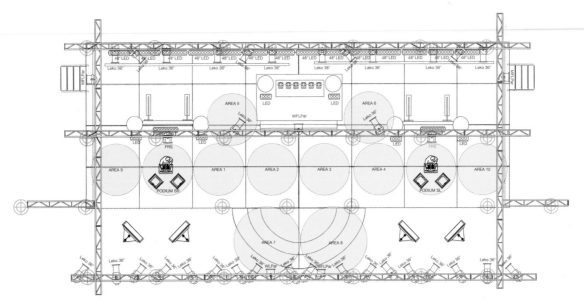

FIGURE 6.13
A basic lighting plot.

drawing the audience's focus to the presenter. Alternately, the entire stage can be illuminated evenly, with all lighting areas being used, to accommodate for a large number of individuals onstage such as a group of award recipients.

Finally, the scenery must be addressed. Although a three-point system can be applied to most scenic elements, the general practice is to use whatever approach looks best for the unique elements of a particular scenic design. Soft goods, for example, benefit the most from a general wash of lights with break-up patterns and gobos being projected from sharp angles. Textured flats and dimensional pieces should also be lit using dramatic angles to accentuate their surface detail and depth. Columns and drapery need little more than uplighting, whereas tension fabric shapes may require a number of lights to capture the unique shape and detail of the material. Working with a lighting designer, you can develop the best solution for your vision and budget.

SO ... IS THAT ALL THERE IS TO LIGHTING?

By no means does this chapter cover all aspects of lighting; in fact, we have only scratched the surface. Fortunately, as a scenic or environment designer, you do not need to delve too deeply into lighting plots and power distribution at this stage of the game. Instead, focus on the design elements of lighting addressed in this chapter and work with a lighting designer and his team of specialists to determine how best to achieve a desired look, and they will handle the rest. That approach may seem like a cop-out, but like rigging, the technical side of lighting can be very dangerous if not executed by trained lighting professionals and electricians. Thus, falling in line with a common theme of this book, rely on industry specialists for ensuring safe installations and use of professional lighting equipment.

Building on this point, make an effort in your career to work with as many different lighting designers as possible and take note of their advice and guidance. Every production you attend will have a unique look and innovative lighting solutions that can be truly inspiring. Furthermore, as technologies begin to blend, such as lighting and video projection, new approaches to event lighting design will develop, and as a designer, you will want to be on the forefront of this evolution.

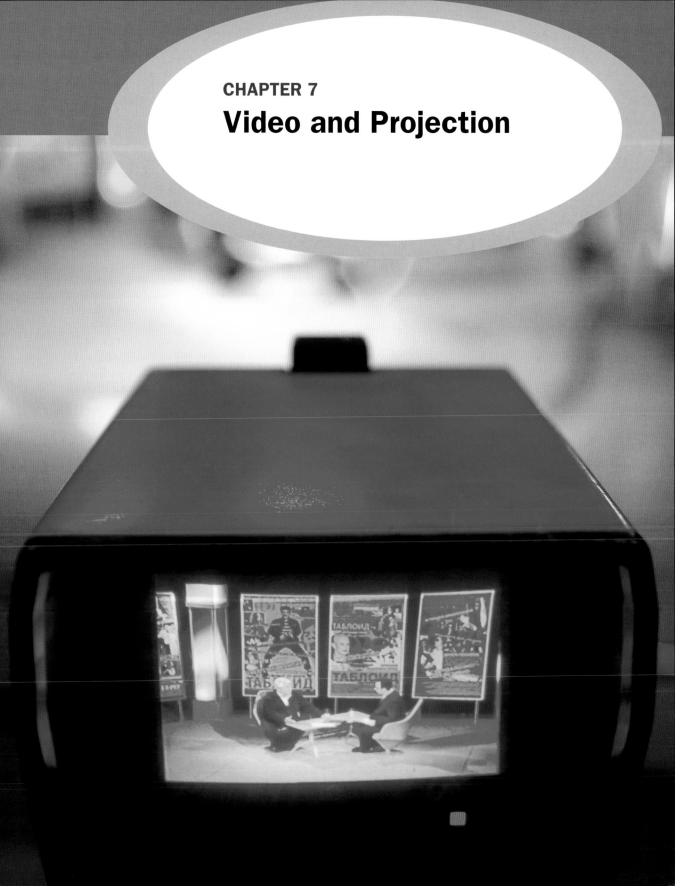

CHAPTER 7
Video and Projection

INTRODUCTION TO VIDEO

In recent years, video has become synonymous with corporate events, and it is safe to say you can no longer attend an event, conference, or seminar without seeing a video screen of some form, whether it is a registration kiosk, digital sign, interactive touch screen display, or of course, projection screens used in a meeting space. Video is used to communicate direction, deliver messages, and provide visual impact. In addition, video serves a practical function of magnifying and documenting events that occur onstage and around the event locale. It is an unavoidable and invaluable piece of the event experience. This chapter will walk you through the relevant basics of video and projection, give an overview of how video cameras and controls are used during an event, and introduce common video elements developed for corporate events.

As an event designer or planner, you will work with video specialists and producers to determine the best technology solutions and approaches for your event budget and objectives. Such collaborations free designers and event planners from needing to understand every nut and bolt of video technology, and instead focus on how to *use* video within an event design. Using the language you will learn in this chapter, you will be able to effectively communicate with the specialists to transform your creative vision into reality.

VIDEO BASICS

Before we look at how video is used or displayed, we need to examine a few relevant basics: namely, the difference between digital and analog video, aspect ratios and resolutions, frame rates and standards, and what is meant by video compression. These basic concepts provide a foundation for understanding more advanced concepts such as high-definition (HD) video, projection blending, and content creation.

Digital vs. Analog

Most videos today are created digitally, but what does that mean exactly? To explain this, we must accept one concept: video signals travel in electrical or electromagnetic waves much like radio. Analog video signals look like the scribbling

FIGURE 7.1
An exaggerated comparison between digital and analog video signals.

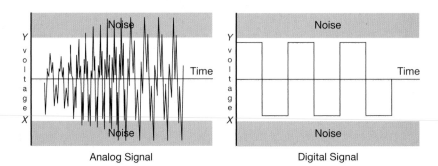

of a child, containing extreme peaks and valleys. These extremes make analog video susceptible to interference or noise, like static on the radio.

Digital signals, on the other hand, have very uniform signal wave patterns in comparison because they use binary code or sequences of 1s or 0s to relay data. So a digital signal is either high or low, on or off, 1 or 0. This simplicity allows for less interference in the signal. Even when small amounts of interference are present, the receiver can still determine if the signal was meant to be a 1 or 0. In addition, binary code can be compressed, which will be covered in a bit, allowing for a greater amount of information to be stored on tape than possible with analog signals. Finally, because computers also use binary code, transferring digital video from a camera or digital tape to a desktop machine for editing is as easy as plugging in a single cable. For these reasons, the reign of digital video has begun, and analog video is slowly being swept under the rug.

Frame Rates and Standards

Frame rates describe how many still images are contained in a video clip per second. This is the core concept of video and film, and the illusion of movement in video or film is possible because of the way our minds work. Our minds like order and try to make sense of the things we see by making assumptions or filling in missing information. So when we watch a video that has 30 images or frames per second (fps), our brains blur the images together as one continuous sequence, resulting in a moving picture.

It takes only 15–18 fps for our brains to perceive smooth movement; anything less and the image begins to look jumpy. Films, the kind you pay to see at a theater, are generally shot at 24 fps, whereas television and video in the United States is 30 fps (29.97 fps to be exact). Video in the United States is roughly 30 fps due to the fact that most power grids transmit AC power at 60 hertz. When broadcast television was first developed, a reliable timing source was needed to sync broadcasted video signals with television receivers. Without getting too heavily into how a traditional TV works, the picture is formed by two interlaced passes across the screen, and just like frame rates, these passes are blurred by our minds to make a complete picture or frame.

Frame Rate (Example of 30 fps)

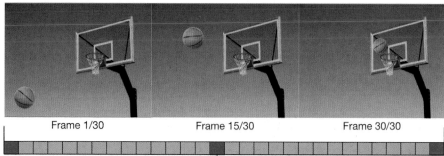

Frame 1/30   Frame 15/30   Frame 30/30

1 Second

FIGURE 7.2
Multiple frames are shown per second to give video the illusion of movement; this is known as the *frame rate*.

By using the beat of the 60 hertz power for the image passes, with two passes per frame, 30 fps became standard in the United States and labeled the *NTSC standard*. The National Television Standards Committee standard describes more than just frame rate; it also tells broadcasters what resolution and bandwidths to send their signals out at for televisions to properly display the received video images. The standard was later reduced to 29.97 fps when color was added to prevent audio interference during broadcast. Because power in most of Europe is transmitted at 50 hertz, 25 fps became the *Phase Alternating Line (PAL) standard*.

Due to their differences in frame rates and resolution, among other differences, the two standards are not compatible with each other. This was a major nuisance when dealing with overseas footage delivered on videotape using the PAL standard because the footage had to be converted and transferred to playback on NTSC production equipment. And even though these standards were developed for analog video systems, they affect digital video and DVD encoding because most television sets and video equipment are still built for specific broadcast standards; a PAL DVD will not play in an NTSC player unless it is designed to play both standards. Thus, standard conversions may still come up on occasion, and clients should be made aware of this when working with footage from around the globe.

As digital video formats evolve, however, these analog standards will become less and less important. Even today, most professional-grade video editing systems

Common Video/Screen Resolutions

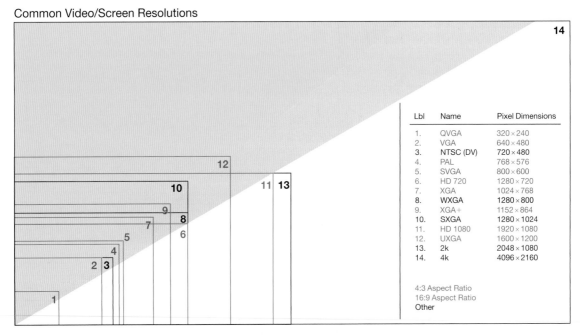

Lbl	Name	Pixel Dimensions
1.	QVGA	320 × 240
2.	VGA	640 × 480
3.	NTSC (DV)	720 × 480
4.	PAL	768 × 576
5.	SVGA	800 × 600
6.	HD 720	1280 × 720
7.	XGA	1024 × 768
8.	WXGA	1280 × 800
9.	XGA+	1152 × 864
10.	SXGA	1280 × 1024
11.	HD 1080	1920 × 1080
12.	UXGA	1600 × 1200
13.	2k	2048 × 1080
14.	4k	4096 × 2160

4:3 Aspect Ratio
16:9 Aspect Ratio
Other

FIGURE 7.3
Common video resolutions and their associated names.

can import and export any form of digital video. As multisystem digital displays, universal video encoders, and region-free Blu-ray Discs become more prevalent, such issues as incompatible video standards may entirely disappear. Until then, be prepared to work with your AV provider to ensure the correct video formats are used for your production.

Aspect Ratios and Resolution

The aspect ratio of a screen describes its width versus its height. Traditional televisions, the kind your parents grew up with, have a 4:3 aspect ratio, meaning the screen is 4 units wide by 3 units high. HD televisions and other newer televisions have a 16:9 aspect ratio – 16 units wide by 9 units high. A common mistake made by newcomers to the industry is to interchange the phrases *16:9 aspect ratio* and *HD video*.

High-definition, or HD, video is called such because of its image resolution. Let's take a side course here for a moment and review what *resolution* means. To keep the discussion simple, we can say all digital images are composed of millions of tiny dots, known as *pixels*. These pixels are composed of three even smaller dots or subpixels – red, green, and blue subpixels to be exact. The brightness and mixture of these three subpixels determine the color of the pixel they make up. To make an image out of pixels, you would line all of them up into a grid. For a standard resolution video image, you would need 720 pixels across and 480 pixels down; HD video, which comes in two common sizes, is composed of either 1920 or 1280 pixels wide by 1080 or 720 pixels high. There are lots of other discussion points when it comes to resolution and high-definition video, but the basics are all you need at this stage in the game.

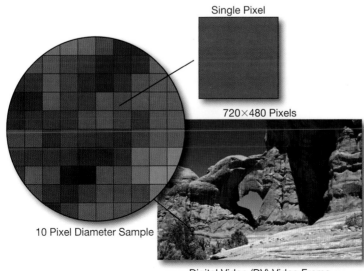

Single Pixel

720×480 Pixels

10 Pixel Diameter Sample

Digital Video (DV) Video Frame

FIGURE 7.4
Multiple pixels are aligned to make one complete image. The number of pixels used is referred to as *resolution*.

Now that we have had a refresher on resolution, it should make more sense when we say just because an image is 16:9 aspect ratio doesn't mean it is high definition. It is not uncommon for standard videos (that is 720×480) to be cropped into a 16:9 aspect ratio. This actually results in even fewer pixels than standard video!

Not all video is limited to specific pixel dimensions, though. HD and standard video resolutions are merely the most common pixel dimensions used by video recorders and players. Videos of any size can be created using graphics and cleverly cropped video sources layered on top of one another like a photo collage. These types of videos are called *compositions* and are becoming commonplace in the event industry. With the development of panoramic projection (the practice of blending multiple video projectors to create one seamless image), pixel dimensions can range as far as the imagination.

Digital Video Compression and File Types

Video compression takes advantage of the fact that there is a lot of repeated or unnecessary information in video images. When this redundant information is compressed or removed, a larger amount of video can fit on a storage device such as a DVD or computer hard drive. There are two approaches to video compression: *intraframe* and *interframe* compression.

Intraframe compression addresses each individual frame of a video clip by looking for common groups of pixel colors. If most of the upper-right corner of an image is blue, the file removes the individual pixel information for that part of the image and replaces it with a collective description, reducing the number of 1s and 0s needed to be written into the file. This is identical to the way still image compression formats like JPEG or PNG work to reduce an image file size. The DV format, used by Sony, JVC, and Panasonic, uses intraframe compression. This compression typically yields better-quality images but requires a larger amount of storage space.

Intraframe Compression

Original Video Image | Intraframe Compressed Image

FIGURE 7.5
Intraframe compression looks for similar pixels within a single frame.

Interframe Compression

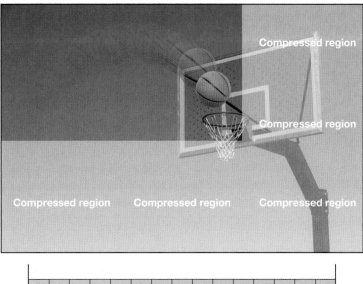

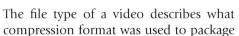

15 Frames

FIGURE 7.6
Interframe compression compares several frames looking for common color groups.

Interframe compression, on the other hand, compares frames and looks for changes in the collective image sequence. If the upper-right corner remains blue for the entire length of a video clip, the information is combined, similar to intraframe compression, until that area of the video sequence changes. The MPEG-2 compression format, or codec, which is used by DVDs and digital television broadcasts, uses interframe compression and allows for a greater compression ratio than intraframe systems. Quick movements in video can cause problems for interframe compression, however, resulting in the occasional appearance of image artifacts or jagged edges.

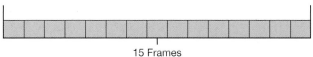

FIGURE 7.7
Overcompressing video can result in heavily damaged and unusable footage.

The file type of a video describes what compression format was used to package the video, so that it can be uncompressed and viewed through a video player, whether on a computer, iPod, or DVD player. Most people are becoming familiar with these concepts due to the widespread use of the MP3 audio compression format with portable music players like the iPod. As with all forms of image compression, you have to find the right balance between image quality and file size. The smaller the file size, the more artifacts and distortion will be present in a video sequence – hence, the advent of so many compression methods, each one striving to do a better job of balancing quality over file size. While MPEG-2 has been the most popular codec for years, the new H.264 codec used by Blu-ray and YouTube is considered by most to be the latest and greatest.

When collecting digital video files from clients, be sure to work with your video specialists to determine what file types are needed for a production. Fortunately, most file types can quickly be converted as needed with a few clicks of a mouse.

PROJECTION

Projection allows for larger-than-life images to be displayed within a meeting space. While video monitors have size limitations, projected images are limited only by the brightness of a projector and the available throw distance in a given meeting space. As an event planner, you need to understand the core difference between types of projectors and how to estimate placement and projection direction. These concepts can dramatically affect an event design and, if not understood, unachievable designs may be shown and sold to clients – a sure way to lose their business. If you get lost in the specifics or details, not to worry; that is why you have a video specialist and AV provider as part of your design team. For now, focus on the general concepts as they apply to event design, and the rest will fall into place as you put your new knowledge to use.

Projector Types

Today, there are two primary projection technologies: LCD and Texas Instruments' DLP. Both technologies produce similar results but get there in different ways. Their differences may be subtle for home and office use, but in larger event environments when projection screens exceed 10 feet in width, these differences become more pronounced. Understanding the basics of both technologies will help you determine which projection system is right for your event.

LCD projectors consist of three liquid crystal display panels, one each for red, green, and blue. Light from the projection lamp is split using a prism and shown through the LCD panels, and then converged and projected as one image. This approach provides excellent color saturation and brightness. LCD projectors tend to produce a sharper image due in part to their low fill factor. *Fill factor* describes how close together pixels are to one another, and by having this small amount of space between pixels, a sharper image can be created. This makes LCD projectors ideal for displaying detailed computer graphics such as PowerPoint or Keynote presentations.

LCD projectors are more affordable than Digital Light Processing, or DLP, projectors but are not designed for use in large event productions due to their limited rigging capabilities and technical limitations for brightness. If your

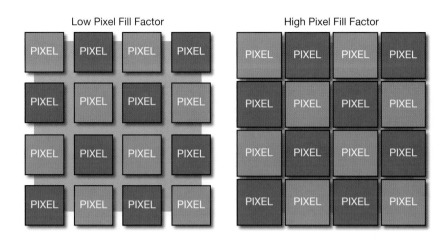

Low Pixel Fill Factor

High Pixel Fill Factor

FIGURE 7.8
LCD projectors tend to use a low fill factor, whereas DLP typically has a higher fill factor.

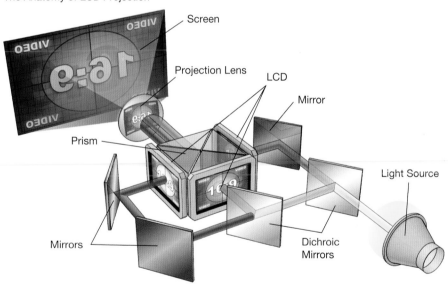

The Anatomy of LCD Projection

Screen

Projection Lens

LCD

Mirror

Prism

Light Source

Mirrors

Dichroic Mirrors

FIGURE 7.9
A simplified explanation of how an LCD projector works.

budget cannot afford a DLP projector, choose the brightest LCD projector available through your AV provider; as of this writing, the Christie LX1500 projector is the brightest of LCD projectors, topping out at 15k lumens.

Large DLP projectors consist of three DLP chips. DLP chips are composed of over a million tiny mirrors, each mirror acting as a pixel. These mirrors either tilt toward or away from the light source, thousands of times a second, with the tilt determining the brightness of a particular pixel. The reflected light from each chip then converges to make one projected image, like an LCD projector.

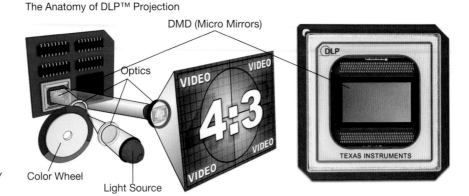

The Anatomy of DLP™ Projection

FIGURE 7.10
A simplified explanation of how a single chip DLP projector works.
Product image courtesy of Texas Instruments

DLP has a very high fill factor and provides higher contrast than LCD systems, meaning deeper blacks and brighter whites. These traits make DLP the preferred choice for moving images such as I-Mag (Image Maginification) and produced video elements. Many movie theaters are also transitioning to DLP projection systems. Such technology isn't cheap, and DLP projectors tend to be significantly more expensive to rent than LCD products. When image quality matters, however, DLP is the way to go.

So what does all this mean? In short, stick with LCD projectors for smaller meeting spaces that will primarily be using projection for presentation materials such as PowerPoint and Keynote. For general sessions that will utilize I-Mag and preproduced video modules, spend the money on a DLP projection system.

Brightness and Redundancy

In regards to choosing the right projector based on brightness, there is a simple rule of thumb to follow. Ideally, you want at least 20 lumens per square foot of screen, lumens being the measure of brightness. So a 12' × 16' screen, which is 192 square feet of projection surface, would require a 3,840 lumen projector. In this case, you might select the Barco RLM R6+ Performer, which provides 6,000 lumens of brightness. Obviously, a larger screen would require a brighter and more robust projector, but the formula is always the same – at least 20 lumens per square foot of screen.

A common practice is to stack two video projectors, one on top of the other, and then converge their images, meaning to shift their lenses so the projected images overlap exactly. This is known as *projection redundancy* and provides a backup image in the event a projector bulb bursts or a connection is lost. So if you are using two projectors on the same screen, wouldn't that screen be twice as bright? Yes, if a single projector gives you 20 lumens per square foot, adding a second projector would indeed make the projected image 40 lumens in brightness. What is interesting, however, is the image will appear only 25 percent brighter. The reason is that our eyes have a limited range for detecting changes in light intensity. If one projector does goes out when redundancy is used, the audience

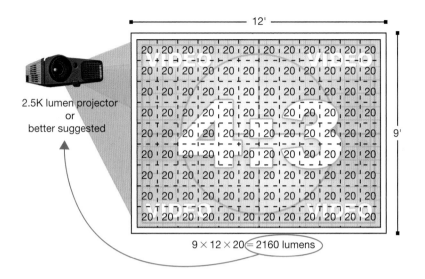

FIGURE 7.11
For ideal brightness,
20 lumens are needed
per square foot of
screen.

FIGURE 7.12
Double or triple stacking projectors prevents a total image loss in the event a bulb burns out.
Image courtesy of Brian Alexander (www.brianalexanderphotography.com)

will notice only a slight dimming of the screen rather than seeing the screen as half as bright. Redundancy is highly advised when your budget can afford it, and adapting Murphy's Law we can say, if you don't have a backup projector, the one you do have will certainly go out.

Lenses and Projection Distances

Projector lenses work just like still camera lenses, only in reverse. Whereas a camera lens uses layers of curved glass to capture light, projectors use these same layers of glass or lenses to control the light beam of a projected image. Zoom lenses consist of additional layers of glass that can shift forward or backward to increase the width of a light beam while maintaining focus.

Projector zoom lenses can range between 0.8 and 8.0 by throw ratios. The numbers are used to define the amount of distance needed between the lens and projection surface based on a screen's width, to produce a focused image. The basic formula is lens ratio times screen width equals projection distance. So a 10-foot-wide screen, using a 0.8 lens would require 8 feet of distance, while an 8.0 lens would require 80 feet of distance.

On a side note, due to the nature of optics, the lower the projection ratio, the more warped the projected image will appear. A 0.8 lens will begin to round the edges of an image, creating an effect known as *fish eye*, a generally undesirable look for projected video. When possible, choose a projection lens that has a ratio between 1.5 and 3 to ensure a proper image shape.

FIGURE 7.13
For a ballpark figure, multiply the screen's width by 1.5 to determine the throw distance required.

Creating one zoom lens that could span this entire range would be nearly impossible due to the amount of glass needed within the lens. In addition, the more glass a lens contains, the less light is able to pass through at full intensity. As a compromise, manufacturers break up this range into several different zoom lenses. To determine what size lens is needed, or the amount of throw distance required, use the following equation:

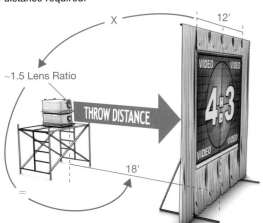

$$\frac{\text{Distance of Throw}}{\text{Lens Ratio} \times \text{Width of Screen}}$$

Simply cover the piece you are trying to find and solve the remaining problem. So for the throw distance, multiply the lens ratio by the width of the screen. To find the lens ratio, divide the throw distance by the width of the screen, and so on. We must point out, however, that this formula was developed for 4:3 aspect ratio screens. Things get a bit trickier when dealing with widescreen or panoramic aspect ratios.

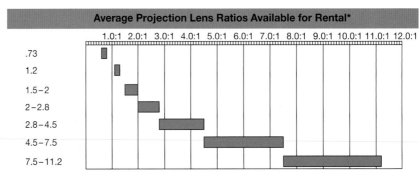

FIGURE 7.14
Common projector zoom lenses available for rental.

*Note: Lens options will vary by brand and model.

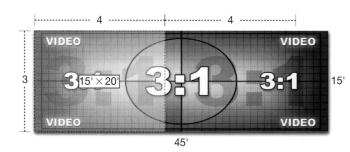

FIGURE 7.15
To determine the throw distance needed for widescreen projections, you must determine the 4:3 equivalent.

To solve this dilemma, you need to find the 4:3 equivalent for the wider screen. Unfortunately, this requires a bit of math once again. Suppose you have a screen 36-foot wide by 12-foot high, and you need to find the equivalent 4:3 size to determine the optimal zoom lens. For this, find the value of X in the following formula:

$$\frac{4}{3} \times \frac{X}{12} = X = 16' \text{ of Screen Width}$$

So we would then use 16 feet as our 4:3 equivalent screen width for determining throw distance or projection lens ratio. This number also helps us determine how many projectors we need to fill the screen. For example, if we divide 36 feet by 16, we get 2.25, so we would need three projectors to make the panoramic image, with the overlap of projectors being blended to make one image. This gets into image blending, which will be addressed later.

Note that several new HD projector models have 16:9 aspect ratios natively, which means the original equation – width times lens ratio yields the approximate throw distance – is no longer valid. To calculate the throw distance required by a given lens for 16:9 aspect ratio projectors, use the following formula:

Screen Height × Lens Ratio × 1.78 (decimal value of 16:9) = Throw Distance

For example, let's assume we are using a 9' × 16' wide screen. Using an HD projector, with a native 16:9 aspect ratio, mounted with a 1.6 lens, would require roughly 26 feet for projection distance or

$$9 \times 1.6 \times 1.78 = 25.632' \text{ of throw distance}$$

As always, defer to the expertise of your AV provider for the exact throw distances required, but these formulas will get you close enough to determine if rear projection is possible, allowing for greater freedom in your scenic and stage designs.

Direction of Projection

The direction of video projection, meaning front or rear, boils down to how much space is available for staging and production after the room has been filled with chairs. Rear projection is always preferred. When the video projectors are placed behind the screen, speakers and presenters can walk directly in front of the screen without being lit by the projected image or casting a shadow on the screen. For these reasons, rear projection allows larger screens to be used. Furthermore, rear projection allows technicians to access the backstage projectors, in the event of a technical issue, without distracting the audience.

Front-projected screens, on the other hand, must be hung above presenters' and speakers' heads, reducing potential screen heights by at least 6 feet. Projectors used in this setup must be rigged over the audience, limiting access by technicians during meetings and increasing load-in time and costs. Thus, front projection is used only when absolutely necessary – which, unfortunately, is often.

In the previous section, lens throw distances were discussed. These distances directly affect whether or not a projected image will be front or rear. If a 16-foot-wide screen is to be used, you know you will need at least 25 feet of distance for projection throw using a 1.6 lens. If you do not have 25 feet of backstage space available, then front projection will be required. Your AV provider will be able to provide additional solutions in some scenarios, but the physics of light and objects cannot be changed. If you have limited space backstage, plan on front projection and using smaller screens hung above the stage.

Projection Screens

Projection screens provide optimized surfaces for projected images to be displayed. Although they may seem like little more than sheets of vinyl or plastic, there is actually an impressive amount of engineering that goes into their construction. As a designer or event planner, however, you can rely on your AV provider for selecting the best type of screen for your event. What you do need to know is what sizes and shapes of screens are generally available for rental and where to put them.

FIGURE 7.16
The three most common aspect ratios used in the event industry.

CHOOSING A SCREEN SIZE AND ASPECT RATIO

Although projection screens come in several shapes and sizes, most rental video screens are rectangular and use one of three aspect ratios: 4:3, 16:9, and 3:1. Both 4:3 and 16:9 aspect ratios can generally be filled with a single projector, whereas larger 3:1 ratio screens typically require multiple projectors and blending technology – read as "they cost more money." Work with your client to determine what aspect ratio should be used during the event. If the meeting consists mostly of I-Mag and PowerPoint slides, then 4:3 screens are probably sufficient. If a good chunk of the video content is high definition, then 16:9 screens should be used. If the client wants to wow the audience with an impressive display of technology, opt for the 3:1 and wider aspect ratios. You can even mix aspect ratios, which requires a bit more equipment and money but creates a very dynamic visual design.

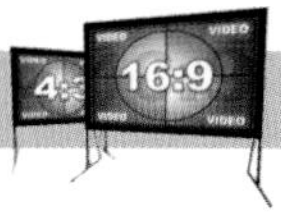

Common screen sizes available for rental*		
4:3 Aspect ratio	**16:9 Aspect ratio**	**3:1 Aspect ratio**
6' × 8'	7'6" × 13'4"	10' × 30'
7'6" × 10'	9' × 16'	12' × 36' **
9' × 12'	10'6" × 18'8"	15' × 45' **
10'6" × 14'	11'3" × 20'	20' × 60' **
12' × 16'	13'6" × 24'	25' × 75' **
15' × 20'	15' × 26'6"	
18' × 24'	20' × 35'6" **	
	28' × 50' **	
	40' × 70' **	

*Note: Available sizes will vary by rental vendor.
** Requires a truss surround.

FIGURE 7.17
Common screen sizes available for rental.

When it comes to screen size, bigger is better. Some will disagree with this method, stating that a screen that is too large for a particular room will make the viewers uncomfortable. This is true for home theater systems, but not when dealing with an audience of thousands who range from 40 to 200 feet from the performance space. So we will stick with the largest screen possible for this overview. Let's begin by determining the maximum screen height possible.

Looking at a side elevation of the room, determine the usable height of the meeting space, meaning the highest point before obstructions are present, such as soffits and chandeliers. For example, say you have a ceiling height of 24 feet with 3-foot chandeliers, then the usable height or trim height is 21 feet. Now subtract 6 more feet, accommodating for the height of a sitting person, which is roughly 4 feet, and space needed for rigging, around 2 feet. We now have 15 feet remaining, which is our maximum potential screen height.

Trim Height − 6' = Maximum Potential Screen Height for Rear Projection

If rear projection is possible, then the rest is easy. We simply find a screen that has the aspect ratio and dimensions we want. If the client wants a 4:3 aspect ratio screen, we could use a 15' × 20' wide rear projection screen. For a 3:1 screen ratio, we might use a 15' × 45' wide screen and so on.

When front projection must be used, as it often will, we must subtract an additional 6–7 feet from the maximum screen height possible for a screen behind the stage to accommodate for speakers and presenters. So our 15-foot high screen is reduced to 8 feet, which is too small to make an impact in a large venue. In this scenario, which uses front projection, a center screen behind the stage would not be advised.

Are these the only screens you need? The answer depends on the distance the audience is from the screen. The rule of thumb for viewing distance is 8 times

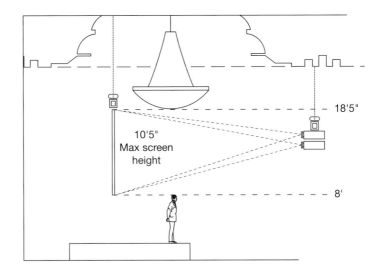

FIGURE 7.18
To determine the maximum screen height that can be used, you must measure all potential obstructions.

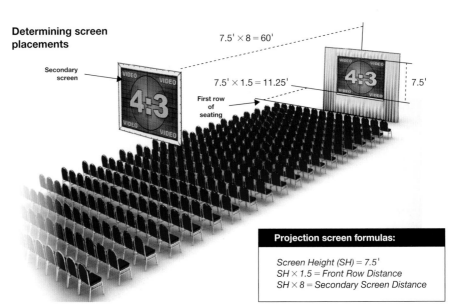

FIGURE 7.19
How to determine screen placements.

the screen's height. So an 18' × 24' wide projection screen will be viewable from up to 144 feet away before a secondary screen, or delay screen, is needed. In addition, the first row of seating should begin no less than 1.5 times the height of the screen in the distance. For an 18-foot high screen, the first row should be 27 feet from the screen's surface.

SCREEN CONFIGURATIONS

There are three main screen placements in general session meetings: primary, outboard, and secondary screens. Primary screens are one or more screens placed in the center of the performance space. A giant 20' × 60' screen behind the stage would be a primary screen, as would two 16' × 9' screens placed side by side. These screens can be used for content such as video elements or presentation graphics, or serve as a background for the stage design. They are not generally used for I-Mag unless hung high above the stage to prevent an infinity loop, in which an I-Mag camera captures its own video feed in the projection screen, causing a psychedelic tunnel effect.

Outboard screens reside on the far left and right sides of the performance space and typically display identical information. Outboard screens are occasionally referred to as *I-Mag screens*, though this term can be misleading because they may display any number of video sources. Several outboard screens might be used for extremely wide audiences, alternating between I-Mag and presentation graphics.

Secondary screens, more commonly referred to as *delay screens*, are placed further into the house and duplicate the video content of the primary or outboard screens. As mentioned in the previous section, projection screens are only viewable up to 8 times a screen's height. Beyond this point a secondary screen must be added for those audience members toward the back of the house. Note that secondary screens are always front projected to prevent the glare from the projector's lens from being visible to audience members.

The arrangement of these screens can vary, and the next few pages highlight several of the more common configurations. As you will notice, not all screens need to have the same aspect ratio. Outboards can easily be 4:3, whereas a primary screen is 3:1. Projection screens can even be rotated 90 degrees to allow for a portrait display. This type of display is becoming more popular for runway shows using 16:9 aspect ratio screens, allowing for a head-to-toe view of the model to

FIGURE 7.20
Infinity effect, also known as video feedback, replicated in miniature.

Common Screen Configurations

Single Center

One Screen Offset

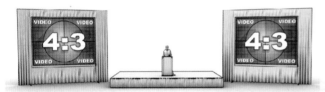

Two Screens Offset

Three Screens

Two Out Wide In

Portrait Outboards

Multiple Outboards

Common Screen Configurations

Widescreen Center

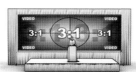

3:1 In 16:9 Out

4:3 and Wide

Circle Screen Center

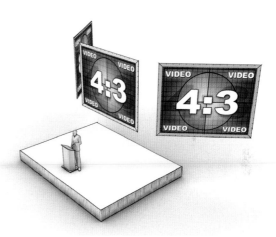

Arena

3/4 Arena

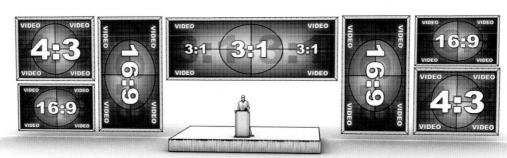

Mosaic

FIGURE 7.21
Widescreen projection allows for dramatic stage designs consisting solely of the screen itself.
Designer: Troy Halsey

be projected as I-Mag. Such configurations may require specific projectors to be used as well as additional video control equipment, so work closely with your AV provider and video specialists to ensure your vision is possible within your client's budget.

Multi-Image Blending and Warped Projection Systems

In the past decade, many advances have been made in projection and video compositing technologies, allowing for several projectors to be used in tandem to create continuous panoramic images. This is possible because of a concept known as *projector blending*. When several projectors are used together, they overlap slightly; this overlap is then controlled by blending software, resulting in an even display across the entire screen. Compositing software can then be used to fill the screen with imagery by layering video sources, graphics, and I-Mag to produce a digital canvas of video. I-Mag can be inserted into the canvas by using Picture-in-Picture windows (PIPs), much like the PIP technology used in televisions. The end result is a visual display unlike any other, and the creative possibilities are limited only by a designer's imagination and the client's budget.

In addition to panoramic images, recent technology advances allow video images to be warped, enabling the use of curved projection screens. Such an effect is quite impressive for entranceways and exhibit displays but tends to be less effective for larger applications when viewed from a distance. This, again, is due to the way our brains try to make sense of the images our eyes capture. A curved panoramic screen will appear flat to observers halfway into the audience of a general session, essentially wasting the additional cost of the image warping technology. This is not to say curved screens should not be used in stage designs. Just be aware that they are best viewed from an angle and are even more effective when attendees can walk right up to their curved or wavy projection surface.

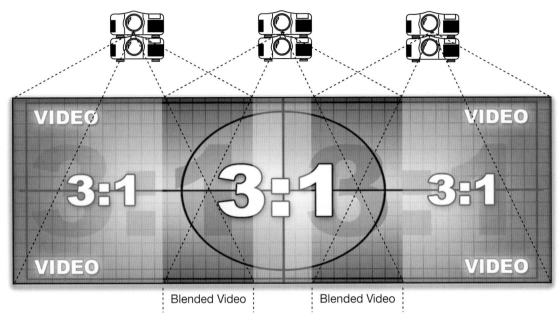

FIGURE 7.22
When images from multiple projectors are blended together, one seamless video image can be displayed.

VIDEO CAMERAS

Video cameras are used during events for three primary reasons: to magnify the presenters and performers onstage, to record the event for later viewing, and to capture raw video footage to be used in video modules edited by video production crews either during the event or afterward. The cameras used within meeting spaces are typically professional-grade broadcast cameras, while hand-held cameras used to capture footage around the event locale can range from consumer-grade digital camcorders to high-end professional HD video cameras. HD cameras will be addressed later because their high-resolution images can impact a design. For the most part, however, rely on your AV vendor to suggest the best camera package and configuration for your event and budget.

I-Mag

The purpose of I-Mag, short for Image Magnification, is to ensure the person in the last row of the audience can see what is happening onstage. In addition, it allows the audience to connect with a speaker on an emotional level by seeing the presenter's eyes and facial expressions more clearly. I-Mag is typically displayed for the duration of general sessions, cutting away to graphics only during presenter transitions. However, when only one or two screens are used, the video feed displayed on the screens will be switched between presentation files and I-Mag.

I-Mag is pretty straightforward, but there are a few things to keep in mind when using it during an event. First, ask your presenters and speakers to avoid wearing pinstriped clothing because such patterns can cause a moiré effect on-screen, a visual distortion created by parallel lines that are too close together to be properly displayed on-screen. Second, ensure that the lighting designer uses backlighting to separate those on camera from the background of the stage design. Finally, consider what will be behind the presenter on-screen. Will it just be an open stage or black drapes, or will you incorporate into your design a branded and visually rich background? The latter is highly advised, but you should keep it subtle, so as not to compete visually with the presenter.

FIGURE 7.23
An image magnification, or I-Mag, camera.

Pinstripe material   As seen on camera

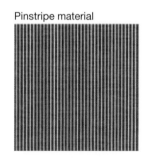 

FIGURE 7.24
Video cameras have difficulty capturing images of pinstripes. Keep this in mind when coaching presenters who will be I-Mag'ed during events.

FIGURE 7.25
A comparison of podium backgrounds. Which would you prefer to look at for hours?

Camera Rigs and Placements

Three primary camera rigs or setups are used in corporate events: stationary, handheld, and jib camera rigs. Stationary cameras are the most common and are mounted on tripods atop a camera platform. The camera is then operated by a camera person who is directed by the camera director backstage. Common uses of this arrangement include I-Mag and show record. When more than one stationary camera is used, a standard practice is to place one camera directly in front of the podium, about halfway into the audience, while placing a second camera off to one side. This configuration allows for front and cross shots, giving the video or camera director a bit of flexibility in which camera to show on-screen. When a second podium is used, an additional camera may be added, similar to the first placement, allowing for even greater flexibility in camera switching and viewing angles.

Handheld cameras are also popular for large events, allowing the camera operator to capture dynamic angles and shots not possible with stationary setups. Award shows and product reveals are common scenarios for which handheld cameras are ideal. As an award recipient is announced, he can be followed to the stage by the handheld camera operator, giving the audience a more personal view of the award winner's reactions. For product reveals, the handheld camera may be used onstage to provide close-up views of the revealed product. Operating a handheld camera requires a special talent for balance and rigidity; otherwise, the resulting video feed will appear amateurish and chaotic. Think of the horror movie *The Blair Witch Project*, which featured two hours of shaky handheld camera movements; this would be an undesirable effect during a corporate event.

FIGURE 7.26
A large jib or crane camera.
Image courtesy of Brian Alexander (www.brianalexanderphotography.com)

Finally, jib or crane cameras are an additional camera setup option. These cameras are mounted on the end of long cranes and are controlled both by manual labor and electronic remote controls. Jib cameras provide audiences with dramatic overhead shots that can swoop down as an award winner approaches the stage or pull way back to show the entire audience. Again, think of the Academy Awards, during which several jib camera rigs are used. Such setups can be quite costly and require skilled operators to use effectively, but their impact on production value is immense.

While stationary rigs tend to serve a more utilitarian function, handheld and jib cameras add drama and excitement to an event. These camera setups, however, are not right for every event. Using a jib camera to capture a financial presentation would just be silly, while trying to shoot an exciting live music performance with only stationary cameras would be tricky. So again, work with your AV provider to determine the most appropriate camera solution for your event.

HD Cameras and Their Effect on Design

With the advent of high-definition video, many clients are beginning to request HD camera and projection packages for their events. Although these packages are significantly more expensive than standard definition packages, they do indeed add production value to an event. HD video provides significantly greater resolution than standard definition cameras, allowing the audience to see more detail in the faces of presenters, actions onstage, and the stage design itself. That last bit is where the problems arise. Scenic elements constructed and finished using traditional methods show their secrets when shot on HD. The seams of flats and brushstrokes of painted scenery become more evident and can dissolve the illusion of an environment design.

As a result, stage designs and scenery created for events using HD video cameras must be built with higher-quality materials such as wood laminates instead of faux wood paint finishes, and seams of scenic flats must be masked by either molding or trim. These adjustments may seem minor, but they can inflate a budget very

FIGURE 7.27
A comparison of standard and high-definition frames, simulated.

quickly. Just remember, if the client is paying for an HD camera and projection system, he will also need to fork out the bucks for an HD scenic design.

VIDEO CONTROLS

As an event designer or planner, you never need to jump behind a video switcher or playback device in any situation. If there is such a situation, the production is in big trouble. This is why AV providers are brought into an event design team. They are the ones who will figure out how to produce your vision and operate video equipment. In your role, you simply need to see video control as the central hub for all things video.

The physical collection of video control equipment and personnel in a general session environment is known as a *video village*. It contains a number of advanced pieces of equipment used to switch camera feeds, play back video modules, operate presentation graphics and prompters, and ultimately send this assortment of content to projection screens and recording devices. And like a jittery kid in an antique shop, you would be wise never to touch or even go near a video village – other than to applaud these engineers and specialists after a successful production. That being said, video control can be organized by sources and destinations.

Sources include I-Mag cameras, video modules, satellite feeds, and presentation graphics. These sources are brought into a central video switching system. Think of any sports game you watch on TV; there are dozens of cameras being switched to keep up with the fast-paced action. Then between plays, the video feed switches to a graphic displaying player statistics or to sportscasters giving their opinions on the game. These switches or cuts are controlled by a team of video engineers. This same model is used during live corporate events, except that instead of a player running down the field, cameras follow a presenter; and in place of player statistics, presentation graphics are shown. The similarities can go on and on, but you get the idea.

FIGURE 7.28
A large production's video control.
Image courtesy of Brian Alexander (www.brianalexanderphotography.com)

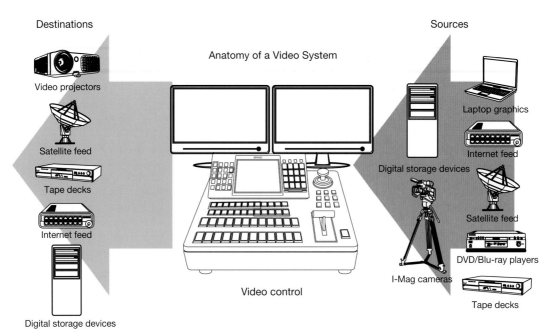

Destinations

Sources

Anatomy of a Video System

Video projectors

Laptop graphics

Satellite feed

Internet feed

Tape decks

Digital storage devices

Internet feed

Satellite feed

Digital storage devices

DVD/Blu-ray players

I-Mag cameras

Video control

Tape decks

FIGURE 7.29
A flow chart of common video sources and destinations.

For these switched video images to have any purpose, they must be sent to a destination such as a projector, video monitor, recording device, or back up to a satellite. When these video feeds reach their destinations, which occur almost instantly, they can be viewed by the live audience on projection screens or by remote audiences via satellite feeds and streaming Internet video. In addition, all the switched video is stored on hard drives or digital videotape to be viewed or edited after the event. This stored footage can then be edited down to only the most important elements, burned onto DVD, and sent to members and employees who were unable to attend the event in person. This practice gives clients the most for their money, transforming a multiday event into a training resource or promotional video that can be reviewed for years to come.

ADDITIONAL VIDEO DISPLAY SYSTEMS

Video projection is by no means the only form of video display used during events. A number of video products are now available for use throughout an event space. LCD and plasma monitors are among the most popular alternatives to video projection and are becoming larger and more affordable every year. Although these products are not viable options for displaying content during a general session, they can be used throughout the event space for displaying directions, schedules, branding, and sponsored advertisements. Many plasma monitors can now be connected and arranged to act as one large video surface or video wall.

FIGURE 7.30
A concept for a seamless video wall composed of several video monitors acting as one.

FIGURE 7.31
Touch screen monitors are becoming commonplace in the event industry and have dramatically increased the usefulness of digital signage and information kiosks.

FIGURE 7.32
High-resolution LED video panels are a breakthrough in video display technology and can greatly enhance a stage design. *Image courtesy of Daktronics. Daktronics Portable PST Display Panel (www.daktronics.com)*

LCD monitors tend to be used more often to display computer graphics due the nature of LCD technology, similar to how LCD projectors work. Many models today feature touch screen interfaces, alleviating the need for keyboards and computer mouses. Such products are ideal for registration and information kiosks as well as interactive exhibit displays.

Finally, LED panels and soft goods are quickly growing in popularity. LED video panels consist of thousands of small LED nodes serving as the pixels of an image. LED panels are available in a variety of resolutions, and their brightness allows them to be used in both outdoor and brightly lit indoor environments. LED soft goods have significantly less resolution than panels but are great options for adding a wow factor to stage designs. It will not be long before projection screens are replaced by LED products altogether. As mentioned in Chapter 1, "An Overview,"

OLED, or organic LED, products are the next step in LED evolution. These products allow video displays to be as thin as a sheet of plastic that can be rolled up for storage between uses. When this technology becomes commonplace, you can be assured it will be applied to almost every aspect of event design. Imagine scenic flats that are covered not with laminate, but an OLED film, allowing for a three-dimensional stage design to change entirely through the use of video images. What an exciting time that will be for designers of every industry. For now, visit www.mainlight.com to view Soft-LED products currently available for rental.

VIDEO CONTENT

All video technology is pointless without content to fill such displays. Aside from live sources like I-Mag, all video content is produced, meaning preassembled, either before the event or during the event by 24-hour production crews. Partnering with a team of skilled video producers and editors is pivotal for developing effective and meaningful video content. Many event design companies and creative agencies include video production among their services, but several vendors and freelancers specialize solely in video production and may be more affordable than all-in-one solution providers. Either source is acceptable, provided communication and collaboration are at the forefront of such relationships. Following are a few examples of the more common uses of video content and suggestions for effective implementation of these elements.

PowerPoint/Keynote

PowerPoint and Keynote are well-known presentation tools but are not always used effectively. The biggest mistake made by clients is to overuse these tools. They create slides full of text, on boring backgrounds, and walk the audience through each slide. This is a mind-numbing approach to a presentation. The answer to effective presentation support is in the name of the programs themselves: Power*POINT* and *KEY-NOTE*. Instead of using full sentences, or even paragraphs to highlight a concept, summarize the idea in a few words.

For example, suppose you are attending an event about how to better manage your time. The speaker walks onto the stage, and the projection screens fade in with the words "STOP WATCHING THE CLOCK" on a nice blue background. The speaker reads the words out loud and lets the audience ponder for a moment. Without changing the slide, the speaker then begins to passionately explain that by watching the clock tick away, you are wasting more time worrying about how much you have to do rather than doing it, or something along those lines. This approach is an effective use of PowerPoint; it makes a powerful point. In contrast, imagine a slide full of text that the presenter reads aloud line by line explaining the same concept. All the life of the presentation is removed, and the audience members spend more time trying to read the convoluted slide than listening to the message being delivered. When it comes to developing support materials for presentations, keep it simple and to the point; anything more detracts from the effectiveness of the entire presentation.

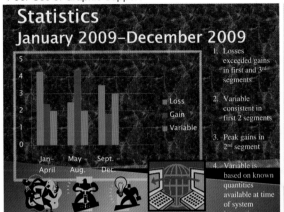

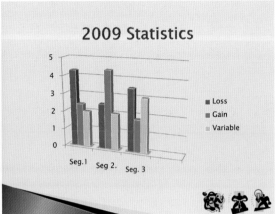

FIGURE 7.33
A comparison of poorly and well-used graphic support. Less is more when it comes to PowerPoint and Keynote slides.

Messaging Videos

Messaging videos help tell the story of the event experience. Opening videos that introduce an event theme are the most common form of messaging video, whether it is a montage of old movie clips to introduce the theme "Hooray for Hollywood" or action shots of athletes in their moments of glory to announce the theme "Achieving the Impossible." Messaging videos tend to be more creative and crafted with higher production values. These are the modules that drive the event message home and can often be quite moving and inspiring. Aside from just opening videos, mini-segments continuing the opening module might be inserted between presenters to keep the flow of the show moving. Closing videos may also be created to reiterate the message and leave attendees with a few lasting thoughts. Regardless of their placement or form, if it is meant to explain or enforce the event's theme and message, then it is a messaging video.

Corporate Videos

Corporate videos focus on the organization as a whole, their current direction and objectives, and an explanation of new policies or products. For example, customer-based events might include a number of video modules highlighting new products and services available from the host; these would be corporate videos. Another example would be a montage of client testimonials explaining why they chose to stick with or leave the hosting company. Finally, a video address from the corporation's president to an audience of salespersons starting off with "Hi guys, I sure am sorry I couldn't be there in person, but…" – this too would be a corporate video. Corporate videos play a pivotal role in events because much of the *meat* of an event is delivered through these modules.

Introduction/Award/Walk-Up Videos

Introduction, award, and walk-up videos are pretty basic and consist most often of dynamic backgrounds, upbeat music, and the name or title of a speaker, award winner, or category. A few great examples are video modules used during the Academy Awards to introduce award presenters – the ones that start off with "Presenting the award for best motion picture...." These elements add excitement and production value to an event. Imagine hearing your name to receive an award and making the long walk up to the stage in complete silence aside from a faint applause; it would be a bit anticlimactic. Filling that time with an upbeat video keeps the excitement flowing until the award recipient or presenter makes his way to the stage.

Event-Based Videos

When event footage is shot of attendees smiling or giving their opinions, then edited to be shown on the last day of the event, the resulting module is an *event-based video*. These elements allow attendees to feel more involved in the event experience. Two common examples of event-based videos include "Person on the Street" and "Smiling Faces" modules. Person on the Street modules ask attendees their opinions on various topics related to the event and are then edited to support a presentation delivered later or as filler video between meeting segments. Smiling Faces modules, on the other hand, are simply montages of attendees enjoying the event and waving at the camera. Such elements are typically shown at the end of an event and accompanied by moving music, basically reaffirming what a nice time attendees had during the event and promoting their return the following year.

Theme or Brand-Based Graphic Content

Theme or brand-based graphic content is pretty straightforward and includes looping logo animations or static graphic artwork used to brand an event environment when attendees enter a meeting space. Projection screens and plasma

FIGURE 7.34
Still frames from an animated theme graphic, one that might be shown while an award recipient walks up to the stage.

FIGURE 7.35
Still frames from a "Person on the Street" video segment.

FIGURE 7.36
A sample theme graphic that might be used as a screensaver as attendees enter a ballroom.
Designer: Marc Vonderhorst

monitors are the typical methods of displaying such content, which might be used as screensavers as attendees trickle into a general session or between presentations. When using graphic content on plasma monitors throughout the event space, ensure that the logo is animated in some way to prevent the image from burning into the monitor's screen. That being said, avoid animations that are too over the top or busy, opting instead for a slow rotation or spin of artwork elements that can be looped continuously for various durations.

ALTERNATE USES OF VIDEO

There are a lot of fun and unique uses for video and projection beyond simply providing content or displaying I-Mag. Video projection can be used to create digital backdrops for staging environments or transform an entire meeting space using multi-image projection systems. Imagine being able to create a virtual backdrop that can display any environment with the click of a button; it's entirely possible today. Add a curved screen and image-warpers, and that custom backdrop becomes visible from every angle of the I-Mag camera. Take it even further and use projectors to create a 360-degree panoramic sky in the registration lobby, complete with drifting clouds, gliding birds, and an occasional airplane. The possibilities for environment projection are limited only by your imagination and budget.

Perhaps you want something a bit more interactive; then gesture-based projection systems like those available from GestureTek (www.gesturetek.com) may be the answer. This system allows observers to affect projected content with little more than the wave of their hand, such as popping virtual bubbles or causing ripples in a simulated pond. The projection system is combined with several motion detection cameras used to alter the projection content in real

FIGURE 7.37
A sample of projection being used as scenery. In this design, two seemingly overlapping screens serve as digital backdrops.
Designer: Troy Halsey

FIGURE 7.38
Gesture-based projection technology allows attendees to interact with a project image in real time. For example, this young girl bounces virtual balloons with a wave of her arm.
Image courtesy of GestureTek and Child's Play (www.gesturetek.com)

time. When this technology is combined with a logo or branded message, an interactive billboard is produced, perfect for event lobbies and lounge areas – an advertisement attendees will actually want to read.

For a more practical interactive experience, consider Internet relay chat (IRC) systems and Twitter casting. These systems combine the infrastructure of popular social networking Web sites and display attendee-submitted content on video walls in lobbies or even on the primary projection screens within a meeting space. When attendees and audience members are allowed to post questions and comments during sessions in real time using a cell phone or laptop, presentations become a two-way communication, allowing presenters to adjust their presentation based on viewer feedback. This approach is not for everyone, but question-and-answer sessions and live user forums benefit from such technology.

Video is certainly a versatile tool in the event industry, and new technologies seem to be spilling onto event floors every year. Three-dimensional displays are no longer science fiction, and as LED displays become more advanced, video projectors may be kicked to the curb altogether. As an event designer, you are responsible for staying informed about these new technologies and how they can be used to enhance your designs and the attendee experience. In time, the idea of alternate uses of video will be laughable because there will be no default use for the medium – it will simply be all around us.

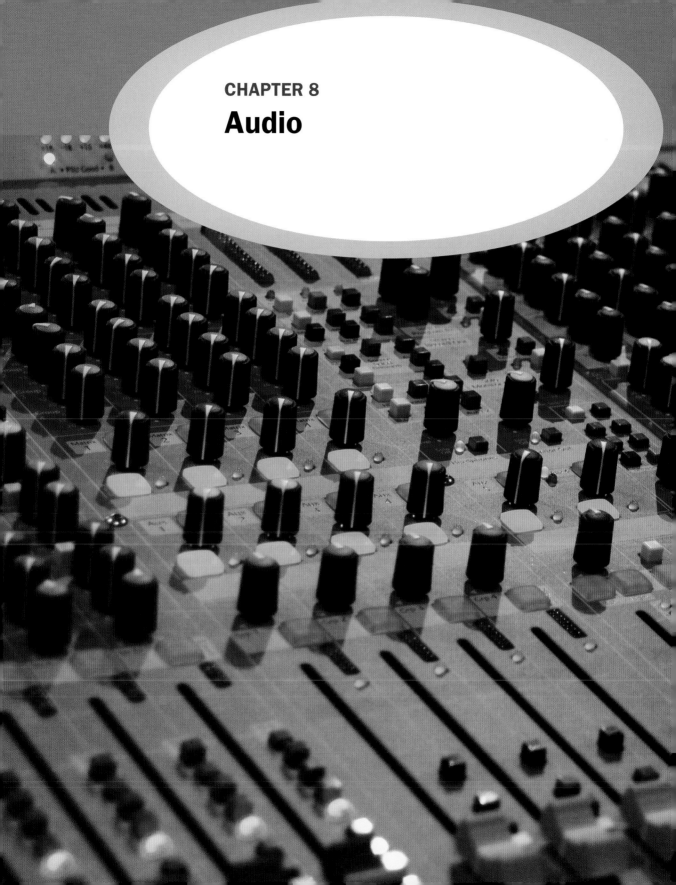

CHAPTER 8

Audio

INTRODUCTION TO AUDIO

Today, it is rare for an audience member to witness a string of presenters without the use of multimedia presentations, video introductions, or even large entertainment acts to break up the monotony. Indeed, elements of visual and especially audio flare have become commonplace in the modern event industry. An experienced audio engineer will approach sound as a crucial design element that, when executed well, adds immense production value to an event. The most basic objective of audio design is to answer a core production question in the affirmative: *can everyone in the audience hear what is happening onstage?*

For a sound system to be integrated into an environment or scenic design seamlessly, it must be included in the overall design from the beginning. Unfortunately, production schedules rarely allow this to happen, leaving sound design to be considered late in the process. As you can imagine, this can cause issues when it comes time to determine equipment selections or ideal speaker placements. This chapter will focus on the fundamentals of audio design to better equip designers and planners during preproduction. There are literally volumes of works dedicated to the art of sound system design and specific technologies should further reading be desired. At this stage of the game, however, it is important for designers and event planners to merely understand the basic purpose of audio as it relates to event design and how to properly incorporate this crucial element into a production.

WHY ARE AUDIO SYSTEMS NEEDED?

An audio system is a collection of electronic equipment that is designed to increase the level and quality of sound. There are two primary reasons sound systems are needed during events. The first and most obvious reason is to ensure that everyone in the event space can hear what is happening onstage or on-screen, whether it be a keynote speaker, opening video, or five-piece band. Through the use of a properly designed and installed sound system, the audience at the back of the room will hear just as well as those who are seated close to the stage. This is referred to as *even audio distribution*, and can be a tougher task than you might imagine.

The second reason an audio system is needed during events is to create atmosphere. Imagine a scenic design that replicates a tropical forest or remote beach. Through use of an audio system, the sounds of a wild jungle or crashing waves with seagulls in the distance can be piped in to create the illusion that the audience has been transported into that environment. Or perhaps low rumblings of bass complement video footage of a jet taking off during an opening video as attendees "Soar Higher" to kick off a session. Sound systems are also employed when there are no live performers on the stage at all. This can include a prerecorded message from a CEO or live content being received via satellite or the Web. The applications of quality sound systems to enhance an event experience are truly limitless.

FIGURE 8.1
A well-designed sound system allows every attendee to hear what is occurring onstage and on-screen clearly without drawing attention to the sound system itself.

PARTS OF A SOUND SYSTEM

Although professional sound systems may seem intimidating to the casual observer, and it is true they are composed of very advanced equipment, they are all constructed on a very basic formula: sound enters the system through input devices, is adjusted and amplified, and then is sent to output devices such as speakers. The system becomes more convoluted when the number of different input and output devices used simultaneously increases. The equipment used to mix the sound, in turn, becomes more complex, resulting in sound boards larger than most coffee tables. We will look at each stage of the sound system in more detail later in the chapter, as well as common audio dilemmas. For now, let's ensure we have a solid understanding of the fundamentals.

Input Devices

When we break down the elements of a sound system, it all begins with an input source such as a microphone, CD player, video source, or computer system. These sources, in essence, capture sound waves, store those waves for later playback, and when prompted, send these same waves to the next step in the system, the audio mixer. Microphones, however, are the exception and do not store sound information but deliver sound waves in real time directly to the audio mixer.

Audio Mixers

Audio mixers receive the waves of sound sent by input devices and route those audio waves or signals to specific output devices. During this routing, the signals

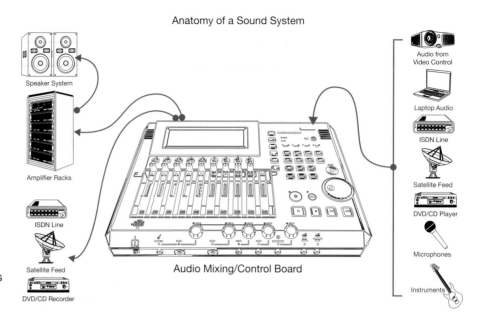

Anatomy of a Sound System

Speaker System

Amplifier Racks

ISDN Line

Satellite Feed

DVD/CD Recorder

Audio Mixing/Control Board

Audio from Video Control

Laptop Audio

ISDN Line

Satellite Feed

DVD/CD Player

Microphones

Instruments

FIGURE 8.2
The basic flow chart of inputs and outputs of an audio sound system.

FIGURE 8.3
Audio mixing boards are a maze of buttons and sliders but can produce amazing results when used by a professional audio engineer.

are adjusted in a number of ways. The reason is that sound is not composed of only one wave, but several waves called *frequencies*.

Every sound made is constructed from several smaller sounds called frequencies. If an input source, such as a microphone, sends a signal that includes a high-pitch hum, the frequency that hum rides in on can be reduced in strength while wanted sound, such as the speaker's voice, can be increased. The most useful feature of a mixer, however, is its ability to combine several audio sources and *mix* them into the clear sounds heard by the audience. After each input and audio source is tweaked, adjusted, and mixed to the best possible quality, it is sent to the amplifier.

Amplifiers

All these audio signals and sound waves are forms of electricity. And during each step of the process, these electrical signals are weakened. For the signals to be strong enough to be heard by the audience through speakers, they must be amplified. Returning to the radio analogy, when the volume knob is turned up, the audio signals are amplified, making the sound emitted by speakers louder. This same function occurs in professional sound systems; the difference is that the speaker systems being used are much larger and require greater amplification.

FIGURE 8.4
Professional event speakers come in a variety of shapes and sizes.

Speakers

In this simple model, speakers are the last link in the chain. When the electricity from the amplifier is received by the speakers, the electricity is converted back into sound and is projected out into the audience. Much like the lenses of a light fixture, speakers project sound in beams or spreads. Depending on the architecture within a venue, these beams can be bounced around in unusual ways, creating less-than-ideal sound quality. This is why speaker placement is so crucial during the planning of an event. Even the best speaker systems cannot overcome poor placement.

BEYOND THE BASICS FROM A DESIGNER'S VIEW

From an event planner's or designer's perspective, understanding the function of each button found on an audio mixing board is not necessary. However, understanding the unique aspects of various microphones and speakers will come in very handy over the course of a career in event design. More specifically, knowing which microphones are appropriate for performers versus amateur award recipients and which speakers need to be placed onstage as opposed to hung from rigging will allow for designs that are functional and affordable. This knowledge will also prevent event planners from being swindled by equipment vendors that recommend only the most expensive products when others may work just as well.

TYPES OF MICROPHONES

A large majority of information is distributed during an event through the spoken word. For presenters and speakers to be heard by the entire audience, they must be *miked*, meaning they are given a microphone. Microphones convert sound waves into electricity and are typically the first link in the audio system chain. There are two basic microphone categories: wired and wireless.

Wired Microphones

Lecterns and panel tables are typically equipped with wired microphones. Wired microphones on stands, as frequently used by standup comedians, are less common onstage. They do often appear, however, in the aisles of audience seating during question-and-answer, or Q&A, sessions, which will be addressed later in this chapter. Wired microphones are simple and straightforward and require little more than long audio cables to reach the mixing board in the back of the event space. The downside to wired microphones is the wire itself. If a speaker wishes to walk the stage, he must constantly fiddle and rearrange this long and twisted mess. A better solution for agile speakers is to use wireless microphone systems.

Wireless Microphone Systems

Wireless handheld microphone systems are composed of two elements: the transmitter, which is built into the microphone, and the receiver, which connects to the mixing board. Each wireless mic must have its own frequency channel to prevent transmitting frequencies from getting mixed up and a unique receiver to deliver those sound waves to channels on the mixing board.

A limited number of frequencies are available for wireless audio, which poses a limitation to how many wireless microphones can be used during a session. Wireless microphones are also battery powered, so batteries should be replaced prior to each session. Furthermore, wireless signals are not always reliable and are susceptible to interference. A smart show director, the individual calling the technical shots during a session, will have backup wireless microphones available offstage in the event of a mic or mics failing … and they will at some point.

When a presenter prefers not to hold a microphone, an alternate option is the lavaliere, or *lav,* microphone. These microphones are made up of two separate pieces: a microphone about the size of a shirt button or smaller that connects to a transmitter pack through a long thin wire. The transmitter pack is about the

FIGURE 8.5
A wireless lavaliere microphone and transmitter.

size of a deck of cards and can be stored in the speaker's pocket, or for women wearing skirts or dresses, clipped to the back of their garment. Lav microphones are also referred to as *lapel mics* because they are typically clipped to a speaker's collar or lapel.

A derivative of lavaliere microphones is the head-worn mic. Head-worn mics are frequently used for musical performances and are becoming more common for professional speaking. These thin microphones extend along the speaker's jaw or eye line and are secured to the head through a wire band, similar to a girl's head band. These systems take a bit of practice to use properly and should not be used for first-time presenters without a rehearsal.

Other Common Microphones

Within the categories of wired and wireless microphones, specialized mics exist for unique applications. Audio engineers can aid you in selecting these microphones when necessary. Two microphone types in particular that may be used more often are hanging and boundary microphones.

HANGING MICROPHONES

Hanging microphones are great for choirs and performing groups. As their name implies, these microphones hang from above and are similar in size to lavaliere mics, reducing their visibility from the audience.

~1.75"

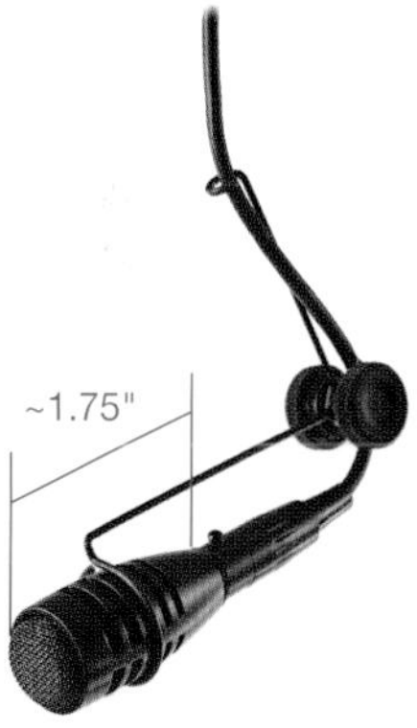

FIGURE 8.6
A hanging microphone is ideal for music performances and group skits.

Hanging mics are also handy for group activities onstage such as team building exercise instruction, where two or more volunteers demonstrate the exercise, or skits. Corporate skits are among those things that make you cringe a bit while watching, but are nonetheless popular among corporate planning committees. Regardless, if the client wants the skit in the show, you had better ensure the dialogue can be heard by the audience.

PZM MICROPHONES

Another microphone that is not often thought of is the pressure zone microphone, or PZM. This unique microphone, and it is indeed unique, takes advantage of an odd characteristic of sound known as the *boundary effect*. Hence, PZM microphones are often referred to as *boundary mics*.

Without getting too technical, the boundary effect allows for capturing of cleaner audio by removing sound reflections. As described earlier in the chapter, sound moves in waves. When sound waves hit a hard surface such as a wall, ceiling, or set piece, they bounce back or reflect. When these reflections make their way back to the microphone, even though they are weakened, they can still muddy the original direct sound meant to be heard clearly, such as a speaker's or singer's voice. If you place the microphone diaphragm, the part that vibrates and captures sound, directly against a hard surface, the reflected

FIGURE 8.7
A PZM microphone looks very different from most microphones and captures sound in a very unique way.

waves bounce right past the mic, allowing the direct sound wave to be captured without interference. This is known as the boundary effect. This explanation is oversimplified but illustrates the basic principle.

PZM mics do not look like traditional microphones because they are built on a flat square plate rather than a cylindrical encasement. The plate allows the microphone to take full advantage of the boundary effect.

These mics work well when placed on tabletops such as in the cases of panel discussions or parliamentary proceedings when each person on the stage is not miked individually. They are also ideal for acoustical performance groups like *Stomp*, which involve heavy bass, reverberations, and loud sounds that tend to echo.

TYPES OF AUDIO SPEAKERS

Most speaker systems used today fall into one of two categories: line arrays and speaker clusters. Each comes with its own advantages and disadvantages. Line arrays are more common in larger events, but there are times when conventional speaker clusters are a better choice or the only option. In addition, designers need a basic understanding of monitor systems and front-fill speakers and how they can impact a design. The following sections cover each type of speaker system commonly used for live events.

FIGURE 8.8
Speaker clusters are best for smaller venues and do not transmit sound waves as efficiently as line arrays.

Speaker Clusters

Clustered speaker systems were the norm for many years. Starting in the 1980s, their use for large sound systems started to fade due to their inability to project

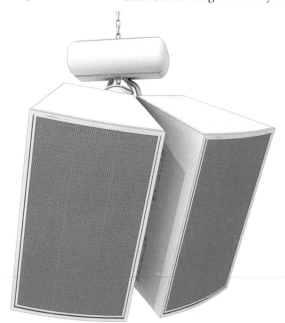

quality sound long distances. The conventional speaker cluster, when used in a small venue, installs quickly and allows for speakers to be focused loosely. Less precision and planning are needed to provide quality sound with speaker clusters than line array systems. The downside to the system, as mentioned previously, is the system's poor ability to project quality sound over long distances. As a result, more speakers are needed to provide quality sound to large and expansive audiences. These additional speakers are called *delays*.

DELAY SPEAKERS

Delay speakers get their name because the sound they project is delayed from the primary speakers. This delay is necessary because sound travels relatively slow, 1130 feet per second to be exact. While this may not seem slow, it is when you consider the size of some venues. Doing some quick math,

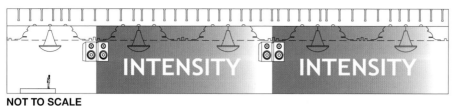

FIGURE 8.9
Delay speakers are needed in larger venues due to the nature of how sound waves travel and dissipate.

NOT TO SCALE

we know there are 1000 milliseconds per second, so sound travels at 1.13 feet every millisecond. If the delay speakers are 100 feet from the primary speakers, they should be delayed 113 milliseconds. This delay allows all the audience members, regardless of their seat, to feel the sound they are hearing is coming from the front of the room. There is some additional science that makes this concept more complicated. The Haas effect has to do with how we perceive sound; therefore, delay speakers should be even further delayed to sound more natural, the added time simulating the distance being traveled. Confused? Don't worry; that is why you have an audio engineer. All that is important from an event planner or designer standpoint is the name of the additional speakers in the back of the room: delay speakers.

Speaker clusters are still solid solutions for smaller venues where rigging is limited. Limited ceiling height may also be the reason to choose a cluster system over a line array. Work with your audio engineer to determine which sound system will be most appropriate for your event.

Line Arrays

Line array speaker systems are hung vertically and form a *J* shape in profile. Their configuration requires high ceilings to prevent sight-line issues and to provide optimal sound. What makes line array systems so popular for today's events is the control they provide in projecting clear sound long distances. Each speaker contained in the array can be focused for a specific area, and the speakers collectively transmit high-frequency sound waves, the ones used by the human voice, excellently. Because most corporate events consist of a mixture of live presentations and motivational speeches, line arrays are an ideal solution for providing clear sound to large audiences.

In addition to providing superior sound quality, line arrays reduce feedback due to the nature in which they project sound waves. Furthermore, the coverage of these units reduces or even eliminates the need for delay speakers. Finally, due to the smaller number of speakers needed for large audiences, installation labor costs are reduced.

Like all pieces of technology, line arrays have a few downsides. First, they are typically hung or rigged and require plenty of ceiling height to prevent sight-line issues. Floor-supported systems are available, but they are not effective for large audiences. Second, to be able to use these systems efficiently, they must be rigged with precision. Fortunately, computer software makes this task a bit easier by

FIGURE 8.10
Line arrays are engineered to transmit sounds waves over a long distance very efficiently.
Image courtesy of Brian Alexander
(www.brianalexanderphotography.com)

determining ideal speaker placements, even before a single piece of equipment is rolled into the venue.

Monitor Systems

Not all speakers used during a live event are intended for the audience. Case in point are monitor systems, sometimes referred to as *fold-back speakers*, which allow those on the stage to hear the same audio as the audience or isolated mixes as used by musicians. Monitor systems are also important during Q&A sessions, allowing presenters to clearly hear the questions posed by audience members when spoken into aisle microphones.

These systems can range in complexity from a few speakers placed downstage to elaborate rigs hung above head and focused for each portion of the stage. Simple monitor systems can be managed through the primary audio board. However, more complex systems, such as those used by bands and music groups, may require an additional mixer. For high-end entertainment acts, it is not uncommon for the monitor mix to be controlled offstage by an audio engineer traveling with the performing group.

An alternative to monitor speakers, and a common choice for musicians, is the in-ear monitor. These low-profile earpieces are generally wireless units, giving performers a free range of motion. Using music groups as the example, these systems can send individual mixes to each performer. This allows lead guitarists to hear their own playing rather than struggling to hear over the rest of band. In addition, using in-ear monitors greatly improves the overall sound quality projected to the audience. Traditional stage monitors have to be cranked up in volume during a loud music performance to allow the performers to hear over the sound projected to the audience. This creates a battle for quality sound between the monitor and audience mixes. In-ear monitoring alleviates this issue by reducing the need for traditional stage monitors, giving the audience one clean audible mix.

Monitor speakers, or wedges as they are sometimes referred, are often overlooked during the design process. Chances are they will be needed in some form, and it is preferred to design staging with these pieces in mind as opposed to adding them at the last minute, which is often the case. Consider how these speakers can be integrated into your design. They can be concealed by adding a lip to the stage or placing them behind potted plants. They can be placed into custom recesses in the stage floor or hidden behind downstage scenic elements. Not incorporating monitor systems into a stage design can ruin an intended aesthetic with visually contrasting speakers scattered across the stage's edge.

Front Fill

The first few rows of audience seating are not positioned for optimal sound from the main speakers. To remedy this situation, front-fill speakers are placed on the downstage edge of the performance area, providing clear sound for those closest to the stage. Ensuring these speakers are balanced appropriately is important because corporate executives and association officers generally populate these rows of seating.

FIGURE 8.11
In-ear monitors allow musicians to hear their own instrument or voice among a barrage of noise.
Image courtesy of Brian Alexander
(www.brianalexanderphotography.com)

UNIQUE CHALLENGES OF AUDIO FOR THE CORPORATE EVENT INDUSTRY

Most people have been to a music concert of some kind in their life. You typically see a curved set of speakers hanging from the roof or perhaps a giant stack of speakers creating monolithic walls on either side of the stage. Depending on the type of music being performed, the sound may be intense or soothing, but all concerts provide clear sound balanced for that unique space and performance. For the audio engineer of a corporate event, the experience and challenges for producing clear sound are a bit different.

The first challenge is speaker placement. Because audio is typically added late in the event design process, optimal speaker placement is not always available due to staging or audience seating. As a result, a common placement for speakers is hanging from the ceiling between the stage and outer screens, just high enough not to cause sight-line issues for the projection screen. While this placement is common, it is typically less than ideal. Incorporating your audio engineer or AV partner early in the design process can prevent such scenarios and find unique solutions for the selected venue and staging design.

A second challenge is that not everyone who will be on the stage is a professional speaker. Amateur presenters who are nervous will often be soft-spoken and mumble-mouthed or speak so closely to the microphone that only a painfully loud static is heard, a practice known as "eating the microphone." Working with these presenters during rehearsal will help give them confidence in both the equipment and themselves.

FIGURE 8.12
Q&A mics placed in the audience permit attendees to interact with presenters at designated times.

Finally, the placement of the audio engineer during the production is most often less than ideal. Audio engineers can do their job most effectively when centered in the audience. This allows them to adjust levels while hearing exactly what the audience hears. More often than not, however, engineers are placed off to one side and against the back wall of the room. Such placement can be referred to as "mixing blind" because the engineer is forced to guess at optimal audio settings.

Feedback

Feedback is the result of a microphone picking up the sound projected by the speakers, creating an infinite loop. This looping sound gets louder and louder until it sends the sound system into overdrive, producing the piercing sound everyone has painfully heard at one time or another.

This annoyance can be prevented if the audio engineer is able to perform a procedure known as "ringing out." By purposely causing the sound system to feed back, the engineer can isolate and diminish problem frequencies without reducing the overall sound quality of the system. In the event industry, this is an important step and requires little more than a few moments of silence before the production to allow the audio engineer to make the appropriate adjustments.

Q&A Sessions

Question-and-answer sessions are often key features of general session meetings. Allowing employees, association members, and customers to openly ask questions and receive immediate answers is a powerful gesture on the part of event hosts. To fully embrace this gesture, however, Q&A sessions should be designed to prevent their inclusion into the meeting's agenda appearing as an afterthought.

The most basic setup for Q&A sessions includes one to three microphones being placed in the main aisles of audience seating. At the appropriate times, attendees can make their way to the microphones, which are placed in microphone stands, to ask presenters or speakers questions. After the question is asked, the questioner returns to his seat and those onstage respond with an answer. Q&A sessions are a simple concept that pays dividends in corporate and association morale, providing a voice for the masses of an organization.

From a logistical standpoint, wireless microphones should be used in the audience because securing several hundred feet of microphone cable through a sea of chairs can be a time-consuming task. In addition, work with the lighting designer to ensure each microphone station is properly lit. Doing so not only allows the questioner to be seen, but also provides enough light for a clear video picture should participants be documented or projected onto I-Mag screens.

Finally, to fully incorporate these sessions into a design, consider elevating microphone stations with scenically designed platforms. Tying these platforms into the design by applying the same textures or treatments as the stage design, provided doing so does not cause sight-line issues, solidifies the perception that the event hosts view the Q&A sessions as an integral part of the event experience. These platforms also give camera operators a clear and unobstructed view of participants. Placing elevated microphone stations toward the front of the audience on either side of the stage is recommended to prevent sight-line issues or audience obstructions.

How the Venue Impacts Sound

As mentioned previously, sound travels in waves or beams. When those waves hit a hard surface, they reflect back. Aside from producing feedback or poor sound quality, the most noticeable result of sound reflection is an echo. Walk into a large, empty hall or event space and clap your hands. The echo of your clap is the result of sound waves bouncing around the meeting space. The volume of an echo and the number of times it repeats can give you an idea of how well the space was designed for sound, a science known as *architectural acoustics*.

For ideal sound quality, echoes and bouncing sound waves need to be reduced as much as possible. To do so, you must add materials that can absorb sound waves to the environment. Professional recording studios use sheets of acoustical foam, which closely resemble egg-carton or mattress padding, to line the walls of their recording booths. This tactic isn't practical, however, for large event halls. Soft materials such as drapery and carpet are more realistic alternatives to acoustical foam for the event industry. Adding carpet padding beneath carpeted walkways and the stage can further improve sound absorption. In addition, finding ways to work soft surfaces into both the scenery and environment can lead to unique and visually dynamic designs, but above all, will aid in providing attendees with a quality audio experience.

AUDIO SERVICES

Audio engineers provide many more services beyond sliding volume controls up and down. Along with designing entire sound systems, they are often equipped with soft skills such as sound editing and recording. Modern audio files are stored digitally and can be edited using sound editing software. This software allows for music files to be trimmed, announcements to be prerecorded, or sound effects to be created or adjusted. In addition, audio engineers are equally skilled at capturing audio known as the *show record*. Following are a few of the additional services skilled audio engineers may offer when contracted.

Walk-In/Walk-Up Music

When attendees walk into a meeting space, such as the general session, it is common for music to be played over the sound system. This music selection is known as *walk-in music*. These ambient music tracks not only fill *dead air*, a radio broadcast term meaning silence, but can aid in setting the tone for the meeting about to occur and build anticipation. This is a common approach used in traditional performance theater as well.

Walk-up music, in contrast, is played when someone is walking onto or toward the stage. When a presenter is introduced onto the stage, a walk-up track might be played to fill the time it takes for that person to reach the podium. In addition, when an award recipient is announced, music is often brought in to add to the excitement and, again, fill the time it takes for the winner to make his way to the stage.

Be aware, however, copyright laws still apply to music used during events. Ensure that the music tracks selected were purchased from royalty-free music libraries or are licensed appropriately before piping any selection into an event space.

Show Audio Record

In most professional event productions, the general session is recorded, capturing both the video feed from the video control switcher and the audio feed from the audio console. However, providing optimal sound quality for both the live audience within the space and for the show record can be a difficult task. Sound within the space must be engineered to accommodate for the venue itself and account for the speed of sound and reflected sound or echoes. These factors, however, do not impact sound being played back on a television or computer. As a result, it is not uncommon for separate audio feeds to be generated, one for the live audience and one for the show record.

Some meetings such as breakout sessions may not be recorded on video, but will instead be distributed on audio CD or streamed over the Internet. Again, these feeds are not meant for live audiences within the space, so a separate feed with different levels is needed.

FIGURE 8.13
Any sound system is useless without a trained audio engineer behind the proverbial wheel.

Often an audio engineer can level the audio for both feeds simultaneously; receiving feedback from the video village means something is awry with the sound quality. Occasionally, a second audio engineer may be needed to ensure optimal quality for the show audio record. Discuss show records with your AV provider and audio engineer early in the design process to ensure all necessary equipment and capabilities are available during the production.

VOG and Speaker Introductions

Although it may not be a politically correct term, *Voice of God*, or VOG, refers to announcements made over the sound system when the speaker is not visible, meaning from backstage or the control booth. A sample VOG might be a preshow announcement by the event producer stating that the event is about to begin or asking attendees to take their seats.

VOGs are also used to announce speakers walking onto the stage. Known as a *speaker introduction*, this is a common practice used during televised award shows. Speaker introductions typically give a presenter's name, the position or company, and the award he or she is presenting. Larger events may prerecord these introductions and possibly preshow announcements as well. Live announcements, however, are still more common in the event industry because they can be rewritten on the fly to adapt to last-minute changes in the production.

On-Site Audio Editing

Audio editing software has become accessible to most anyone who owns a computer. The capabilities of these software packages can be truly remarkable, allowing many of the same audio mastering tools once limited to professional sound studios to be used on a portable laptop. Such a resource often proves invaluable on-site before and during productions.

When selecting an audio and video provider, ensure that the audio engineer who will be working during the production has such software available and is proficient in using its features. Last-minute edits to music selections, voice-over recordings, and sound effects are common and should be expected. As a meeting planner or event producer, you should be prepared for such situations.

FINAL THOUGHTS ON AUDIO

Audio design is possibly one of the most underrated specialties in the event business. The reason is that sound quality is not noticed unless it is subpar. The moment the audience is bombarded with the piercing screech of feedback, everyone turns in his seat to stare daggers at the audio engineer. Rarely will an audio engineer be approached after a show to be complimented on a job well done. Taking the time to understand how scenic and environment designs can impact or support an audio system is the responsibility of every event designer. For event design to be complete, all elements must work together, and these elements are not limited to the visual arts. Quality audio design is an important key to producing a successful event experience and requires careful planning and the support of experienced audio professionals.

CHAPTER 9

Speaker Support

INTRODUCTION TO SPEAKER SUPPORT

Those speaking and presenting at a corporate event will vary greatly in both their experience and comfort level with large audiences. Event speakers range from professional inspirational orators to corporate executives and product specialists to subcommittee chairpersons.

As a freelance designer, you may have little contact with those utilizing your environment and scenic concepts when the project moves into the realm of production and execution. However, it is crucial that you understand the experience through their eyes to ensure that your work is not only functional but, when possible, also strives to provide an ideal performance space.

From the designer's perspective, the environment you design is not the only piece needed for creating a positive presentation experience. Even the most experienced speakers will occasionally be affected by nerves and have concerns of fumbling their speech or presentation. Therefore, it should be the goal of every production team to remove as many stresses as possible by providing speech management services, rehearsals, prompters, and comfortable speaker-ready rooms. This chapter will focus on providing hospitality for speakers and presenters, a service known as *speaker support*. Although this topic may not seem crucial for a designer to delve into, it is pivotal for the overall success of an event and should be understood by everyone involved in a production.

TYPES OF SPEAKERS AND PRESENTERS

To state the obvious, not every speaker will be the same. Furthermore, each will serve a different purpose during an event. Some speakers will inform, whereas others will inspire. There are two broad categories for speakers and presenters at events: internal and external. Internal speakers include those who are employed by or members of the hosting company or organization, such as CEOs, committee chairpersons, and award recipients. External speakers include professional speakers who are hired by the event planning committee, those giving client testimonials, and product or service specialists. To better understand how to support speakers, let's first look at the different types of speakers in more detail.

External Speakers

External speakers have an advantage over the internal speakers that are featured during corporate events. To begin with, they have been asked to present, implying that they have something to offer that the audience will enjoy or benefit from. That kind of buildup makes them poised for success before they even step foot onto the stage. They are also outsiders of the company or organization. As outsiders, they can make tongue-in-cheek statements about the company or management to relate to the audience and get a chuckle. This practice is especially popular with motivational speakers. A CEO doing the same thing, in some circles, could be considered offensive and off-color.

If an external speaker is a client or customer, his opinion is more meaningful when presented before a live audience and can have a greater impact than an executive reading the same testimonial. Product vendors and specialists, on the other hand, are typically invited to corporate events only when the product is already or is about to be used by the majority of the audience and are thereby providing a training service rather than giving a sales pitch. Each group is discussed in more detail in the following sections.

PROFESSIONAL SPEAKERS

Professional speakers can be, at times, a mixed bag. Former sports coaches and star athletes, retired CEOs, and book authors are a few of the more common professional speakers booked for corporate events. Even these credentials, however, do not guarantee that a former quarterback or corporate bigwig will be a good speaker. In fact, the situation can be quite the opposite. Many attendees have been drawn into a presentation, lured by a famous name, only to leave the meeting disappointed.

Many professional speakers acquire clientele through word-of-mouth. Ask meeting professionals who have been in the business for a while whom you should recommend to your client as a speaker; that will steer you in the right direction. Keep notes of which speakers were truly good speakers and for which audiences they would be ideal.

CLIENT OR CUSTOMER TESTIMONIALS

When a company is customer service driven, corporate management may invite clients to share testimonials of their experience from a customer's perspective. Such speakers may be varied in their public speaking experience and may require

FIGURE 9.1
Former Vice President Al Gore, one of the more skilled celebrity speakers, speaking on global warming.

additional support and encouragement. Taking extra time during rehearsals to ensure that customer speakers are comfortable will prove most beneficial. As a reward for this extra care, the audience will be given an insight into what customers want from a service provider.

PRODUCT AND INDUSTRY EXPERTS

In today's technology-driven world, the daily activities of companies often revolve around a software package of some kind. Corporate gatherings and events are an opportune time to train employees in ways of using said software more efficiently. As a result, it is not uncommon for hosting companies to invite representatives of the software manufacturer to present during general sessions. Such presentations may require additional audio and video equipment and should be rehearsed repeatedly to ensure a flawless execution of all technical aspects because the software representative will not be pleased if there are technical issues while demonstrating his product.

Internal Speakers

An important element of internal speakers to keep in mind is that they work for the hosting company or organization. As a result, they may exude a sense of ownership of the event and rightfully so; it is, in essence, their show. There are three tiers of internal speakers: executives, management, and submanagement. When translated to association or organization meetings, these tiers can be renamed executive officers, chairs, and members. Each has unique traits, but all have the added pressure of speaking in front of an audience of their peers, a daunting task indeed.

EXECUTIVES: CEOS, PRESIDENTS, AND VICE PRESIDENTS

Top executives vary when it comes to their ability for public speaking. Generally, they are relatively good speakers and know how to address the masses of their company effectively. After all, this quality aided in their rising through the ranks of the business world. Executives typically travel with a support staff of their own, including an assortment of secretaries, administrative assistants, presentation designers, and even on occasion speechwriters. Be prepared to assist as needed because these teams will vary in their comfort level and knowledge of presentation preparation.

MANAGEMENT/CHAIRS: MANAGERS, CHAIRS, AND SPECIALISTS

Managers, chairpersons, and specialists are notorious for being show stealers, meaning they speak for much longer than scheduled. Most often this is due to nerves and the desire to impress their superiors. On the flipside of show stealers, however, are those who provide abruptly short presentations. Nerves are also to blame for such scenarios. As a result, it is a good idea to have subsequent speakers waiting backstage and ready to take the stage at any given moment.

SUBMANAGEMENT/MEMBERS

General employees and members, the majority of people attending events, are less likely to speak onstage during large events. During award presentations, for example, most recipients simply take their award and either return to their seat or stand off to the side for a group picture. If a group picture is intended, it is a good idea to have someone onstage to direct recipients after they have received their award. Occasionally, top award winners are given an opportunity to speak at a podium. These speeches are rarely more than a few minutes long and no additional preparation is needed, but you should always be prepared for the unexpected.

PREPARATION SPACES

Speaking before an audience of peers can be stressful, but preparation can aid in reducing the intensity of that stress. Preparation can come in the form of making last-minute edits to speeches, reviewing presentation files, or just having a moment to collect one's thoughts and relax. You should consider providing these spaces within a production design for an event of any significant size. Modern corporate events typically have one of the following, if not both, types of preparation spaces.

Green Rooms

A *green room* is traditionally a space offstage or backstage where performers wait before walking onto the stage. The origins of the room's name vary from source to source, but one of the most commonly accepted theories is that the room gets its name from Shakespearean theater. During this era, actors would wait before a performance in a room full of green plants, believing the moisture the plants exuded aided in relaxing their vocal cords. Another theory states the space was named the *green* room because the limelight, a type of stage lighting used in the

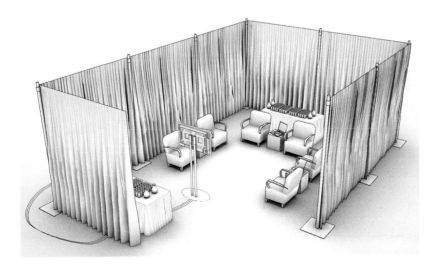

FIGURE 9.2
Backstage green rooms provide presenters with a comfortable waiting area before walking to the stage.

early nineteenth century, from the performance space cast a green glow into the offstage room. This is also where the phrase "step into the limelight" originates. Regardless of the room name's origin, the purpose of the space hasn't changed: to provide a relaxing environment to choral performers and speakers before they are needed onstage.

Today, green rooms are still used in traditional theater and in a simplified form during corporate events. Most corporate green rooms are merely designated spaces backstage consisting of a few chairs or couches. Water bottles are typically available to the speakers as well as a video monitor displaying a live feed of the stage. These spaces not only provide a place for speakers to mentally prepare for their presentation, but also allow the stage manager (a production crew member who manages backstage activity during a meeting for event) to ensure speakers make it to the stage on time.

Speaker-Ready Rooms

Speaker-ready rooms can be viewed as green rooms for the modern era, equipped with computers to make last-minute presentation edits or to check email, and luxurious lounge areas with catering services and even cable television.

FIGURE 9.3
Speaker-ready rooms provide presenters a home base for last-minute presentation edits and relaxation.

In addition, speaker-ready rooms allow breakout session presenters to meet the technicians who will be operating any audio and video equipment needed in their rooms to discuss the flow of the presentation and any unique technical needs.

Another benefit to speaker-ready rooms is the ability to keep tabs on presenters. As mentioned previously, the combined number of presenters for general and breakout sessions during large events can be close to a hundred if not more, and not all presenters will be as concerned with promptness as some event planners and attendees. To combat this potential dilemma, for larger events, presenters may be asked to sign in and out of the speaker-ready room so that production staff knows who is prepped and ready for their presentations and who needs to be tracked down.

During general sessions, all speakers who will be presenting during a session can wait comfortably in the speaker-ready room until directed by production staff to the backstage green room. It is a good idea to have speakers backstage at least one presentation before they are needed onstage in the event the previous speaker finishes more quickly than expected.

PRESENTATION MANAGEMENT

Presentation management is becoming a necessary service for shows and events of all sizes and is available from most reputable audio/video companies. This service takes the pressure of ensuring a presentation file will function properly off the presenter and onto the production support staff where it belongs.

In a nutshell, presentation management permits presenters to upload their digital presentations, such as PowerPoint files, to a designated Web site weeks before traveling to the event location. Once on-site, should they wish to make last-minute revisions, they can download the file from the server, make their edits, and upload the file again all from the comfort of their hotel room. When they make their way to the speaker-ready room, they can view their files on the exact machine that will be used during their presentation and ensure that embedded video files and fonts are displayed correctly.

This service is most useful when breakout sessions are a key element of an event. Breakout sessions are the smaller, topic-specific meetings that occur in between general sessions. These sessions are a primary source for attendees to acquire education specific to their own interests or professional needs.

FIGURE 9.4
Presentation management systems allow presenters to make last-minute edits to their presentation from the comfort of their hotel room and then send the updates to a central server.

For larger conferences, as many as 30 breakout sessions can occur at the same time. The presenters of those breakout sessions will undoubtedly have some form of digital presentation. With several sessions per day, and up to 30 sessions at a time, the total number of presentations that need to be managed during an event can quickly exceed several hundred. This is when presentation management is a must.

Instead of relying on each presenter to set up his own laptop and connect to a sound system and video projector, one computer is used for each room designated to host a breakout session, and each session's presentation files are loaded remotely. All the presenter has to do is walk into the session, click the computer mouse, and he is ready to present.

Presentation management is not limited to large shows. Even smaller events with only a few speakers can suffer from corrupt presentation files, missing video clips, or misplaced storage devices. With presentation management, as long as the file was uploaded before the show, the production staff will ensure that everything runs smoothly.

PROMPTERS AND CONFIDENCE MONITORS

Prompting is, in essence, the practice of providing public speakers with a line-by-line visual or audible cue of their prepared speech. The primary benefit to using a prompting system, as opposed to printed copies, is the speaker does not have to look down to read sheets of paper and thereby draw attention to the fact that the speech was prewritten.

FIGURE 9.5
Presenting onstage can be quite intimidating for first-time presenters.

There are two methods of prompting a speaker: visually and audibly. When visually prompting a speaker, either teleprompters or cue cards may be used, though the latter approach is a bit antiquated. When audibly prompted, the speaker wears an earpiece receiving a closed-circuit broadcast from backstage where a staff member reads the speech, word by word, following the speaker's tempo.

Confidence monitors are video monitors, typically plasma screens, that face the stage and allow a speaker to see what is currently being displayed on the room's primary projection screens. Confidence monitors are so named because they give speakers *confidence* that the topic they are discussing correlates with the presentation slide or graphic currently being viewed by the audience without having to turn their back to view the projection screens for themselves.

Teleprompters

Teleprompters primarily come in two forms in the event industry: presidential teleprompters and video displays. Both provide the same service, which is a visual representation of a prepared speech. In fact, both methods are fed by the same source.

The source of modern prompter systems is a computer installed with unique prompting software. Prompting software allows for text files to be loaded and formatted so that they can be scrolled from bottom to top of a display device. The pace at which text is scrolled is controlled by an external control device composed of a rotating dial. The more the prompter operator rotates the dial, the faster the text scrolls; reversing the direction of the dial reverses the flow of text. This manual control allows for quick adjustments if the speaker reading the speech stumbles or misses a line of text.

The output of the computer is then sent to either video monitors or presidential glass teleprompters or both. Video monitors can range from small LCD screens embedded into a podium to large plasma screens placed on the floor in front of the stage. The downside to video monitors of this nature is the speaker is forced to either look at the podium or down at the plasmas in front of the stage, destroying the illusion that the speech is spontaneous rather than carefully crafted.

Presidential Glass Prompters

A presidential prompter system, also referred to as a *beam-splitting prompter*, is composed of a tilted panel of glass or acrylic, mounted atop an adjustable stand, which reflects the speech text from an LCD monitor lying flat at the base of the stand. The glass or acrylic panel is specially coated with unique reflective and nonreflective films that allow the reflected text to be visible from only one side while the reverse appears as clear glass. The monitor at the base of the unit displays a mirrored image of the prompter feed so that it appears correctly when reflected by the glass panel.

FIGURE 9.6
Beam-splitting glass teleprompters give speakers a cheat sheet of sorts while allowing them to look directly at the audience or camera.

Typically, this method supplies a prompter on either side of the podium, just below eye level, allowing the speaker to naturally direct his attention to either side of the audience without appearing to be reading. Although it is true the audience will be aware that prompters are being used, the clear glass prevents the system from being distracting. As the name implies, this method of prompting is popular during presidential speeches, allowing the president to look directly at the audience and television cameras. This same technology is frequently adapted for television broadcasts in which the speaker focuses his attention at the camera the entire time. For such applications, the prompter system is installed directly in front of the camera lens.

A Few Last Thoughts on Prompting

For clients who are more comfortable onstage and prefer to control the speed of the prompter themselves, remote controls and foot pedals are available. However, such tools take the control away from the technicians backstage, so a backup plan should be put in place in the event of remote control failure.

A less traditional method of prompting is to project the prompter feed onto the back of secondary screens. This method reduces the amount of equipment needed onstage and takes advantage of the screens already in place. If the secondary screens are too high above the audience, however, the speaker may appear to be looking beyond the audience and disconnected with the speech.

Regardless of what system is used, keep in mind the objectives of prompting: to provide the speaker with a visual or audible backup in the event he forgets a portion of his speech and allow the speaker to appear as though he is not reading and thus is more sincere. Prompting systems are great tools for improving the quality of lengthy presentations and speeches, but ensure that each speaker has time to practice with the system before he or she is in front of an audience.

THE VALUE OF REHEARSALS

Rehearsals are practice or dry runs of a presentation or performance, and they are invaluable for ensuring a successful show. They also give speakers and performers a chance to get more comfortable with the stage and their surroundings. There are a few key issues experienced and inexperienced speakers alike will be concerned with the most: How do I get to the stage? Where do I stand? Can I read the prompter? And how will I cue the AV techs to change slides or roll video?

The Presenter's Experience

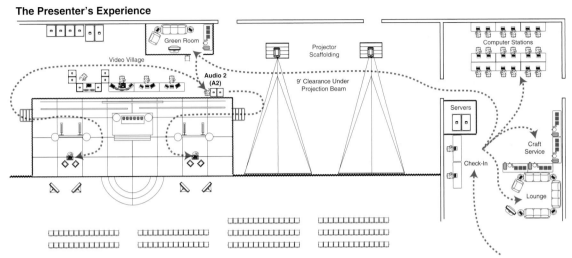

FIGURE 9.7
A common backstage layout for events.

To answer these questions and put your speakers and performers at ease, arrange specific times before the meeting, when the room is empty with the exception of tech crews, to physically walk them from backstage or the speaker-ready room to the stage and podium. Have speakers run through their entire presentation using all audio/video technology. Doing so not only gives the speakers confidence in the support staff behind the scenes, but also gives that staff a chance to learn the speakers' unique styles and quirks. If speakers are to use a teleprompter, this is the time to ensure the font is large enough for them to read and for the prompter operator to learn the speakers' pace. You may be surprised how many oversights will be discovered during rehearsals. But that is okay! This is the time to find solutions.

Professional performers, on the other hand, will be more likely to run their own rehearsals. They have enough experience with their routine that they need to merely adapt their choreography or planned movements to the event's stage. If they sent a rider when contracted, a document detailing their performance requirements, they will use rehearsal time to ensure that all those requirements are met. If it is a musical performance, they will ask for a sound check and may install their own sound boards and equipment. It is important to remember that your client is paying a good chunk of change for these performers, and it is important that the performers' needs are met in order to give the client his money's worth.

SPEAKER SUPPORT EQUALS CUSTOMER SERVICE

Speaker support, including the various pieces that comprise this service, will have one of the greatest impacts on your client. When the client thinks back to whether or not the production staff that produced the event took care of his needs, the people involved in speaker support will be remembered and evaluated. Whether you are a show producer, event planner, or even a designer visiting a show site, providing customer service to the client in every way should be a top priority to ensure the relationship continues. Through speaker support, a production team is able to provide face-to-face assurances to top-level executives and premier public speakers of the event's success as well as cater to any need. In essence, keeping the speakers happy and comfortable will do the same for the hosting event committee, who ultimately decide whether your services will be needed on future events.

CHAPTER 10

Design Teams
and Processes

INTRODUCTION TO DESIGN TEAMS AND PROCESSES

A tremendous number of pieces must come together before a successful event can be produced. Specific roles, positions, and specialties are needed within an event design team to ensure all pieces are addressed. From the account executive who receives the bid request or Request for Proposal (RFP); to the graphic designer who creates the event logo; and finally ending with the production manager who oversees the event installation, production, and strike, each individual plays a significant part in producing the event. When collected, whether a salesperson, artist, or production specialist, all these roles make up the event design team.

If you are new to the industry, you may wonder where and how the process begins. The answer depends on perspective. If you are the client or a member of an internal event planning committee, the event design process begins as a directive from the organization executives stating that the event is needed. An example of this might include a vice president of sales determining there is a need for an internal sales conference. A committee chairperson or team is selected. This team determines the venue and event structure and organizes the event agenda. The initial planning and development lead to the creation of an RFP, which is sent to potential production companies for bidding. A vendor is chosen, and the event details and designs finalized. Finally, the event is produced and generally repeated several times a year or annually, depending on the type of event. This is, of course, an extremely abbreviated description of the process from the client's perspective.

When a creative agency or production company is hired to produce an event, the process begins after an RFP is received. We have alluded to RFPs throughout this book and will reference them frequently in the remaining pages. So why are these documents so important? From a vendor's standpoint and for a freelance producer or designer, RFPs are the starting point and perhaps the most crucial step in the event design process. These documents contain an overview of the event and provide the requirements needed to be addressed by vendors to win the business. A well-drafted RFP clearly states how vendors will be selected and by what criteria. The creation of proposals that respond to these criteria, therefore, is a primary objective of event design teams.

Because this book is targeted toward freelance designers and event planners, this chapter will focus on the proposal process and the roles necessary to develop the event designs proposals contain. Because it is common for freelancers to be hired temporarily within corporate design teams to offset workloads, it is important to understand the corporate design model as well. Although the specific titles and responsibilities vary between organizations, their fundamental function is universal. Understanding these roles and structures allows you to be seamlessly integrated into an existing team when necessary – a characteristic required to be a successful freelancer.

THE PROPOSAL RESPONSE PROCESS

When clients decide to host an event, they require assistance from specialized vendors and creative partners to ensure the event is produced safely and effectively. During the preplanning and production of an event, clients and vendors are in constant communication, developing event details and making adjustments as each client's message is revised and focused. For communication to be efficient and objectives to be achieved, strong relationships must be formed between clients and vendors. These relationships begin with the proposal process, during which vendors and creative partners are selected. Although various forms of proposal processes exist, the most common begins with the sending of an RFP document to select vendors. Vendors, in turn, create their proposal responses, which aim to persuade a client to select them, over any competitor, to produce the event. This process is known as an *RFP response* and will be encountered by corporate and freelance designers alike. Following are the basic steps comprising this process.

RFP Received

RFPs can be received in a number of ways. Many industry organizations and visitor bureaus allow RFPs to be posted to their Web sites, requesting responses

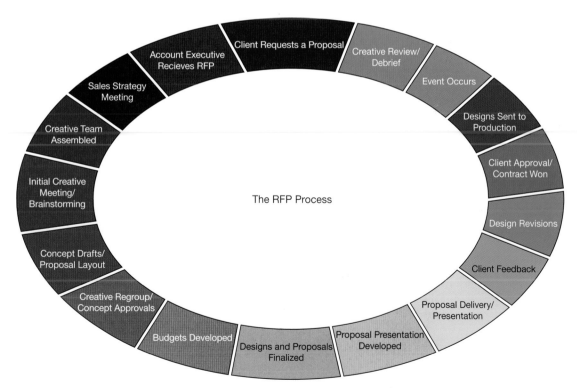

FIGURE 10.1
One interpretation of the RFP process, beginning at the top and moving counter-clockwise.

by any and all interested vendors. This cattle-call approach is less common for larger events, but a healthy amount of business can be collected through such avenues. For larger productions, the kind described in this book, RFPs are typically received by an account executive or manager directly from the potential client. Being selected as a potential vendor in this manner is the reward for successfully networking and building relationships with potential clients – a process that can take a number of years.

The RFP process can be draining on clients, and as a result, selected vendors are often contracted for several events at a time. As with all business relationships, however, clients will eventually shop their business around to ensure more affordable or effective solutions are not available. These windows of opportunity are what account executives or event salespersons are seeking to gain new clients. By continuously visiting with potential clients and showcasing services, vendors eventually make their way onto the short list of vendors asked to bid on an event. This bid comes in the form of a proposal and is typically generated by a vendor's event design team. The same process applies to freelance event producers; the difference is that they act as both the salesperson and creative lead during the proposal process.

Research

The most obvious function of research is to gather information, and it is a broad step in the proposal process. To simplify things, research can be broken down into the categories of technical and design research. Both categories are equally important but serve entirely different functions within the process.

Technical research collects known data such as venue dimensions, audience sizes, talent requirements, and any number of unique criteria requested by the client. Designers and technical specialists use this information to determine what is possible within the event space before time is dedicated to developing full production concepts.

Design research focuses on the intangible characteristics and objectives of an event. Experience directors and designers must understand for whom and what they are designing. Who is the audience? What is the vibe of the event? What should the client gain from hosting the event? How can design make the event experience more meaningful and effective? The derived answers to these questions will lead a creative team to develop a strategic response within their proposal. Design research will be covered in greater detail in Chapter 12, "Developing a Design Palette."

Initial Client Meeting

The initial client meeting, sometimes referred to as a *discovery meeting*, is not a guaranteed step within the proposal process. Many clients are unable to meet with each individual company bidding on their event and limit communication to only a few phone calls or emails to answer specific questions not addressed within the RFP. Therefore, when a client meeting is available, especially a face-to-face meeting, it is wise for the proposal team to take full advantage. Having completed basic research, teams should come prepared with well-thought-out questions and leave with an in-depth understanding of the client's objectives and event message.

After a relationship has been developed with the client, discovery meetings have the potential to become creative brainstorming sessions that allow design concepts to be developed with the client. Doing so allows creative and production teams to elevate their status from that of vendor, an entity that can easily be replaced, to an integral creative and strategic partner, a more stable and longer-lasting relationship.

Creative Design and Proposal Development

The bulk of creative design for an event occurs during the development of a proposal. Within this document, often accompanied by a live presentation, production companies and creative agencies propose to clients their event solutions in hopes of winning the clients' business. If the business is won, the creative solutions detailed within the proposal move off the page and into production and fabrication. Because of this, great care must be taken to ensure the designs contained within the proposal can be reproduced in reality.

A common business practice among creative agencies, however, is to impress clients with amazing concepts at the proposal stage and then rework the concepts to adjust for reality after a job has been won. This strategy does have its advantages. Namely, it frees designers from the annoyances of reality such as venue sizes, technical limitations, and budgetary confinements. Without these barriers, designers can focus their energy toward creating innovative designs that support the client's message.

The downside to this approach is many clients are very literal-minded. In other words, when they see a staging concept sketched or rendered in detail, they assume that is what they will be getting when they sign the contract – a logical assumption. As a result, confusion and frustration on behalf of clients arise when produced elements and environments do not closely resemble the concepts shown in proposal artwork. Clients may be further frustrated when learning the designs shown in the proposal could never have been reproduced in reality to begin with.

The flipside to this is focusing only on designs that have been proven to work in reality. Concept sketches are replaced by photorealistic

FIGURE 10.2
A solid event design team is crucial for proposal success.

renderings, and CAD drawings are used to ensure the design will work within the venue. This approach solves the problem of selling clients unattainable designs but at the same time limits designers to what has been done before and is conceptually safe. As a result, designs contained within these proposals may appear less imaginative or deficient of innovation. Therefore, this approach can lead to a loss of potential business due to a lack of creativity.

So what is the balance of the two strategies? Unfortunately, the balance lies in more work for the creative design team during proposal development. Begin with creative brainstorming sessions and keep reality at bay for now. Focus on developing new concepts that have never been seen before and environment designs that are not limited by budget. When these concepts have been documented through sketches and rough diagrams, proceed to investigate the limitations of the venue and technical capabilities.

Call for another design meeting, but this time focus on adapting the initial out-of-the-box concepts to the confines of reality. The end results are designs that are creatively original and functional solutions that can be reproduced in reality. These are the designs that should be included within a client proposal. Include the initial brainstormed concepts as part of your design research. This hybrid of the two approaches shows clients the creative engine behind a design team while offering products that are practical.

Along with solutions provided by the design team, budgets must be derived for these concepts and the equipment they require. Labor must be estimated to produce the event, and logistics must be mapped. A company history or samples of previous work might also be included within the proposal. All these elements are then laid out in a logical manner that can easily be understood by clients while they determine which vendor will be contracted as an event partner. The proposal document is then packaged and shipped to clients according to requested specifications or hand-delivered during a live presentation.

Presentation

Client presentations come in two forms: live and delivered. Live presentations are much more intimate, with designers and creative directors explaining their proposal through printed boards, PowerPoint slides, and even animated visualizations. During these presentations, clients are able to interact with the design team and pose questions, while in turn design teams are able to expound on the effectiveness of their proposed solutions. This fluid interaction strengthens client relations and generally improves the odds of winning the project. Chapter 16, "Presenting Your Design," will delve into live presentations in greater detail.

FIGURE 10.3
A client presentation is the pinnacle of the RFP process.

Although live presentations are typically preferred by design teams, they are not always an option provided by clients. Many clients accept only proposals formatted to their own specifications and received through email or postal delivery. For these delivered presentations, the appearance and design of the proposal document itself is nearly as important as the information it contains. Creative packaging and supporting elements may also be included when appropriate. A produced highlights reel of past productions, for example, might be included on DVD in the back of a printed proposal. A link to a customized proposal Web site could also be included, allowing for an automated interactive presentation to be viewed at the client's own convenience.

Unfortunately, from a designer's perspective, many event designs end at this stage of the game. Event design is big business, and a lot of competitors are gunning for the same business as your own design team. The time and effort put into proposals that are not won can pay off in other ways, however. For example, a proposal may not have won for several reasons unrelated to design: a competitor may have offered cheaper pricing or discounts, or a local vendor may have been chosen to allow for easier face-to-face communication. In these scenarios, though not ideal, the client has been informed of your design abilities, and you will likely be considered for future events or you may be recommended to the client's peers looking for similar solutions. All is not lost when a proposal does not succeed.

If the project was not won and the client specifies the loss was due to design, the event design team should review with the account executive what caused the loss specifically and how it can be prevented in the future. The purpose of these meetings is to review strategy and is not intended to place blame or find fault. Clients are not always forthcoming with their reasoning behind vendor selection, so when clear feedback is given, it should be appreciated as a valuable learning opportunity.

Revisions, Sign-Off, and Production

After a proposal has been presented to clients, they may request revisions be made to the designs per their own feedback. Although revisions are the bane of every designer, such requests are generally a good sign that your proposal is being considered. As a designer, you need to remember that the designs developed for an event are not works of art created for self-expression. They are solutions intended to serve a purpose and support a client's brand or message.

From the clients' perspective, they must ensure the event, and the elements it contains, falls in line with their own branding guidelines as well as organization objectives and policies. In addition, event planning committees may be dealing with changes in their own organization, such as a new CEO or president, business restructuring, or rebranding – any of which can drastically affect the message and design of an event. It will not always make sense to the designer why a client suddenly wants a brown color scheme or an entirely new scenic design. It is the designer's responsibility, regardless of personal opinion, to revise the designs as

FREELANCE CONTRACTS

There are many joys to being self-employed, but there are of course many chores that come along with such a business model; namely negotiating contracts. Not every project you work on will require a contract, such as quick, one-day turnarounds. Be forewarned, however, it is usually the simple ones that come back to haunt you. So it is a good idea to set down your rules and expectations before beginning a project; both for your peace of mind and to hopefully prevent lawsuits.

First you must decide how you will estimate a project, meaning what you will charge. There are two approaches, billing by the hour and project bidding. Billing by the hour can cause issues because there is no way for the client to know you really worked a certain number of hours when you are based from a home office. Thus, when they receive your bill, they may question the total hours listed. The second approach is to bid on the project as a whole; I can do this for you for X amount of dollars, everything included. This method is risky on your part, as you may underestimate the project's value and lose money on the deal. However, it makes clients happy because they know what to expect on your bill. Learning to estimate a project will take time and lots of practice, but after a while you will be able to confidently listen to a client's needs and comfortably determine a price.

But what happens if there are revisions? Explain in your agreement that the client gets one or two free revisions before you begin charging X amount for additional revisions. This of course does not include revisions needed due to your own mistakes, those should always be free. Also, be very clear as to what format your design will be delivered in, whether or not you will help present the idea, your expenses and accommodations for travel, etc. Be as specific as possible before you even begin the project to avoid frustrated and surprised clients when your bill arrives. Ironically, the larger the company, the longer it often takes to get paid. Typically, this is due to more complex accounting procedures. You can combat this a bit by declaring a specific NET, meaning when you expect payment. Many clients will demand no less than a NET 30 (meaning you should receive payment within 30 business days). If you have a good relationship with your client, however, you can negotiate a NET 15 or even Due on Delivery. But be careful with this, you don't want to come off desperate!

In the end, contracts benefit both parties, they protect you and give your client confidence they won't be tricked into hidden costs. For smaller projects, include the specifications covered above within your estimate document and have the client agree to the terms before you begin work. Keep it friendly and professional and contract negotiating will soon become second nature to you.

requested and ensure the results of these adjustments can be produced safely within the event environment. In simpler terms, you provided a solid design and now it is up to the client how to use it.

The reward for the many hours and days spent revising and polishing concepts is the contract signature signifying that your team has won the client's business. Now it is time to bring these concepts into reality. After a client has signed off on a creative concept and agreed to the terms of a proposal, the event design process shifts from the creation of conceptual solutions to production implementation.

In corporate event design models, the team that developed the initial designs contained in the proposal will often hand over the project to production teams after a job has been won. Designers may guide or oversee the aesthetics of fabrication or make an appearance on-site during the event, but for the most part their time on the project is complete. They now shift to a new proposal and begin the process all over. In a freelance model, designers play a much more integral role in communicating designs to fabrication houses and, working with the production manager, may even oversee the installation of elements on-site during the event. After an event has been completed, both corporate and freelance design teams should reconvene to review what elements were successful within the event design and which require further development before use on future events.

DIFFERENCES BETWEEN FREELANCE AND CORPORATE EVENT DESIGN TEAMS

So what are the real differences between a freelance and corporate event design team? Corporate teams exist within a larger production company that may have several specialized branches, including equipment rental, production logistics, fabrication, and transportation. An alternate scenario includes teams within a creative agency that focus strictly on developing design solutions and strategies and contracting equipment rentals and labor for clients. Finally, large production houses that specialize in equipment rental and labor may have a few designers on staff whose designs are used as sales tools to rent additional equipment.

Freelance design teams, on the other hand, are typically pulled together for a single project at a time. An event producer or executive producer, for example, who is wooing a new client or has been hired directly, in turn hires individual freelance designers to develop a proposal or design an event. Stand-alone event producers abound and function as one-person creative agencies supplementing a full-time staff with contract freelancers. In this model, the client for the freelance designer is the event producer, who is then working for the end client hosting the event. Successful event producers commonly maintain an inventory of freelance designers who are used on a regular basis.

A hybrid freelance scenario, which is equally as common, involves corporate teams supplementing their labor force with temporary freelance designers. This

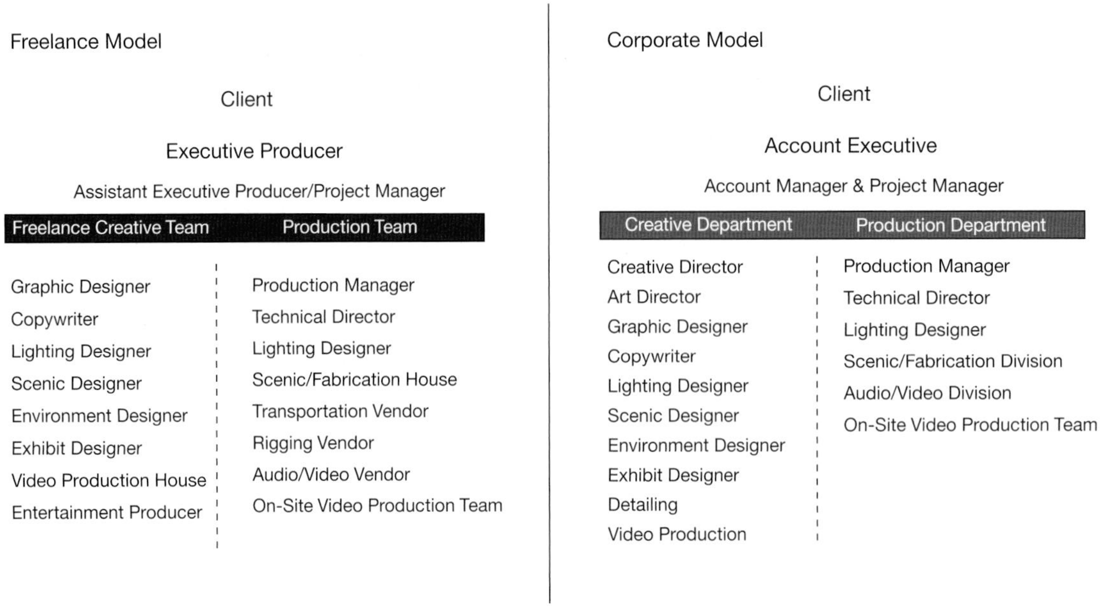

Freelance Model

Corporate Model

Client

Client

Executive Producer

Account Executive

Assistant Executive Producer/Project Manager

Account Manager & Project Manager

Freelance Creative Team	Production Team
Graphic Designer	Production Manager
Copywriter	Technical Director
Lighting Designer	Lighting Designer
Scenic Designer	Scenic/Fabrication House
Environment Designer	Transportation Vendor
Exhibit Designer	Rigging Vendor
Video Production House	Audio/Video Vendor
Entertainment Producer	On-Site Video Production Team

Creative Department	Production Department
Creative Director	Production Manager
Art Director	Technical Director
Graphic Designer	Lighting Designer
Copywriter	Scenic/Fabrication Division
Lighting Designer	Audio/Video Division
Scenic Designer	On-Site Video Production Team
Environment Designer	
Exhibit Designer	
Detailing	
Video Production	

FIGURE 10.4
A comparison of common corporate and freelance design teams.

arrangement is very beneficial for the hiring company or agency because contract labor is typically more affordable than full-time employees requiring benefit packages. A common example of this is a creative agency hiring a freelance exhibit or scenic designer when full-time employees are overtaxed by workloads. This scenario works best when freelancers provides their own equipment and work from a home office or design studio. The downside to bringing freelancers into an existing office environment is the time needed to teach the proverbial ropes of a particular business environment and having to arrange for equipment and workspace to be available.

ADVANTAGES AND DISADVANTAGES OF FREELANCE AND CORPORATE EVENT DESIGN TEAMS

As with all things in life, there are advantages and disadvantages to both models of event design teams. Corporate design teams are supported by a number of dedicated resources, including full-time designers and specialists as well as larger budgets for proposal creation. Full-time corporate designers are exposed to hundreds of projects a year, generating trial-and-error experience quickly. There is also the brand recognition provided by larger companies and agencies. In addition, corporate design teams are typically supported by a sales team dedicated to bringing in new clients and managing existing relationships. These sales representatives serve as central client contacts, ensuring consistent communication and, it is hoped, eliminating miscommunication between the client and design team.

The downsides to corporate design teams are mostly inherent in the nature of all large corporate environments. Namely, politics and red tape run rampant in office environments, distracting designers from their primary function. These politics and protocols lead to additional stresses that can reduce the enjoyment of design and potentially extinguish the relaxing environment necessary for creative minds to thrive. Although working on a large number of projects a year does increase the speed at which designers gain experience, it can also reduce clients to meaningless account numbers rather than individual organizations with unique needs.

In stark contrast, freelance teams come with considerably less bureaucracy. There is no stress of coming into an office, wearing corporate attire, dealing with administrative procedures, or working predetermined office hours. Freelance designers have a stake in whether projects are won because a negative outcome may reduce their potential pay or prevent their being hired for future projects. Thus, there is a need to provide top-of-the-line work every time. Freelancers also have the benefit of being critiqued as individuals rather than being included in a company's potentially negative public image. In essence, freelance designers are their own bosses and have the option to turn down less-than-ideal opportunities – though doing so frequently is not advised.

There are naturally downsides to freelance work as well. Most obvious is that work is not guaranteed, and freelancers must constantly be on the lookout for their next paycheck. Equipment and healthcare must be provided by the individual, and it is difficult to declare standard working hours for freelance work. As a whole, freelance design teams do not have the deep pockets of larger event companies for proposal creation and have fewer resources readily available when in a crunch. There is also limited to no brand recognition for freelance design teams, which rely only on the reputation of the event or executive producer by whom they were hired. Finally, many clients prefer the reassurances provided by an established company as opposed to the unknown patchwork of talent associated with freelance design teams.

Although there are pros and cons to either arrangement, freelance design work can be very rewarding, but so can a guaranteed paycheck provided by a corporate employer. As an individual, you must decide your own preference. As an event planner or client, you must weigh the cost savings of using an event producer and associated freelance team, which is typically cheaper and potentially more dedicated, against the reliability and automation of an established event production company.

ROLES WITHIN AN EVENT DESIGN TEAM

Event design teams come in many forms, and individual roles may be known by very different names. This is the result of a lack of universal structure for design teams, with each company or freelance team developing its own processes and role responsibilities. Although each team will have its own unique spin on the creative or design process, the positions and roles collected here

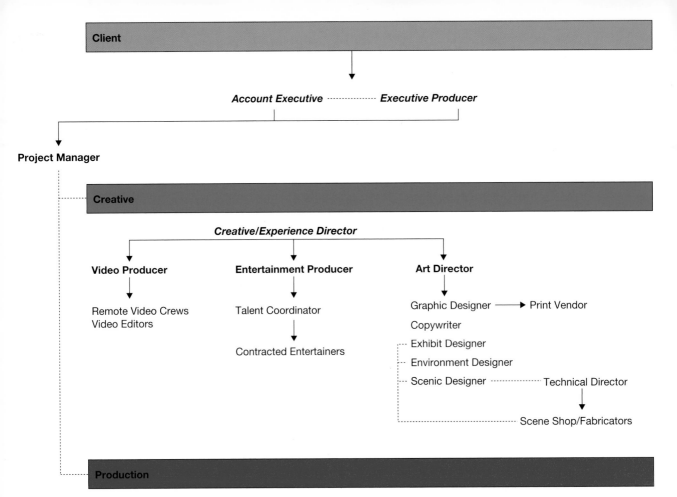

Client

Account Executive .... Executive Producer

Project Manager

Creative

Creative/Experience Director

Video Producer

Remote Video Crews
Video Editors

Entertainment Producer

Talent Coordinator

Contracted Entertainers

Art Director

Graphic Designer ⟶ Print Vendor
Copywriter
Exhibit Designer
Environment Designer
Scenic Designer .... Technical Director

Scene Shop/Fabricators

Production

General Session Producer/Show Producer

Production Manager .... Stage Manager

Technical Director
Head Carpenter .... Scenic Crew/Hands
Rigging Master .... Rigging Crew/Hands
Lighting Designer/Director .... Lighting Crew/Hands
Audio Engineer .... Audio Crew/Hands
Camera Director .... Camera Operator(s)
Video Engineer .... Graphics Operator
.... Prompter Operator

Environment Producer

Head Carpenter .... Environment Install Crew
Rigging Master .... Rigging Crew/Hands
Lighting Designer/Director .... Lighting Crew/Hands
A/V Technicians

Exhibit Floor Producer

Head Carpenter .... Exhibit Install Crew
Rigging Master .... Rigging Crew/Hands
Lighting Designer/Director .... Lighting Crew/Hands
A/V Technicians

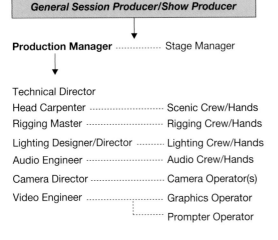

Breakout Session Producer

Speaker Ready Room Manager/Technicians

Breakout Room Technicians

represent common trends within the industry. As a freelancer, you would be wise to understand the function of each role and how your position fits into the team as a whole.

Account Executive or Manager

The account executive (AE) or account manager is the client's primary point of contact in the corporate model. In this sales role, account executives are charged with seeking out new RFP opportunities and growing existing client relationships. As the primary point of contact, account executives and managers often filter design concepts based on their own conversations with the client. The AE is also held responsible for the outcome of a proposal, meaning a win or loss, and therefore has the ultimate word in decision making related to proposals and design concepts.

Event or Executive Producer

The event or executive producer (EP) is a position typically reserved for the freelance design team structure. Along with acquiring the business from the client, this person is responsible for ensuring all the pieces of the event fall into place and accomplish the client's goals. As described previously, the EP acquires a team of freelance designers and may assist the client in selecting an AV partner. Many of the management roles described in the following sections are undertaken by the executive producer in the freelance design team model.

Project Manager

Project management is a necessary evil for artistic talent in a corporate environment. Project managers (PMs) keep designers on a schedule and keep a line of communication open with account executives, who are always eager for updates on their projects. In addition, a PM manages the creation of the RFP document and any supporting materials. When a show is won, the project manager works with the show producer and production manager to ensure all creative elements promised are delivered.

In a freelance model, project managers may be full-time employees working for an event or executive producer or a preferred freelancer. From the EP's standpoint, it can be difficult to find a project manager who can juggle all the elements necessary and communicate well with the EP and freelance team. Thus, when a successful pairing is made, the relationship often lasts for several years.

Creative or Experience Director

The creative director ensures that the look and feel of design concepts, and the proposal as a whole, respond to the client's requests. He guides the design team during brainstorming sessions to develop a strategic direction. If the proposal is to be presented in person, the creative director most often presents the creative concepts to the client directly. Generally managing several projects at a time, creative directors are hard to pin down at times when specific direction is needed.

In a freelance situation, do not be surprised if a person comes barking orders at you and then disappears for a large majority of the project, returning only to review the final proposal; this person is more than likely the creative director. Within the freelance model, the executive producer typically fills this role.

The term *experience director* is relatively new to the industry and can be used almost interchangeably with *creative director*. The differences are slight, but experience directors focus on the big picture of a proposal and, as the name implies, the overall experience of the event. Furthermore, experience directors aim to discover the most effective and innovative ways to deliver the client's message to event attendees.

Art Director

An art director typically manages a creative team under the creative or experience director. Referencing again the large number of projects a creative director may be managing at a time, art directors serve to fill in the gaps of creative guidance related to specific project details. In addition, art directors develop a proposal style guide based on the direction determined by the team and creative director during brainstorming sessions. A *style guide* is similar to a design palette but focuses on graphics and proposal layouts. If not laying out the proposal themselves, art directors oversee the final details of a proposal before presenting to the creative director, to ensure that the final deliverables are of good quality and in line with the creative direction. They remain in close communication with the creative director during the design process and inform the team of alterations to the creative direction or when revisions are needed.

Designer

Several design specialties might be included within a freelance or corporate event design team. The specific roles filled in the corporate model, of course, depend on the services provided by the company or agency. A full event production company may have on staff hundreds of designers, whereas smaller agencies may rely on freelancers or a small team of designers capable of responding to any design need. The primary structural and environment design roles within a corporate team are exhibit, environment, and scenic designers. The remaining designers provide some form of content, such as graphics, proposal layouts, Web sites, and interactive presentations.

The scenic designer is responsible for creating one or more designs to serve as a physical backdrop during the general session or keynote meetings. During the proposal process, the scenic designer provides the layout artist with scenic renderings illustrating staging concepts. This designer also works with scenic fabricators to estimate the cost of these concepts, which will then be included in the show budget for the proposal. When a show is won, the corporate scenic designer works with fabricators to ensure all necessary diagrams and schematics are provided to ensure the design is executed correctly. Depending on the size of the event, the scenic designer may oversee the on-site installation. Exhibit and environment designers function in much the same manner, designing for their assigned areas of the event.

Graphic and layout artists are often combined into one role, providing both customized graphics for the creative concepts as well as laying out the proposal for printing. This role produces much of the content used by the other players in the design team. Some teams may refer to graphic designers as *art directors*, but this is a less common use of the title. Like structure and environment designers, graphic designers work with printing houses and fabricators to ensure all printed goods are provided as presented with the proposal. The remaining content designers, such as layout artists and Web site designers, function much the same way as graphic designers. Their participation in an event, however, is typically completed at the end of the proposal stage.

Detailer

Detailers may or may not be involved during the proposal stage. Their role is to provide detailed CAD drawings of the concept elements for use by fabricators. This detail work is especially important for fabricated products such as multi-year exhibits and kiosks that must be built with longevity in mind. Detailed drawings provide fabricators with exact instructions of how a concept should be built, including every nut and bolt location. Furthermore, detailers may also create instructional guides for units requiring on-site assembly. In the freelance model, these responsibilities most often fall to the designer who developed the initial concepts.

Video Producer and Editor

Video production plays a key role in corporate events, and video producers and editors are involved with a project from the proposal stage through the completion of the event. During the proposal phase of a project, the video producer develops video concepts for opening videos and elements supporting the theme. He also estimates the associated costs of these video elements to be included in the event budget proposed. Video producers and editors are often combined roles for smaller event companies and freelance teams, especially since the advent of nonlinear editing systems. During the event, producers and editors often work late into each evening, creating highlight video segments showcasing the previous day's events as well as making any last-minute adjustments to existing video elements.

Copywriter and Copy Editor

Copywriters and copy editors ensure the text included within a proposal document is intelligible, grammatically correct, and well written. More often than not, this position is vacant and the task is divided among the design team to look over copy for obvious errors. This practice is less than ideal and can result in poorly received proposal documents if textual errors run rampant or the copy is hard to read and comprehend. Freelance copy writers are readily available and should be considered for either freelance or corporate design teams lacking the role.

Talent Coordinator

Full-time corporate talent coordinators are less common, and the position is typically filled by an outside consultant or booking agency. This position provides suggested talent and entertainment options, when requested, to be included in event proposals. In addition, talent coordinators check availability, book, and negotiate contracts of talent after a project has been won. Successful talent coordinators maintain vast databases of talent options for both national and regional locations.

Producer

There may be a variety of producers during an event. In fact, each main segment of the event may have its own producer or manager. For example, the exhibit floor may have a floor manager, while all the breakout sessions might be managed by a breakout manager. The general session or keynote meeting, specifically, requires a show producer. Show producers, sometimes called show directors, are a combination of traditional theater directors and broadcast television producers. This role both directs speakers and presenters as to how the stage is to be used as well as calls the show flow for a particular meeting. The *show flow* is a second-by-second rundown of what should occur during a session, including speaker order, video segments, and entertainment cues. The show producer uses the show flow as a detailed script to inform talent and technicians of what should be occurring on the stage at a given time. In simpler terms, the show producer is the boss after the meeting begins, whereas the production manager is in charge during load-in and strike. For larger events, show producers are introduced to the design team very early in the design process to ensure technical and logistical considerations are included with the design concepts. Again, the executive producer of the freelance team typically fills this role as well.

Specialist

Specialist is a blanket term used to describe any technician related to areas of production such as rigging, audio, video, lighting, and fabrication. In a corporate model, these individuals provide guidance for designers during the proposal stage and work with the production manager to ensure the design is reproduced accurately in reality. Specialists ensure that necessary equipment is acquired for the production, and each manages a specialized labor team on-site. Fabrication specialists, whether corporate or stand-alone businesses, work with designers and detailers to produce the physical structures depicted with conceptual artwork. This task often requires clever problem solving and quick engineering to accomplish. The industry would truly not be possible without these individuals and the crews they manage, and as a designer, you should heed their guidance when provided.

Technical Directors

Technical directors, or TDs, act as a communication bridge between scenic and environment designers and fabricators. When TDs are brought in for larger productions, their responsibility is to ensure the proposed design is executed and done so safely. In addition, TDs stay abreast of new technologies and techniques across various industries and determine how such elements can be incorporated into event production. It is a good idea to add a TD to your design team if the event production requirements fall outside the expertise of your own design ability or the experience of the on-site production manager. In addition, working with technical directors early in the design phase can elevate the production value of a design in many ways, introducing technologies and approaches that may have otherwise been left on the table.

Production Manager

Production managers (PMs) are responsible for taking a design from the conceptual phase and bringing it into reality. Much of the detail planning created by this role occurs during CAD drafting, in which all production elements for a specific meeting space are mapped out, such as seating layouts, staging placement, rigging, and the location of video control and production stations. The production manager also ensures that the layout of the event complies with local regulations and fire codes. Chapter 11, "Designing from the Ground Up," will delve deeper into the CAD layout process.

In addition, this role typically manages labor coordination and on-site production schedules. With crews often exceeding 50 or more individuals, the management of labor can be a daunting task. To make matters even tougher, strict labor regulations such as working hours, break and meal times, and task assignments are provided by state and national laws as well as labor unions. With the limited amount of time typically given for loading in an event and striking it, the ability to juggle crews and abide by all regulations requires a seasoned veteran to accomplish successfully. It is not an exaggeration to say every event that is produced successfully is due in very large part to the hard work of a production manager. As with project managers, when freelance executive producers find skilled production managers, they generally become staples of the EP's event team.

A FEW ADDITIONAL THOUGHTS

Whether you are working within a corporate team or as a freelancer, understanding the fundamental process of event design and the development of proposals is important to ensuring the longevity of your career. Respect the importance of each role and make an effort to learn from the specialists you encounter. Doing so will broaden your capabilities as a freelancer and provide more work opportunities. Finally, observe which roles you aspire to fill later in your career, such as becoming an event producer or creative director. Such aspirations will keep you motivated and inspired during the many late nights of your early career.

CHAPTER 11

Designing from the Ground Up

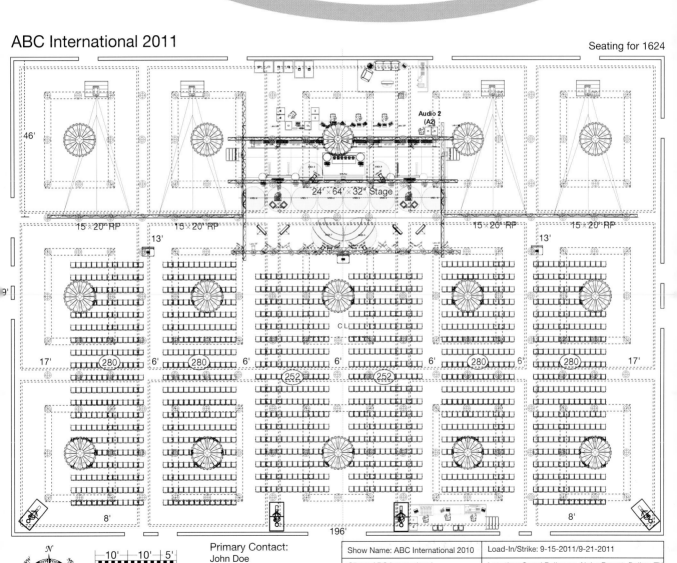

ABC International 2011

Seating for 1624

46'

9'

13'   13'

17'   15' × 20" RP   15' × 20" RP   24' × 64' × 32" Stage   15' × 20" RP   15' × 20" RP   17'

Audio 2 (A2)

CL

17'   (280)   6'   (280)   6'   (252)   6'   (252)   6'   (280)   6'   (280)   17'

8'   196'   8'

Primary Contact:
John Doe
Production Manager
Acme Production Company
jdoe@email.com
1.555.123.4567

N E S W NE SE SW NW

10' 10' 5'
Scale: 1" = 25'

Show Name: ABC International 2010	Load-In/Strike: 9-15-2011/9-21-2011
Client: ABC International	Location: Grand Ballroom, Alpha Resort, Dallas, TX
Version: 003	Drawn By: A. Drafter 3-5-2010

INTRODUCTION TO DESIGN

So you have the concept rendering of your design and everyone has signed off on your creative vision up to this point. What now? Now you begin transforming your vague vision into a practical design that will work within the parameters of the space and the client's budget. To begin, you need to create a scaled floor plan of the venue. Although floor plans are typically produced and managed by a production manager, it is not uncommon for such drawings to be requested of the designer. Event planners and producers may even draft floor plans themselves, to determine what is possible within an event space before bringing in an entire design team. Understanding how such a document is crafted and used is a requirement for any member of an event design team.

Floor plans are schematic top views of an event space that are used to organize and ensure all the necessary elements will fit into the room or environment. When laying out a floor plan, you may feel as if you are working on a jigsaw puzzle, trying to get all the pieces to come together. Taking each element one step at a time, however, makes the process a bit more manageable. The end goal is to produce a visual document that is quickly and easily understood by clients, venue representatives, fire marshals, and most importantly, your own design and production teams. Furthermore, a completed floor plan will serve as a road map for installing the event on-site and help discover potential dilemmas that remain to be resolved.

DRAFTING SOFTWARE

The practice of creating a floor plan or scaled drawing is traditionally known as *drafting*, and several software packages allow even first-time users to quickly generate accurate drawings. AutoCAD and Vectorworks are among the more popular software packages that can be used to view, create, and edit floor plans. Both packages offer similar features, but for first-time users, Vectorworks may be a better buy because it is a bit cheaper and targeted more toward the event and entertainment industry. Free drafting software programs are also available and can be tracked down with a quick web search. These programs have very limited capabilities, however, and are not advised for professional production planning. The samples contained within this chapter were created using Vectorworks.

VENUE FLOOR PLANS

Floor plans and capacity charts provided by venue web sites can often be misleading. As described in previous chapters, the capacities of event spaces listed on venue web sites generally do not take into account the staging and production elements. A good rule of thumb is to subtract a third of the listed seating capacity to get a ballpark figure of actual seating capacity for a meeting space after production elements have been added. At this stage of the game, however, planning has moved passed ballpark estimates and into exact measurements. To begin drafting an accurate floor plan of your event, you must acquire a scaled drawing of the meeting space.

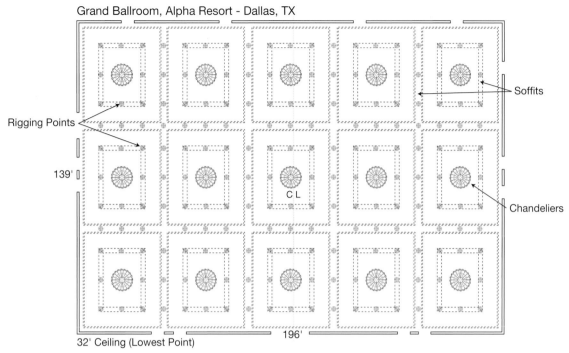

FIGURE 11.1
Blank floor plans with a reflected ceiling are the starting point for designing an event.

Tracking down scaled venue floor plans can be a frustrating and time-consuming task. In the best case scenario, a quick phone call to the venue lands you a *computer-aided drawing* (CAD) of the event space, complete with a reflected ceiling. Reflective ceilings were mentioned in Chapter 5, "Rigging," but as a refresher, they are standalone documents or a layer within a CAD document showing where potential rigging points and structural steel beams are located.

In a slightly less ideal situation, the venue has a contracted rigging company that can provide you with scaled venue drawings. In the worst case scenario, you will need to visit the location and take detailed measurements using conventional and laser measuring tapes. Although visiting the location is advised either way, it is far easier and desirable to spend your site-survey time double-checking ceiling heights and basic dimensions rather than creating a floor plan from scratch.

CREATING A WORKING FLOOR PLAN

So now you have your clean scaled venue drawing and are ready to start laying in elements unique to your event. Begin by adding known elements, such as seating, front of house, staging, and backstage spaces. These pieces must be included in the environment and have the least amount of flexibility as to location. The order in which these elements are added to the drawing depends on the client's priorities.

If the client specifies from the beginning that an exact number of seats must fit into the space, the seating is the first place to start. Or perhaps the stage design takes precedence and seating is added after the stage has been placed. This is where the juggling and jigsaw puzzle sensation ensues – determining which is the most important element and then building around that piece. Following are a few considerations for each element that should be included in a working floor plan.

Stage

If your budget requires the use of house risers, make a quick phone call to the venue to confirm the sizes of risers available; they typically come in 6' × 8' or 4' × 8' sections. If seating was placed first, place the stage at least 8 feet from the front row of chairs to accommodate for confidence monitors and step units. Otherwise, determine which is the best wall to place the stage against, leaving room for rear projection if necessary and backstage areas.

Because most stages are built from house risers and are therefore rectangular, draw a rectangle the width and length of your desired performance space in 4-, 6-, or 8-foot increments. If your scenic concept was modeled in 3D and to scale, use these dimensions to determine your ideal stage width. If you are working from pencil sketches, try to use standard scenic elements, such as rented backdrops, as size references to estimate the stage size needed. The exact stage placement and size may be reworked a few times until rigging points and projection distances have been determined by your production specialists and scenic designs are finalized.

Seating

Seating was covered heavily in Chapter 4, but when you're laying seating into a floor plan, always shoot for maximum capacity, meaning add as many chairs allowed by the venue and local fire code. Clients frequently request additional seating as the event draws near, and determining the maximum seating capacity early in the design process will prevent clients from overbooking the event space. When using venue-provided chairs, confirm chair widths because they can range between 17 and 20 inches wide, and a few incorrect inches per chair can add up quickly when seating gets tight.

FIGURE 11.2
A stage layout using house risers.

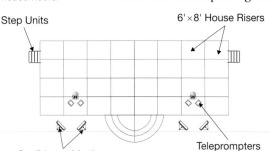

Step Units

6'×8' House Risers

Confidence Monitors

Teleprompters

Be on the lookout for columns and architectural elements that cause sightline issues and avoid placing chairs directly behind such obstructions. Keep seating at least 8 feet from the walls and include plenty of aisles and walkways. Theater seating should consist of 20 rows of 14 chairs with a 4- to 8-foot aisle between each section. Rounds should be placed at least 11 feet apart from center to center. And classroom tables should have one and a half to two seat depths between rows. Confirm these measurements with the catering manager before finalizing your drawing because some venues may install seating differently.

Grand Ballroom, Alpha Resort - Dallas, TX

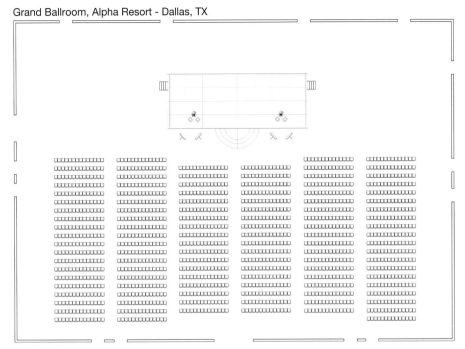

FIGURE 11.3
Seating added to the
floor plan.

Front of House

A few specialists must have a clear view of the production as it occurs, seeing exactly what the audience sees: the show producer, lighting director, and audio engineer. The space provided for these specialists, known as *front of house* (FOH), serves as a command center for the production. The FOH would ideally be placed in the middle of the meeting space, allowing each specialist a perfect view of events onstage and lighting cues, as well as providing the optimal location for acoustical monitoring. Because event audience seating is typically flat rather than raked like a traditional theater, placing the FOH in the middle of the room would cause a number of sightline issues. Therefore, it is typically placed in the back of the room, read front of the house, and off to one side – the side opposite of the primary entrance or catering pathways.

The FOH typically consists of an 8' × 24' section of 24- or 32-inch risers, just enough space for two 8-foot tables and an audio console with processing racks. Audio controls take a majority of the FOH space with the audio console and engineer requiring a 4' × 4' space, and processing racks making as much as a 3' × 4' footprint. The remaining two tables are shared by the show producer and lighting director and lighting console. Pipe and drapes, just tall enough to reach the top of the 8-foot tables, are then placed around the perimeter of the FOH to mask the mess of wires and cabling running from the lighting and audio consoles.

FRONT OF HOUSE (FOH)

Audio Engineer   Show Director/Producer   Lighting Director

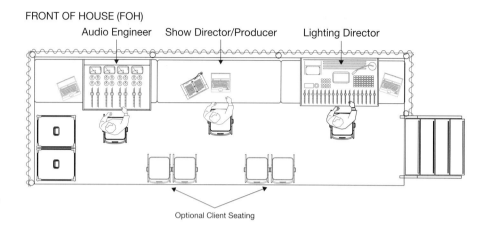

FIGURE 11.4
The parts of front of house (FOH).

Optional Client Seating

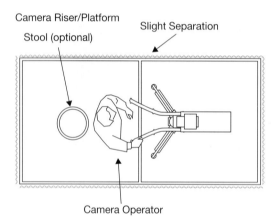

Camera Riser/Platform

Stool (optional)

Slight Separation

Camera Operator

FIGURE 11.5
An Image Magnification, or I-Mag, camera platform.

Camera Platforms

Camera platforms are required only if the event is being documented on video or when presenters are I-Mag'ed onto projection screens. More often than not, corporate events require I-Mag, so it should be assumed that at least one camera platform will be required. A common practice is to place one camera platform in the middle of the room, directly in front of the primary podium, with a second camera being placed off to one side, allowing for both a cross and direct shot of speakers and presenters.

Most camera platforms have a 4' × 8' footprint and are elevated to the same height as the stage. Many platforms consist of two separate pieces: one for the camera tripod and one for the camera operator. This separation prevents the camera operator's movement from shaking the camera when the tripod head is locked. Take full advantage of columns when present by placing camera platforms in front of them to reduce the number of seats blocked by the camera platform. Otherwise, select locations that create the fewest sightline issues.

Cable Paths and Exits

Ensuring clear pathways to emergency exits are present must be a constant concern for all event planners and designers. Not doing so will lead to fire code violations and place your production crew and attendees at risk. A lot of potentially dangerous equipment and technology is used during event productions, including high-voltage amplifiers, overhead rigs weighing several tons, and lighting fixtures emitting immense heat, any of which can lead to disaster and tragedy if precautions are not put in place – namely, a number of clear evacuation routes.

In addition, miles and miles of cabling are used during events. Efforts must be made to secure cabling in a manner so as not to cause tripping hazards for attendees and catering staff or prevent emergency exit doors from opening. Consider using trussing or floor-supported pipes to build cable bridges over doorways when necessary and use cable protectors, such as Yellow Jacket cable protectors (www.yjams.com), or wide gaffer's tape to secure cabling across walkways.

Primary Truss Lines

The location of the primary truss line, the main trussing used to hang downstage lighting fixtures, is dependent on available rigging points and stage placement. More often than not, the placement of this truss line dictates the exact placement of the stage and not the reverse. Again, we run into the jigsaw puzzle sensation. The trick is to find a line of rigging points, parallel to the stage, that allow truss-

FIGURE 11.6
A cable bridge over a doorway.

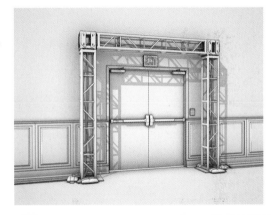

ing to be hung so that a 35-degree angle is created between the light fixtures and the elements being lit onstage. A side elevation or section is the most efficient view for determining the angle and location of primary trussing. From there, you begin adding any additional trussing for projectors, secondary screens, drapery lines, etc.

While laying in additional trussing, consider how you will run lighting and audio cables from fixtures and speakers to their corresponding backstage racks. A common practice is to rig a line of trussing from the primary truss line, spanning over the stage and ending backstage. This additional line of trussing

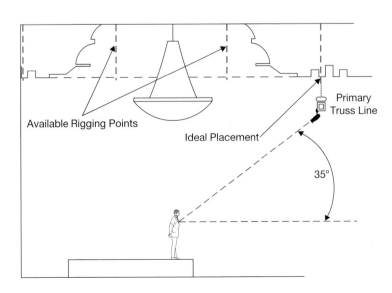

Available Rigging Points

Primary Truss Line

Ideal Placement

35°

FIGURE 11.7
Primary trussing should be hung 35 degrees from the lighting focus. Finding a line of rigging points at that location is the challenge.

allows the masses of cabling to be run overhead and dropped down to dimmers and amps backstage. An alternate solution is to use pick points, in which cabling is hung directly from rigging points using wire rope, in place of trussing. Fortunately, this process is typically accomplished in collaboration with the technical director and lighting designer, and it is best to rely on their expertise.

Screens, Projectors, and Speakers

Screens, projectors, and speakers typically are added by a corresponding specialist, making the finalization of working floor plans a collaborative task. However, to get the proverbial ball rolling when a specialist is not available, you can use a few basic formulas to initially place these elements into your floor plan.

FIGURE 11.8
A cable pick point.

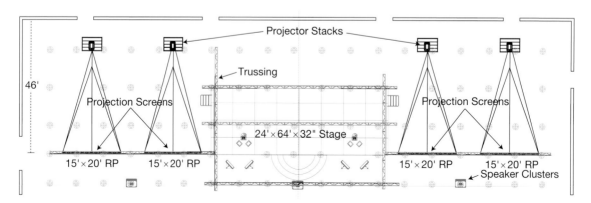

FIGURE 11.9
Projectors, screens, and audio speakers are added to the floor plan.

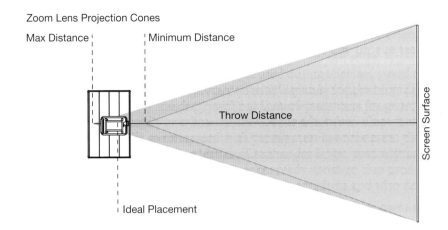

Zoom Lens Projection Cones

Max Distance | Minimum Distance

Throw Distance

Screen Surface

Ideal Placement

FIGURE 11.10
The projection cone explained.

In regards to screen placements, the rule of thumb for viewing distance is eight times the screen's height. So an 18' × 24' wide projection screen is viewable from up to 144 feet away before a secondary screen, or delay screen, is needed. You may encounter this rule being described as six times the screen's width. This model still applies to 4:3 screens but, with the addition of various new aspect ratios, no longer works as a general rule.

Projector placement is dependent on the lens used within the projector, and unless a fixed lens, a range will be determined. For example, an adjustable zoom lens of 1.6–2.0 requires 16 feet of throw distance to fill a 10-foot wide screen at a minimum and 20 feet at maximum. This placement is typically illustrated on a floor plan by two cones, starting at the front of potential projector placements and extending to the edges of the screen, one cone representing the shortest possible throw, whereas the other shows the maximum throw distance. A rigging point within that range would then be selected as the location for the projector to be hung. Review Chapter 7, "Video," for more in-depth explanations of screen placements and sizing as well as projection specifics.

Placement of audio speakers varies greatly depending on the sound system used. For use as placeholders, until an audio specialist is brought onto the team, place a speaker cluster or array 5 feet out and over from each downstage edge of the performance space. If your stage is particularly wide, place an additional cluster or array 5 feet in front of the downstage center.

Backstage Spaces

A number of stations and areas are needed backstage behind the performance space. A video village, consisting of a 10' × 12' footprint for video bays and switchers, provides a central location for all things video related. Also included in a video village are two 8-foot tables for graphics control, meaning PowerPoint or Keynote, and teleprompter computers and their corresponding operators and engineers.

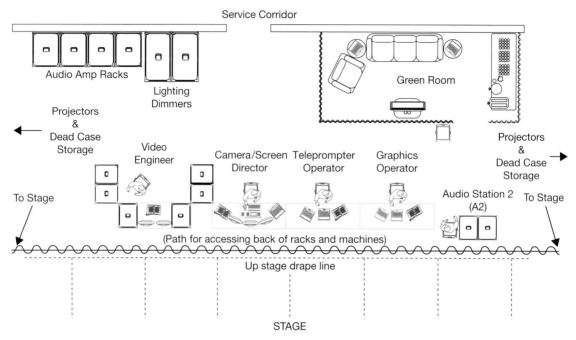

FIGURE 11.11
The parts of backstage.

When rear projection is used, projector stacks, supported by 5' × 7' scaffolding, can be found directly behind each projection screen. This configuration allows technicians to access projection equipment in the event of a technical issue without disturbing the audience – a task that would be impossible with projectors rigged for front projection.

A secondary audio station, referred to as A2, is generally placed to one side behind the stage. This station is manned by an audio specialist in charge of wireless microphones who preps presenters and speakers before they walk onto the stage. Audio amplifiers are also stored backstage, requiring at minimum a 4' × 12' space, as well as lighting dimmer packs with roughly a 6' × 6' footprint. Rounding off the space required for equipment and operators is dead case storage. Dead cases are empty equipment cases, the equipment being used during the production, which can take up a surprising amount of space. For larger productions, it is not uncommon for an entire meeting space not being used by the event to serve as dead case storage. Think of the closing scene from *Raiders of the Lost Ark*.

Finally, space must be allotted for green rooms. Green rooms were addressed in Chapter 9, "Speaker Support," but as a reminder, consider dedicating enough space for a few couches, chairs, and tables for presenters to wait prior to entering the performance space. Depending on the size of the show and number of

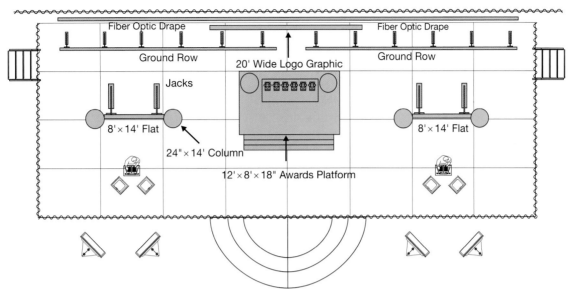

FIGURE 11.12
Scenery added to the floor plan.

presenters, green rooms can range in size from a few banquet chairs behind the stage to full lounge areas complete with beverage stations and video monitors providing a continuous feed of stage activity. Work with your client or event producer to determine the extent of green room requirements before finalizing your floor plan. Again, if you feel overwhelmed, do not worry; your technical director or production manager will generally manage this task with you.

Scenic and Environment Elements

Scenic elements should be added in the performance space and include any necessary supports such as jacks and vertical trussing. Drawing elements in as accurately as possible, meaning showing the actual thickness of flats and footprint of dimensional pieces, is important to determine how much space is left for stage entrances and performance space. Include any trussing or rigged piping needed to hang soft goods and ensure rigging points are available above these locations. Next, draw in all drape lines, usually shown as wavy lines, to determine how many linear feet of drapery will be required from rental providers. Providing detailed locations and sizes of scenic elements and soft goods also helps lighting designers develop accurate lighting plots and inform specialists where cabling can be run.

FRONT ELEVATION AND SECTIONS

Although front elevations and sections fall outside the realm of floor plans, they are very useful tools for determining trim heights and sightlines. If the floor plan is drawn in 3D, creating elevations can be as easy as changing views within your drawing software; otherwise, a scaled 2D drawing must be created similar in detail to the floor plan.

Sightlines

The term *sightline* describes what audience members can see from their location in the audience. Since it is dependent on location, the sightline varies from seat to seat. As a designer, you must view your design from every angle to ensure sightlines are addressed and that the design works from various angles. There are two kinds of sightlines; we will call them *positive* and *negative sightlines*.

Positive sightlines are what you want the audience to see clearly, such as projection screens, speaker entrances, or the performance space as a whole. Negative sightlines are those areas you do not want an audience member to see, such as upstage rigging and areas offstage. There are a few ways to check for both positive and negative sightlines to ensure the audience is seeing only what you intend to be seen.

If you are modeling your design in a 3D environment, it is very easy to check sightlines. Simply move the virtual camera around the space from about 4–6 feet off the ground. Target the stage and use a wide-angle lens. Check for areas you intend to mask from view. Again, a 3D scaled model makes this task very easy.

A more traditional approach is to draw front and side elevations of the environment. In the side elevation, draw an *X* 48 inches above the ground plan to represent a seated attendee's eye level. Now draw diagonal lines, starting at the *X*, to the top of the elements in your design. These lines represent potential focal points.

FIGURE 11.13
An explanation of positive and negative sightlines.

What you want to see (Positive Sightlines)
What you don't want to see (Negative Sightlines)

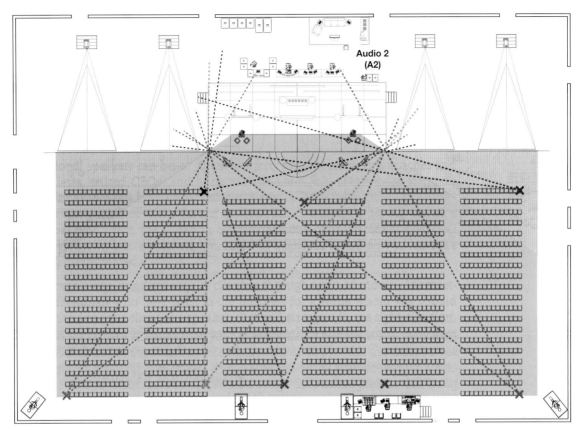

FIGURE 11.14
A method of checking sightlines and determining less-than-ideal seating.

If the lines reach elements that are not intended to be seen without crossing an obstruction, then that item will be seen by the audience. Consider lowering your teaser drape or masking the undesirable elements in some way. Repeat this process using the floor plan created earlier, drawing Xs in the nine extremes of the space. Draw sightlines from each of these points and again check that elements offstage will not be seen by the audience.

Finally, repeat the process checking for positive sightlines, ensuring that columns or speakers do not block the view of video screens or the key performance spaces. It may not be possible to create a perfect environment in regards to sightlines in some venues. These exercises, however, allow you to confidently inform your client of which areas of the seating are preferred and which should be used only in the event of a packed audience.

Trim Heights

In a theatrical environment, *trim height* describes how high masking drapes can be hung before exposing lighting equipment and rigging to the audience. In a

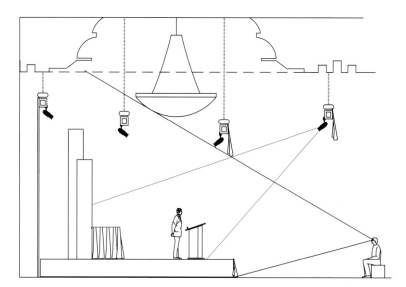

FIGURE 11.15
A method of checking sightlines and trim heights.

corporate event environment, trim height is typically used to declare how high production elements can be within a given environment. For example, an event producer might inform a scenic designer that the room's trim height is 21 feet, which lets the designer know the design cannot exceed 21 feet from the venue floor to the highest point of the stage design, including masking drapes and the top bar of trussing.

Trim heights can be determined from either front or side elevations, though side elevations tend to be easier to read when multiple lines of trussing and secondary screens are used. Determining trim heights is especially important when you are working in venues that contain ceilings with soffits or low-hanging chandeliers. In such scenarios, checking trim heights is similar to checking sightlines, and ensures that projection and lighting are not blocked by structural elements. As in the previous exercises for sightlines, using the side elevation, draw diagonal lines from the front of a projector lens to the top and bottom of a screen to ensure a clear line of projection is available.

PREPARING YOUR DRAWING FOR FIRE MARSHAL APPROVAL

Most venues require that your production floor plan be approved by the local fire marshal to ensure all safety codes and regulations are followed. Fire-marshal-approved floor plans also reduce the venue's liability in the event of an incident related to the event. Work with the venue representative to determine if he will deliver your floor plan to the fire marshal or if your team needs to work directly with the fire marshal's office and pay any associated fees; typically, the venue handles this task to ensure compliance. Before the floor plan can be sent

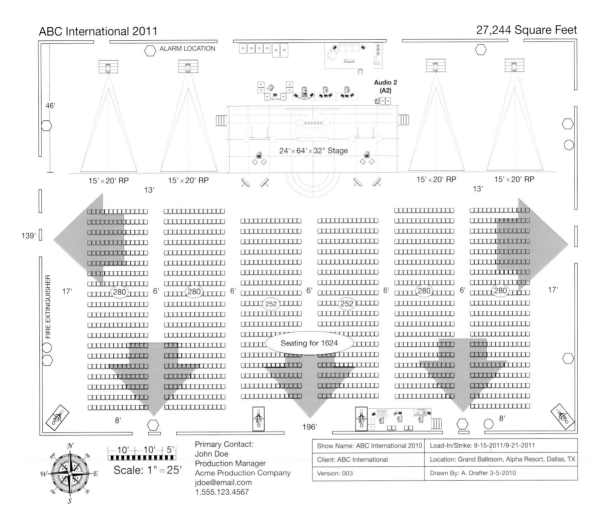

ABC International 2011

27,244 Square Feet

24' × 64' × 32" Stage

Seating for 1624

Primary Contact:
John Doe
Production Manager
Acme Production Company
jdoe@email.com
1.555.123.4567

Scale: 1" = 25'

Show Name: ABC International 2010	Load-In/Strike: 9-15-2011/9-21-2011
Client: ABC International	Location: Grand Ballroom, Alpha Resort, Dallas, TX
Version: 003	Drawn By: A. Drafter 3-5-2010

FIGURE 11.16
A floor plan prepped
for fire marshal
approval.

for approval, however, it must be prepped according to that county's specific regulations. Following are a few common elements that should included in or removed from an event floor plan before submission.

Ensure that the floor plan includes basic event details such as the event name, room and venue names and address, and event dates, including load-in and strike. In addition provide a production contact name, typically the production manager, and a phone number where he can be reached before and during the production. If haze or fog is used, requiring the smoke detection system to be disengaged, this is the phone number that will be called when the fire marshal arrives on location during the event. A return mailing address or email also needs to be included in order to receive a copy of the approved floor plan.

Next, remove any information that is not related to fire evacuation – the primary purpose for this approval process. Remove rigging, lighting, and audio symbols unless they are floor supported or block an exit. Remove production notes and projection lines as well, leaving only seating, staging, and floor-supported elements such as drapery lines and projection screens. Anything that might impede an attendee's path to an exit should be included; all else can be removed.

Now add the basic venue dimensions and a total square footage, information needed to determine maximum occupancy. Ensure that aisleways are at least 4–8 feet in width and rounds are 11 feet apart from center to center. For theater seating, make certain that a walkway is placed between every 20 rows of chairs and that a row does not contain more than 14 chairs. Place a total number of chairs over each section and a combined total of chairs for the space in bold.

Finally, make clear notations of all exits and egress pathways and highlight fire extinguisher and alarm locations. Blocking an exit with draping is hit or miss, depending on the fire marshal reviewing the production plan. If allowed, hang internally lit exit signs from the drape piping to make clear to attendees that an exit is available behind the draping and notate these solutions in your drawing.

After the document has been filed with the fire marshal's office, it will be reviewed and approved, or the contact listed will be notified of necessary revisions. If submitted directly, the approved floor plan will be stamped and mailed to the contact listed on the document or returned to the venue representative. Make certain that the approved floor plan is followed during production because fire marshals frequently visit production sites to ensure compliance and are authorized to shut down an event if violations are found. Event safety is nothing to take lightly, and there is no contest between design aesthetics and the safety of attendees and production crews.

ADDING THE FINISHING TOUCHES TO A WORKING FLOOR PLAN

Before a floor plan can be useful, a few finishing touches must be added. For one, a title block should be included in the bottom right or left corner, including show name, client name, event date(s), location and room, name of the drafter and contact info, date of latest revision to the drawing, and event producer or company name. In addition, the scale ratio of the drawing should be noted, such

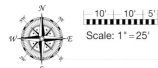

Scale: 1" = 25'

Primary Contact:
John Doe
Production Manager
Acme Production Company
jdoe@email.com
1.555.123.4567

Show Name: ABC International 2010	Load-In/Strike: 9-15-2011/9-21-2011
Client: ABC International	Location: Grand Ballroom, Alpha Resort, Dallas, TX
Version: 003	Drawn By: A. Drafter 3-5-2010

FIGURE 11.17
A title block and scale bar example.

as 1/4" = 10'. This ratio defines for others how to take measurements from your drawing when printed in full size. Including a scale bar is also helpful because your floor plan may be printed in various sizes. Finally, notate key dimensions of the stage, screens, projection distances, backstage space, and any additional measurements that will be referenced frequently during production planning, such as ceiling and platform heights.

Now that you have a working floor plan, distribute this document to your design team so everyone can work on the same literal and figurative page. However, be prepared for several revisions to be made to your floor plan as elements are changed and specialists determine technical approaches to the event – hence, the name *working* floor plan, as in a work in progress, as opposed to *final* floor plan, which will not exist until the event has ended.

CHAPTER 12

Developing a Design Palette

INTRODUCTION

Let's be honest, every designer, regardless of experience level, will at some point hit a creative wall. Professional designers, however, do not have this luxury and are required to meet deadlines that often seem unreasonable. There is no question deadlines are indeed becoming shorter due to the fast-paced communication technologies that are now commonplace in America's workforce. So what is the creative mind to do when told to be creative between the hours of 9 and 5?

To begin, successful designers build themselves a toolkit. Every designer's toolkit varies in form, but most include common features such as reference manuals, inspirational materials, and drawing supplies or software. This chapter will make a few suggestions that you, as a designer, may find helpful to add to your arsenal of creative tools. Adapt these suggestions to your own style and preferences, but make a sincere effort to begin building your own toolkit early in your career because doing so will pay dividends as your projects grow more complex and creatively demanding.

Having a variety of resources within your toolkit, however, is not the be-all and end-all of design. To create a successful design, you must understand what it is exactly you are designing and for whom. While the obvious answer may seem the client, it is often the client's audience that determines whether an event was successful or a failure. To answer the questions of what you are designing and for whom, you must be aware that client, audience, and event research must take place for every project, regardless of the size or complexity of the event itself. The steps laid out within this chapter will guide you through the research process, providing you with the raw data needed to create your design palette.

The design palette is a visual representation of your research and creative decisions unique to each event, scenic, or experience design. The fundamental elements of color, texture, line, and mood or vibe will guide your design process toward targeted concepts that will aid in delivering your client's message and enrich the attendee experience. As mentioned previously, you are encouraged to try out the methods and techniques listed within this chapter, but are strongly urged to adapt them as needed to be realistic and functional for your own unique workflow and creative process. Before we delve into the design techniques and tools, however, let's review the fundamentals of design.

THE FUNDAMENTALS OF DESIGN

All forms of design consist of the same building blocks known as *design elements*. When combined, these elements form the *principles of design*. The successful use and arrangement of these elements and principles are what separate quality designs from the mundane. If you are a novice designer, you have more than likely been using these elements all along but were simply unaware of their names or specific functions. If you are an experienced designer transitioning to event design, the following definitions will show how these fundamentals are applied specifically to corporate scenic and environment designs.

Design Elements

Design elements are found in nature and have always existed, even before they were labeled and categorized. They are the shapes of clouds, the textures of rocks and trees, and the colors and compositions of the horizon. While these poetic examples may seem like fluff, similar observations drove early designers and artists to put order and structure into what they saw around them by giving these elements names and definitions. These same definitions are still used today and cannot be avoided in design. The moment your pencil touches paper, you have a design element. It is understanding how to use these elements together in a complete composition that adds value to your designs.

LINE

A line can be either the mark made by a pen or brush or the edge of two shapes or spaces meeting. In scenic design, lines exist all over the place. The side of a box on stage is a line. The curve of the proscenium arch is a line. Even the top of a stage set against the void of backstage is a line. And, of course, if you paint a big wave on the flats making up your set, that is another line. Later in the chapter, we will determine what type of line should be used in your designs through research and the development of a design palette.

SHAPE

When connecting lines create a closed space, a shape is created. If you have a cube on stage, each side is a shape. If that box is at an angle to you, the entire outline or silhouette of the cube from that angle creates an entirely different shape. Here is something to contemplate under an apple tree: for every shape you create, you are also creating a negative shape. If you have two wavy flats on stage with space between them, the space between them becomes a negative shape. The void above the stage is the negative shape of the set. Negative shapes can come in quite handy when using multiple layers of flats and soft goods. Even replicating a logo with a negative shape is possible and can be more visually interesting than hanging a foam cutout.

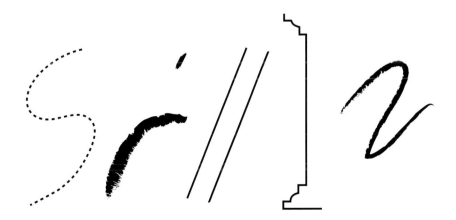

FIGURE 12.1
Examples of line.

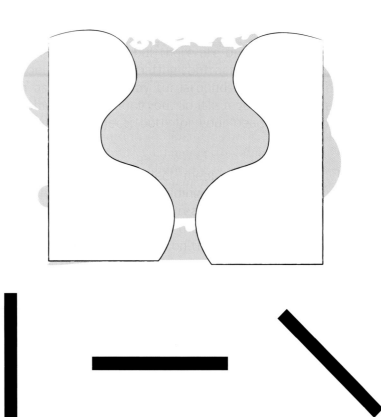

FIGURE 12.2
Two shapes also create a shape in the void between them, known as a negative shape.

FIGURE 12.3
How lines give direction and are interpreted subconsciously.

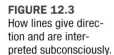

Vertical
(Balance, Formal)

Horizontal
(Calm, Stability)

Diagonal
(Movement)

DIRECTION

All lines have direction – horizontal, vertical, or diagonal (sometimes referred to as oblique). The direction of lines can create emotion in the observer or give the design a sense of movement. A horizontal line, for example, can imply calm or stability, but lack movement. Vertical lines create a sense of balance and formality, but also lack movement. Diagonal lines, on the other hand, imply movement and action. It is the use of direction that can make a design seem exciting and modern, or muted and plain. For example, giving stage flats a slant or casting light patterns from steep angles creates a motion in a stage design. Obvious direction, however, must be used sparingly; otherwise, the design risks being too busy.

SIZE

The space of a shape is its size. For a shape to have size, there must be another shape to compare. There is, however, always another shape. The proscenium opening itself is a shape and therefore gives the shapes within it a size. The size of a shape or object directly relates to its visual dominance in a design, but larger does not necessarily mean dominant, as we will discover later.

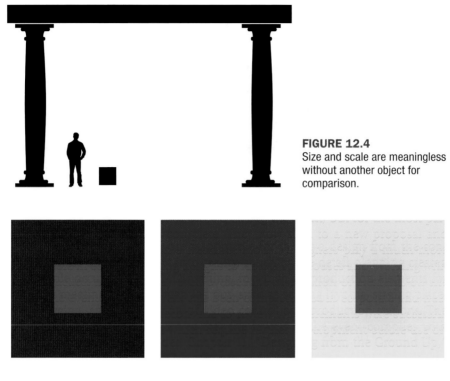

FIGURE 12.4
Size and scale are meaningless without another object for comparison.

FIGURE 12.5
The appearance of a color relies on the colors that surround it.

TEXTURE

Texture in the physical world is determined by how light reacts to a surface. A glossy surface reflects light; a smooth, flat surface absorbs light; and a rough surface both reflects and absorbs light. In the 2D world of graphics and hand sketching, texture describes the edge of a line or fill of a shape. A solid square has a smooth texture, whereas a jagged line drawn with charcoal has a rough texture. Texture plays an important role in determining the finishes to scenic elements and contributes to the vibe of an event as a whole.

COLOR

The color, sometimes referred to as the *hue*, of an object is what your eyes see when light reflects off the object's surface. This topic was addressed in Chapter 6, "Lighting," but as a refresher, remember that color can dramatically affect an attendee's emotional response to a design. Blue, for example, tends to calm observers, whereas bright red can subconsciously cause alarm. In addition, the colors selected for a design are dramatically affected by the color of stage lights used during an event. Again, review Chapter 6 to delve into this topic to a greater degree. Finally, understand that the appearance of a color is determined by the colors surrounding it. A shade of green against a blue background appears very different from the same shade applied to a red background. Keep this fact in mind when placing a Pantone®-specific client logo against various color backgrounds.

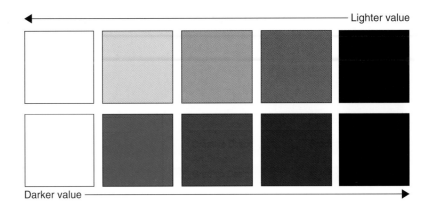

FIGURE 12.6
A study of color value.

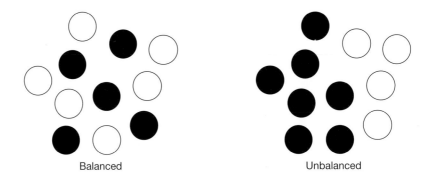

FIGURE 12.7
A comparison of a balanced and unbalanced composition.

Balanced   Unbalanced

VALUE

The brightness of a shape is its value, or tone. The void above the set usually has a dark value, whereas a white box has a light value. Similar to color, value is determined by how much light is reflected or emitted from an object versus how much is absorbed or filtered.

Principles of Design

When the elements described in the preceding sections are combined within a composition or design, they create the principles of design. These principles take the raw materials of design and apply theory and rationale to their use. When a design feels off or just isn't working, review these elements to determine what exactly is not working and how it can be remedied.

BALANCE

Balance in design is just like balance in the physical world. Think of your design as a seesaw with the center of the stage or environment being your pivot point. Our minds like balance, but balance doesn't necessarily mean symmetry. The darker the value of an object, the heavier it is visually. As the illustration in Figure 12.7 shows, a large object with a lighter value can be balanced by a smaller object with a darker value. Distance can also balance objects. A large object close to the center can be balanced by a smaller object of the same value placed at the edge of the visual space or stage.

GRADATION

Gradation is a method of showing movement within objects and shapes. Think of them as ramps for the eye: your eyes roll down the slope from darkest value to lightest. Compare the two scenic flat treatments in Figure 12.8 for movement. The flat on the left appears stationary, whereas the flat on the right shows a rising movement from bottom to top.

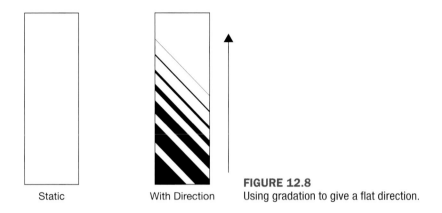

Static   With Direction

FIGURE 12.8
Using gradation to give a flat direction.

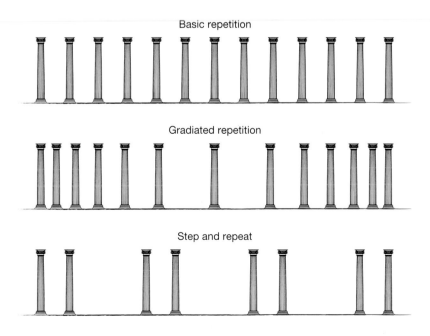

Basic repetition

Gradiated repetition

Step and repeat

FIGURE 12.9
A combination of repetition and gradient repetition to add visual interest.

REPETITION

Repetition is an easy one and understood by most. Be wary of uniform repetition, however, as such a use creates a very static and monotonous design. Combining repetition with gradation can create movement and physical interest, especially for background imagery and scenic treatments. Also, the placement of identical scenic elements, such as columns, can be enhanced by a gradient repetition as opposed to equal spacing across the performance space.

CONTRAST

Contrast is the comparison of opposing elements. Contrast can occur with any of the elements. The colors red and green are contrasting because they lie opposite from each other on the color wheel. White contrasts black, a large circle contrasts a small circle, and a field of circles contrasts a single square. In addition to size, color, and shape, other forms of contrast include direction, transparency, and reflectance or texture. If your design is relatively uniform with one large exception, make sure this contrast is intended and is the center of focus. Sporadic contrast scattered throughout a design can create chaos and make your audience uncomfortable – even if they don't know why.

FIGURE 12.10
By using contrast, an unexpected object can become the focus of a composition.

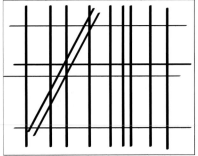
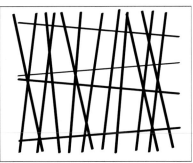

Inharmonious   Harmonious

FIGURE 12.11
A study of harmony.

FIGURE 12.12
The largest image is not always the dominant focus as illustrated in this example.

HARMONY

Harmony is a little tougher to put into words, but you know when it is not present. Similar shapes, textures, and tones create harmony. Direction can also affect harmony. Contrasting elements disturb harmonious designs; an example in nature might be a jagged boulder in the middle of a grassy field, but it could also be argued that these elements are still in harmony because they are both natural elements. Perhaps a better example would be a busted television in the middle of a grassy field in place of the boulder. The use of contrast within a harmonious surrounding is a popular design approach for both print and physical design.

DOMINANCE

Dominance creates interest by emphasizing one or more elements in a design. Similar to contrast, dominance can be shown through size, shape, direction, and tone. As alluded to earlier, a larger object does not necessarily mean it has dominance within a design. A scenic design consisting of several monolithic elements is dominated by a disproportionately smaller element placed center stage. This element becomes dominant, not only because it is center stage, but because the audience is drawn to the object, pondering why it is so small in comparison.

UNITY

Unity applies to many aspects of design. A scenic design that is meant to excite may be united by energetic elements such as fully saturated colors, extreme tones, and movement in line and gradients. In contrast, a subdued design might combine horizontal lines, muted tones, and smooth textures. Connecting elements within the design visually also contributes to unity. Sounds a bit like harmony? They are very similar, but while harmony describes the subconscious connections or feel of elements, unity defines their tangible or visible similarities.

FIGURE 12.13
Texture in 2D graphics is achieved with various uses of line.

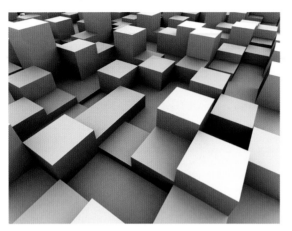

FIGURE 12.14
An abstract image illustrating unity within a composition.

Applying the Fundamentals in Your Design

The elements described in the preceding sections will naturally work their way into your designs, but you will occasionally run into designs that are just not working or seem less than par. In such situations, consider the principles of design and how they are used in your design – whether used intentionally or not. Is the design lacking unity or are there unjustified uses of contrast? Have you created a boring repetitive pattern or are the wrong pieces dominating your design? Taking time to review these elements and principles on a regular basis will keep your designer's eye sharp and will allow you to quickly articulate why a design is not working. Often, only a few slight adjustments will get you back on the right track. If you decide the design you have been working on for days is a lost cause, your deadline is approaching, and you are stumped for creative inspiration, do not fret; that is what the rest of the chapter is all about.

A DESIGNER'S TOOLKIT

All designers have a variety of tools they use on a regular basis, plus resources and assets that allow them to do their job efficiently. These tools may include a color wheel or paint sample catalog, helpful Web sites, or trade magazines. These resources allow for quick reference to keep the design process moving. When the design process is halted by lack of creative inspiration or clear direction, these tools can help restart the creative engine. The following sections will describe a few sample tools you should begin building and continue to contribute to throughout your career.

Sketchbooks

Inspiration comes at unexpected times, so, as a designer, you should welcome these moments and capture them in a logical manner for later review, whether in a scrapbook, elaborate file system, or just a notebook of scribbled ideas and doodles. Read trade magazines for live event and theatrical design, as well as architectural digests. Cut out pictures and images that interest you or designs that catch your eye. Collect material and texture swatches. Use random objects to make ink impressions or rubbings in your notebook. Make an effort to see things differently and appreciate design of every form.

After you have filled one notebook, purchase another and another and keep adding samples and clippings. Sketch ideas that you have or shapes that interest you. Use the pages to experiment with illustration styles. Take notes of technologies that interest you and how to use them in new ways. If you scribbled an idea onto a napkin, copy that artwork into your notebook. Collect everything: your thoughts, ideas, inspirations, and images. You should keep renderings or photos of designs you have completed and those produced by your competitors or mentors, not to copy or steal from, but to see what design means to other successful designers and how to diversify your palette. Review your own designs and make note of what elements were successful and which were lacking.

With time you will build your own library to pull from when you are feeling less than creative. Such a resource is especially helpful during the incredibly short timelines of event design proposals or brainstorming sessions. Often, flipping through the pages a few times will get the creative juices flowing again and have you back on track.

Literature and Resources

As mentioned earlier, it is a good idea to subscribe to various trade magazines for live events, theater, as well as graphic design and architectural literature. Many innovative designs are born from cross-pollinating similar crafts. Reference materials are also handy to have around, such as Pantone® chip books and vendor catalogs. Because we live in a computer age, collect Web sites of vendors you use on a regular basis or may consider using on future projects. Books related to the field of design (*especially this one*) should never be discarded because forgotten volumes are great refreshers when rediscovered and the nuggets of wisdom they contain are generally timeless.

Design Deck

Creating a deck of design cards is a great way to build a quick palette of materials and shapes at the beginning of a project or when you have a creative block. This tool can even be used with a client to collaboratively develop a design, a task that can be both extremely challenging and rewarding.

Build yourself a set of flash cards sorted by four categories: materials and textures, mood, line, and color. For the first category, collect 20 images of various materials and textures such as old and new brick, plastic, glass, stone, metal, wood, etc. Next, select 10 images that represent different moods and atmospheres; the lights of Las Vegas, a shadowy alley, a breezy field, and a circus are a few examples. Now set aside 10 cards and draw various shapes and lines on each, some representing clean and straight lines and others more whimsical or aggressive. For more visual interest,

FIGURE 12.15
Design and trade magazines are handy for creative inspiration when your creativity has hit a wall.

The Design Deck

Hue: Orange | Tint | Tone | Shade

Hue: Black

Hue: Red | Tint | Tone | Shade

Hue: Green | Tint | Tone | Shade

Hue: Cyan | Tint | Tone | Shade

Hue: White | Tint | Tone | Shade

Hue: Yellow | Tint | Tone | Shade

Hue: Purple | Tint | Tone | Shade

Hue: Magenta | Tint | Tone | Shade

Hue: Blue | Tint | Tone | Shade

Circle/Sphere

Square/Box

Calm/Stability

Movement

Balance/Formal

Elegant

Watercolor

Grunge

Clean

Knot

Offset Circle/Donut

Triangle/Cone/Pyramid

The Dark Alley

The Carnival

Mystical Forest

Nostalgia

Bright Lights

Paradise

Adrenaline

Corporate Clean

The World Traveler

A Futuristic Vision

Rubber

Liquid

Stucco

Paint Splatter

Silk

Brushed Metal

Droplets

Glass Acrylic

Elegant Wood

Found Wood

Brick

Concrete

Extruded Metal

Metal

New Wood

Organic

Chiffon

Dry Brush

Gold/Bronze

Plastic

use three-dimensional shapes drawn with varying levels of shading and form. These cards represent the lines and shapes of future designs. Finally, color 12 cards according to the primary and secondary hues of the color wheel. To make this category more useful, divide these cards in four and add each color's tint, tone, and shade.

You should now have 52 cards in the deck. Feel free to add additional cards over time and replace images when better examples become available. You will learn how to use this tool later in the chapter.

Drawing Software

Although drafting and hand illustration abilities are extremely useful, especially during client meetings and brainstorming sessions, computer illustrations or renderings have become the norm for presenting concepts. Familiarize yourself with several different software packages and determine which is ideal for your own style. Several products are available for download with a free 30-day trial, allowing you to give each a test run. Although cheaper packages are available, Autodesk Maya and 3ds Max are among the more popular applications. Google™ SketchUp Pro is a more affordable solution that is great for creating and sharing early design concepts. This ability to quickly visualize a concept in scale and from multiple perspectives is invaluable during the design phase of a production and for concept direction approvals from your clients. Presentation and illustration styles will be addressed in much more detail in Chapter 16, "Presenting Your Design."

RESEARCH

An effective event and scenic design is not meant to broadcast the client's message on its own; rather, it should aid in creating the mood and atmosphere needed to effectively deliver that message. To accomplish this goal, a designer must research the client and his audiences, fully understand the client's objectives, develop an appropriate design palette, and finally apply that design palette to a successful design. There is not one agreed-upon and foolproof procedure that guarantees a finished design will be successful. Each client and project will come with unique challenges that must be overcome in equally unique ways. There are, however, a few methods that can stack the odds in your favor and can be included in your design toolkit. Ultimately, these methods will lead to the creation of a solid design palette that will serve as the backbone of your entire event design.

Defining the Client

As the business world moves quicker and the proposal process becomes shorter, the part of design in which the client is defined is often skipped or thought of as being less important than just getting something in the client's hands. So let me make this point clearly: the most elementary step in event and scenic design is to truly understand your client and his audience through research. When a client has two proposals with equal budgets in front of him, he will always choose the design he feel understands his company or organization and the true meaning of his message. Thus, it behooves every designer or design team to know the client better than any potential competitor.

VISIT THE CLIENT'S WEB SITE

Web sites are not always the best place to pull design inspiration from, but they are a great starting point when researching a client. The downside to using Web sites as research is that companies often change the branding and message of their Web site to reflect a current trend, and this will not always reflect who the company is as a whole. That being said, you will likely find some fundamental elements of use.

First, take a good look at the Web site's home page. This is the page the client wants everyone to see and can give a great glimpse into where the client is at the moment. Look for the feel of the design. Is it exciting or informative? Are there images of youthful people running and jumping in a park or of executives sitting behind desks? What shapes are used in the layout's design? What do the menus look like; are there glossy glass buttons or flashy drop-down menus? Does this

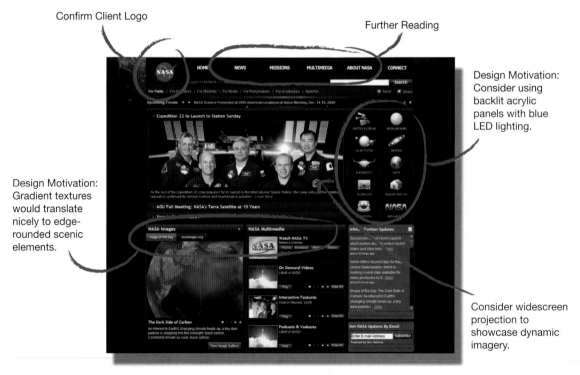

FIGURE 12.16
NASA's Web site; a great exercise for finding design inspiration in a client's Web site.

design represent who the company truly is or is it a momentary campaign? To determine the answers, you must dig a little deeper.

Look for the About Us page and read all of it. This is your opportunity to learn about the client from his own well-thought-out and edited words. This isn't necessarily who the client really is, but this is who he wants his audience and clients to think he is. Does the client's company have a long history or tales of rags to riches, or it is a relatively young organization just beginning its story?

Every company and organization offers a product or products of some type. For associations, those products are generally networking opportunities and further education, but these are still products. Products produced by corporations and companies range from tangible items found in retail stores to consulting services. Regardless of the form these products take, however, they provide a service and are purchased by customers and members for a reason. Understand these products and how they are used.

If the Web site is composed of numerous pages and links, take the time to study them. You may be surprised with what you find. Perhaps even photos of past events can guide you to what the client likes or has already seen. Most importantly, this research will give you insight into the client you are designing for and bring you closer to a meaningful design.

DECONSTRUCT THE CLIENT'S LOGO

Effective logos visually describe a company or organization and its personality. All successful logos are composed of similar elements such as color contrast, memorable graphics and shapes, and font design. If the event you are designing does not have a brand or fully developed theme but is instead based solely on the corporate brand, these logo elements should be used to influence your design.

Color is an obvious design element, but look beyond the actual color. Focus on the energy the colors reflect and what they say about the company behind the logo. Are they high contrast, lively colors, or desaturated and conservative? What kinds of shapes make up this corporate or organization icon? Is the font wacky and lighthearted or powerful and bold? As corny as it sounds, what does the logo say to you: "I am a buttoned-down no-funny-business company" or "I like to laugh and make my clients smile"?

FIGURE 12.17
Three sample logos for observing usable design elements.

In addition, the shape and line of the logo can tell you a lot about your client and his company or organization. You should use these shapes and lines as inspiration in your design, but do not feel you must use them literally. Many logos do not translate well to physical designs. Look for unique features that can be highlighted within your design abstractly. Leave unusable elements for projection screen graphics and printed pieces.

COLOR SCHEMES/BRANDING GUIDELINES

Studies have shown that color increases brand recognition by up to 80%. However, not all corporate color schemes translate well to environment design. Colors are powerful and can greatly affect an audience's mood and emotional state. An entire set painted in bright red can quickly create panic subconsciously because it is associated with warning signs, danger, and chaos. Similarly, too much light green can create discomfort and conjure up images of emergency room hallways. As a designer, you sometimes will have to guide your client to the best color scheme for large applications such as in a scenic environment.

In addition, remember certain colors simply cannot be re-created using conventional stage lights. If you sell a design that shows a lighting effect with exact corporate colors, you may be setting yourself up for hours of headaches with your lighting director.

LISTEN DURING CLIENT MEETINGS

Client meetings can be difficult to arrange if you are hired by a third-party entity such as a creative agency or event producer. When such meetings are available, take full advantage. Let someone else take the lead on your team so you can just observe. If you have to lead the meeting, compile clear questions based on your research. When the client speaks, listen carefully and note every piece of information – even tangents that may not seem directly related.

These meetings are your opportunity to see the event from the inside out. The clients attending these meetings will likely be members of an event planning committee. They in turn will present design proposals to their superiors who approve their budgets. Keep these meetings respectfully casual. If clients want to talk about a movie they saw the previous weekend, let them and appear entertained by their stories. This chitchat loosens up everyone in the room a bit and allows clients to relax. In doing so, they will often reveal more information than they intend, such as what competitors have submitted, their true objectives, and hints at internal politics they must navigate. Although this information may seem to have little to do with design, it will provide a big picture view of the event and focus the true objectives that may not be apparent on the surface.

Defining the Audience

Knowing who to design for can be more complicated than you might think. While the client may be signing the check at the end of the day, it is the audience that will be giving the client feedback as to whether or not the event was

FIGURE 12.18
Client meetings are the best way to zero in on the client's needs and design objectives.

successful. With this thought in mind, you, as a designer, have two parties to impress with your concepts and their execution: the client and his audience.

DEMOGRAPHICS

Audience demographics include the average age of attendees, ratios of gender, and their professions. The reason this information is needed is to tailor your design to a specific audience. For example, a hip nightclub environment may not be appropriate for an audience of 50-year-old men. Likewise, creating a nostalgic scene with oversized black-and-white photos for an audience of 20-year-olds may not hit a homerun because most of their childhood photos were in color. Understandably, these statements hinge on stereotypes, and there will always be exceptions within an audience. Thus, the audience must be treated as a collective whole – as one person representing the average interests of the entire body of attendees. This idea will come into play later.

ATTITUDE

What is the attitude of the audience? Are they franchisees who are upset with their parent company? Are they pharmaceutical salespersons who had a great year and want to celebrate? Did the company have layoffs throughout the year and the audience of employees just wants stability? Understanding where the audience is starting from emotionally when they enter an event environment is important.

For example, if a company has had major layoffs during the year, a flashy stage design that looks expensive is not an appropriate choice – that is, unless the message is, "The hard times are over; everyone here is safe!" Association events, funded entirely by membership fees, are another type of event in which pricey-looking sets may not be appropriate. The concept of *looking expensive* is used on purpose here because a common request from clients is a great design that doesn't look overly costly. In sharp contrast, an equally common request is an exciting and dynamic design that doesn't cost a lot of money. Returning to the point, be aware of attendee attitudes and consider how your designs will be perceived and reviewed.

BACKGROUND

The background of the audience is similar to attitude but focuses more on their collective interests such as their professions, social and political views, or religious affiliations. An environment design for medical doctors will look entirely different than one for a convention of school teachers. Social organizations will have very different wants than organizations built on causes. Ensuring that the correct religious iconology is used is an obvious concern. The background of audiences will affect a design and should be known and understood.

Defining the Event

Defining the event is perhaps the easiest of research steps. For the most part, this information is provided to you by the client through theme selection when predetermined and the Request for Proposal (RFP). While the theme represents the client's message, the RFP explains what is needed technically and logistically. Review these documents carefully and refer to them often throughout the design process.

DISSECT THE RFP

Requests for Proposals are documents drafted by clients requesting bids by production companies and agencies to produce their events. Within these RFP documents are event production requirements, event schedules, branding guidelines, venue locations, and possibly a theme overview.

Read over these documents thoroughly and highlight all references to specific elements of design as well as areas that need clarification. Clarify unclear requests during client meetings or by submitting your questions in writing to the client contact provided within the document. Make a list of items that need to be addressed within your design such as general session staging, registration areas, entrance units, etc. Before submitting your design or proposal, review the RFP to ensure all required elements have been addressed.

THEME

Many events have a theme as discussed in Chapter 1, "An Overview." When present, themes typically act as a unifying force for design. Entrance units, directional signs, registration counters, exhibit floors, and general session environments can all be tied together visually through the use of a theme. Things can get a bit muddled when it comes to interpreting the theme. For example, a theme titled

FUNCTION SPACE REQUIREMENTS:
All meeting space under one roof is preferred for all offices, scientific and general sessions and exhibit/poster areas. Nearby or adjacent hotel may be used for committee and special functions.

General Session (1 room): Used for Saturday night Keynote and may be divided into two concurrent Symposia Sunday – Tuesday afternoon (or room to be divided in thirds for 1,200, 1,200 and 1,400 on each side, depending on flexibility of room at Center). On Wednesday, for the concluding Keynote, can use on half of the room for the Symposium for 2,000. The Opening Keynote is set theater style for 4,000-4,500, staging, screen, data/video projection, VLan from Speaker Lounge to General Session room, laser pointer (or laser pointer in mouse), 6' or 8' head table, lectern with light and microphone, lavaliere microphone, speaker timer, stands for projectors or cameras. Pipe and drape with nice background setting for stage. One guard is provided 24 hours from set up to take down to watch equipment. A projectionist and Sound person are in the room during sessions. The ▮▮▮ does not accept responsibility for lost or stolen property.

Exhibitor Showcases (2 rooms): Two rooms set theater style for 300 Sunday, Monday and Tuesday from 7:00 am -11:00 pm. These rooms are set with staging, screen, data/video projector, PC, confidence monitor, video switchers, 8 port hub, laser pointer, 6' or 8' head table, lectern with light and microphone, lavaliere microphone, aisle microphones, table microphones, speaker timer, stands for LCD. A projectionist is in the room during these sessions. A sound person will float between the rooms. Speakers are allowed to use their own laptops, which most may be MAC's.

Subgroups (12-20 rooms): Theater set for 80 to 1,300 on Saturday. Minisymposia rooms will be used. These rooms are set with staging, screen, data/video projector, PC, confidence monitor, video switchers, 8 port hub, laser pointer, 6' or 8' head table, lectern with light and microphone, lavaliere microphone, table microphones, speaker timer, stands for LCD. A projectionist is in the room during these sessions. A sound person will float between the rooms. Speakers are allowed to use their own laptops, which most may be MAC's.

Tutorials (12-20 rooms): These rooms are used on Tuesday evening and are set theater style for 50-250. Floor plans will show staging, screen, data/video projector, laser pointer, 6' head table, lectern with light and microphone, lavaliere microphone, aisle microphone, table microphone, speaker timer, and stand for LCD. The ▮▮▮ does not provide sound or AV for these sessions. Instead, we put the organizers in contact with you to find out their needs. They are to be billed directly by you as the provider.

FIGURE 12.19
A sample Request for Proposal (RFP).

"Soaring Above the Rest" can conjure images of eagles, fighter jets, parasailing, or any number of activities. Determining how the theme will be interpreted universally is crucial to maintaining a cohesively themed event. If the theme is provided by the client, ensure that the implementation of the theme is clear. Conversely, if you or your creative team are suggesting themes, show clear examples and choices regarding how the theme will be visualized.

FIGURE 12.20
Three theme graphics interpreting the same theme, highlighting the need for an agreed-upon design palette.

TRANSFORMING DATA INTO DESIGN RESEARCH

Now that you have thoroughly dug into the background of the project, it is time to begin developing your design palette. To do so, you must first transform the mass amounts of data you have collected into useful pieces of design inspiration or visual summary. The following two methods can aid in this transformation of raw data to useful design elements.

The Design Cube

On a clean sheet of paper or digital canvas, draw a grid of three rows and four columns. In the first row, write one of following words in each box: *person, color, TV show, texture*. On the next row, fill in these words: *object, element, graphic, color*. And finally, on the third row, use these words: *color, car, sound, taste*. Your grid should look like the one in Figure 12.21.

Imagine the entire audience being combined into one average attendee. Of course, there is no such thing as an average attendee in the real world, so some liberties must be taken to view the audience as one entity. Fill in the squares of your grid using images that represent this average attendee. Take your time and really think about your choices because they are the foundation to your design palette.

For the first box, find a photo of a person who represents your average attendee. The three color boxes should be filled using the client's brand color scheme, which should be available in the RFP or from the marketing department. The graphic box is usually reserved for the client's logo or theme artwork. Sound can

The Design Cube

PERSON	COLOR	TV SHOW	TEXTURE
OBJECT	ELEMENT	GRAPHIC/ LOGO	COLOR
COLOR	CAR	SOUND	TASTE

FIGURE 12.21
The design cube is a useful tool for determining design inspirations.

be represented by an image of a boom box, wind chime, ticking clock, or any item that might have meaning for your attendee. Element refers to the elements found in nature: water, gold, iron, dirt, sand, etc. Like sound, taste should be represented by images of foods that would have significance for your attendee.

When you have all the boxes filled, print out this grid and study the images you have collected. What types of materials are common in the images? What forms of lines are present: straight or curved, circles or squares, clean or jagged? What is the feel of the images: happy and fun or cold and down-to-business? As you analyze the images, begin to collect pieces that can be used within your design palette.

In addition, this diagram is a great presentation tool for showing your client you have really thought about his audience. Using it can be risky because you may be way off base on your image selections, but that is the nature of the business – you must trust your instincts. If your client likes being part of the creative process, you can minimize some of the risk by filling out the grid with him.

The Design Deck

Using the deck of design cards referred to earlier in the chapter, begin selecting cards that represent the event experience as a whole. Choose three images from the category of textures and materials. From the tone cards, select two images that represent the vibe or atmosphere of the event. Next, determine which shape or line should be used within your design. And finally, select three colors that closely match either the client's brand color scheme or theme artwork. The selected cards now represent the fundamental elements of your design and will be used to guide selections within your design palette.

FIGURE 12.22
The design deck in use.

Like the design cube, a deck of design cards can be used with a client to collaboratively select a palette representing the emotion and experience the client wants to convey through his message. Use your design expertise and experience to aid the client selections to ensure the elements selected are cohesive visually and thematically rather than a collage of random images and textures. As mentioned a few times throughout this book, involving the client in the creative process strengthens his connection to the concepts that are ultimately developed.

DEVELOPING A DESIGN PALETTE

The concept of the design palette is not original. The template proposed within this chapter, however, was developed specifically for the creation of physical design elements such as entrance units, registration counters, environment peripherals, and scenic designs. It is built from similar templates known as brand guidelines, graphic style guides, and material boards. All these different approaches serve the same function: to provide guidance throughout the design process.

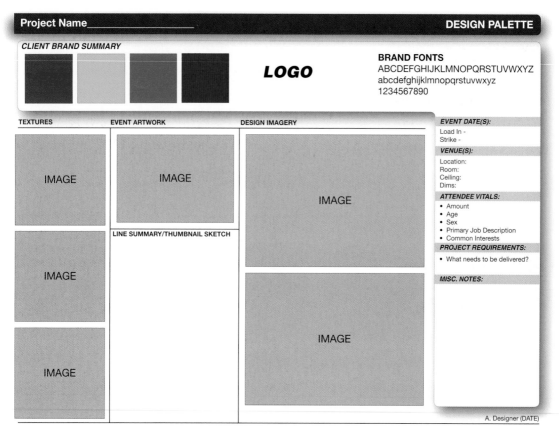

FIGURE 12.23
The design palette is a great tool for staying focused during the design process.

It must be stated, however, that a design palette is not a foolproof method and offers no guarantee in regards to winning creative proposals or ensuring the creation of a successful design. With time and practice, however, the benefits of constructing carefully thought-out design palettes will become undeniable. Utilizing a design palette will keep you on track when projects become convoluted with several rounds of concepts and revisions and will eliminate the need for creating several fully developed concepts for a single proposal. Instead, you can create two to three design palettes based on your research and can then review with your design team or client to determine which palette is selected to guide the design process.

A design palette is a collection of decisions you, as a designer, have made, such as color schemes, materials, textures, and the general shape and mood of your design. Often, during condensed design timelines, such selections evolve alongside physical structures and environment designs. However, there are obvious advantages to clearly making these decisions early in the design process to

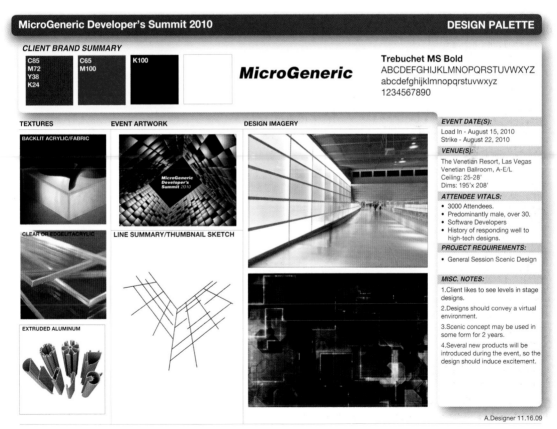

FIGURE 12.24
A design palette using a fictitious computer company as a subject.

ensure uniformity in elements of the event experience. Instead of allowing your decisions to exist only in a few emails between your production team and client or in a sketch notebook, get in the habit of physically collecting them in a visual document. This document should be frequently reviewed as you develop environment, scenic, and experience concepts. Furthermore, this document must be laid out in a way that it can be clearly understood by both nondesigners and late arrivals to the design team. Once your design palette template is created, it can then be populated by the decisions you have made using the design cube or deck of design cards.

Keep your design palette fluid and revised as new discoveries are made during your design process. While you're developing one design palette, additional solutions may come to light. Embrace these revelations or moments of inspiration and create a second or third design palette. Work with your design team or client to determine which palette best represents the essence of the event. If you are working alone and time allows, review these options over the course of several days until a clear choice becomes apparent. This palette, built from your research and creative inspiration, will serve as a solid foundation that your designs will be built upon for the remainder of the design process.

CHAPTER 13
Scenic Design

INTRODUCTION TO SCENIC DESIGN: CORPORATE VS. THEATRICAL

Although traditional theater and corporate events may seem worlds apart, they are more similar than you might think. In theater, the story or message is organized within a play's script. With corporate events, this same script comes in the form of RFPs, meeting agendas, and marketing materials. Both the director and event designer must understand their audiences and attendees thoroughly. Scenic designers in either field must determine what is needed for each scene within a play or meeting during an event. Most importantly, both trades aim to deliver a message. An understanding of this core message is crucial because it ultimately provides the tone for the entire production. Scenic designers then take this tone and develop a staging environment accordingly.

A successful scenic design in either field is not meant to broadcast this message on its own. It should, however, provide an environment or atmosphere that supports the delivery of that message. Furthermore, for a design to be effective, it must serve a purpose. Each design choice made should be weighed against its overall value in supporting that purpose; otherwise, it results in frivolous and pointless design. If a designer chooses a specific material or texture to be used onstage, justification in some form must be available for such selections. The design palette created during preproduction provides this justification and should be adhered to throughout the design process.

USING YOUR DESIGN PALETTE

A common frustration for readers of design literature is that little direction is given for the actual design process or that there is a lack of logical steps that lead to a completed design. This book may be guilty of the same vagaries, but there is reason for this lack of concrete procedure. All design, even design for hire, is subject to the observer's own likes and dislikes. What is a remarkable design to one client may miss the mark altogether for another. Thus, a foolproof process is not possible when the results are subjective, and they are always subjective.

All designers are guilty, at some point in their careers, of spouting off that their clients don't know a good design when they see one. Of course they do; in fact, they are experts of what good design is – to them. The real challenge for designers is providing designs that are good in the eyes of the clients while supporting their clients' messages. This is where the design palette comes into play.

The creation of a design palette is the most important step toward developing a successful design because it provides an accurate understanding of the client, the audience, and the message. When this foundation is in place, the physical elements of a staging environment can be designed with confidence. Use your design palette for determining material and texture choices, color palettes, and the general shapes and lines of your design. Each area of focus discussed in this chapter must be addressed using the design palette. If an early design concept fails in the client's eyes, re-examine how the design palette should be applied to the event and rework your design. Regardless of the number of revisions necessary, rely on the research and thought behind your design palette.

AREAS OF FOCUS

According to Darwin Payne, author of *The Scenographic Imagination*[1], there are four primary areas of focus in scenic design: the stage floor, the background, scenic elements, and furniture. These four areas translate well to scenic and stage design for the event industry with a bit of tweaking. An additional area is needed, however, to fully adapt this methodology to the event industry: technology. When developing a scenic design, consider how to address each of these areas while maintaining a cohesive design.

FIGURE 13.1
This design takes extra care to address the stage floor with accent lighting and paint texturing.

The Stage Floor

The first area of focus is the floor or staging. This area includes ramps, steps, stage surfaces, stage levels, and fascia. In a traditional theater setting with raked seating, meaning the audience is looking down at the performance space, the finish to the stage floor is very important. This is less true for corporate scenic design because most audiences are seated below the stage line. Fascia, step units, ramps, and levels, however, remain valid areas of focus for the corporate scenic designer.

The Background

The background includes the general elements that are behind a presenter or speaker. Examples include backdrops, drapery, scrims, cycloramas, etc. Corporate scenic design must approach this area from both a theatrical and broadcast mindset. Due to Image Magnification (I-Mag), the act of using video cameras to project a close-up of the presenter onto large video screens, the audience see the stage as they would in live theater and on television at the same time. As a result, designers must create visually dynamic backgrounds that are pleasing from a distance of 20–40 feet and not so busy as to distract from the speaker when magnified on-screen.

FIGURE 13.2
A design that provides a dramatic background.
Image courtesy of Atomic Design, Inc. (www.atomicdesign.tv)

---

[1]Southern Illinois University Press; 3rd edition (April 29, 1993)

FIGURE 13.3
Rental scenic elements, like this miniature White House, can give designers a head start and are typically cheaper to rent than to design and construct from scratch.
Image courtesy of Freeman (www.freemanco.com)

Scenic Elements

Scenic elements include columns, tension fabric shapes, art pieces, and any number of scenic structures. Scenic elements can contribute to the general background but stand out as features that make the design unique for a specific event. For example, a cyclorama lit with moving lights and gobos provides a generic background, while fluted columns, marble steps, and a 12-foot high model of the United States Capitol building are scenic elements that create a patriotic American environment. If the same backdrop is to be used, sans Washington, D.C. properties, and chiffon drapery is added as well as cascading flats, an entirely different scenic environment is produced.

Furniture

Podiums, stools, couches, and tables used for expert or legislative panels are all furniture. What separates furniture from scenic elements is that they can be removed from the staging environment without affecting the visual impact of a design. A panel table may be used for only one meeting during a conference while the scenic elements comprising the design remain throughout. Podiums may seem misplaced because they may be heavily designed thematically, but they can still be struck from the stage without affecting the general design.

FIGURE 13.4
Podium and head table placements are important and should be factored into a design.
Designer: Troy Halsey

Technology

Projection screens, video displays, and LED panels are the most obvious examples of technology in a design. Although little more than screen surrounds can be added to projection screens thematically, their size and visual real estate make them an undeniable focus. The content displayed on these systems must tie in thematically with the combined design of the space. Lighting accents such as LED rope light also draw focus in a design. In essence, imagine the design with all stage lighting turned off, leaving only video displays and lighting accents; all that is left is technology and it can be quite visually dominant.

SCENIC DESIGN BY ADDITION

Here is an approach for adding that something *special* to your designs. When you have a basic look and fleshed-out concept, consider how you can add the following: levels, depth, texture, and something unique. Some of these elements will make their way naturally into a design, but fresh and experienced designers alike occasionally get stuck on a design that just isn't working. When these situations arise, ensure that each area of focus is addressed; then consider how the following elements can enhance your design. In doing so, a new solution will come to light, breathing life in a stagnant design.

Add Levels

Levels refer to vertical surfaces or landings within a design. Staging, however, is not the only way to introduce visual levels into a design. In fact, as mentioned in Chapter 3, "Staging," many clients prefer only one level of staging. The key is in the word *landings*.

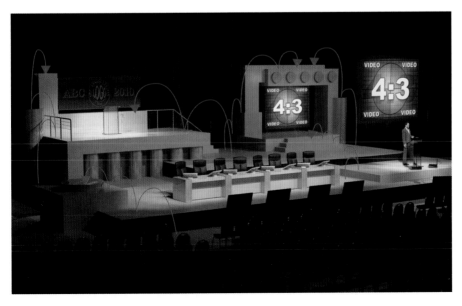

FIGURE 13.5
Levels within a design act as a visual playground for observers, but multilevel staging is not always desirable to clients.
Designer: Troy Halsey

Levels provide visual landing points for viewers, giving the eye a playground to jump from point to point. Using this understanding of levels, you can more easily envision how to introduce visual landing points into a design. Three columns of different heights, for example, provide visual levels, as well as an assortment of dimensions in scenic flats.

Custom graphics can also introduce levels within the printed design. A logo hanging in the center of the stage provides a level, and stair-stepping scenic elements toward the center of the stage naturally draw the eye to the hanging logo as well as provide additional levels. Visual checkpoints leading to an element of focus are a great use of levels and add visual interest to a design.

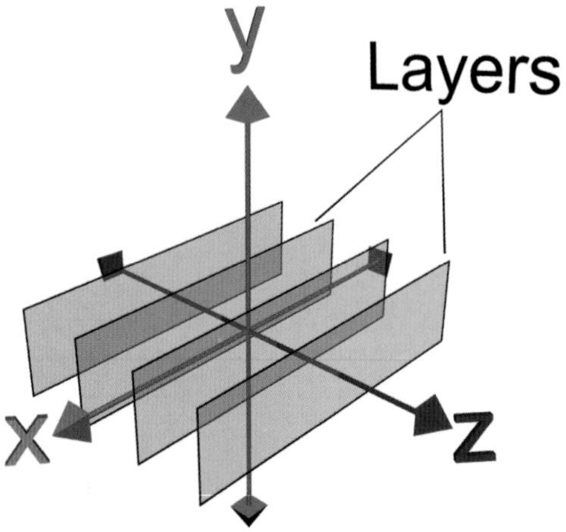

FIGURE 13.6
Depth in a design is achieved by layering elements on the Z-plane.

Add Depth

Depth in a design is achieved through the use of layers. Similar to adding visual levels in the vertical plane, depth adds layers in the Z-plane. Cascading flats, layers of scrims and cycloramas (cycs), scenic elements, and printed goods all add depth to a design.

Keep in mind, though, a design with depth does not require a cluttered stage. For example, depth can be achieved using only three elements: a piece of furniture downstage, such as a podium; an element center stage, such as a hanging logo or projection screen; and a cyc,

FIGURE 13.7
The vertical dimensional drops give this design desirable depth.
Image courtesy of Atomic Design, Inc. (www.atomicdesign.tv)

or drop, on the upstage edge. Alternately, adding a scrim a few feet in front of a cyc creates depth and is heightened when a gobo is projected onto the scrim, spilling onto the cyc behind.

Depth can also be achieved using color. Imagine a stage with six 4' × 10' flats spaced evenly apart from one another across the center of the stage, spanning from stage right to stage left. The two outside flats are painted light blue, the two flats closer to the middle are painted a medium blue, and the center two flats are painted dark blue. The gradation of color in these flats creates the illusion of depth despite all six flats being on the same plane.

Add Texture

All textures are created by light reacting with an object's surface. This reaction can be seen as either surface highlights or shadows. Raised surfaces and peaks within a texture are highlighted while their shadows are cast onto depressions and pits in the surface below. If the origin of a light source is changed, the direction of shadows is shifted accordingly, giving a sense of height or depth within the texture. This fundamental understanding of texture is important to remember when applied to scenic design.

Two forces work against a designer when adding texture to a stage design. Stage lighting is the first; its intensity and various origins illuminate shadows, thereby diminishing a surface's visual texture. Second, the audience's distance from the stage and scenery reduces a texture's impact. As a result, textures applied in theater and live events have to be larger than life and overstated. However, a careful balance must be made between realistic and overstated textures to accommodate for both the live audiences and video. Textures closer to the audience and presenter locations should be scaled more realistically, whereas textures further upstage and away from the audience and camera should be more contrasted and exaggerated.

Using dimensional drops and dramatic gobo patterns is a great way to add texture to the general background of a design because they do so on a grand scale. Realistic textures such as stucco, brick, and stone should remain downstage to be fully appreciated. Simulated textures are also possible using print, such as a photorealistic brick appliqué. The downside to printed goods, however, is they do not react to lighting, and the illusion of realism will be destroyed when light sources are moved.

FIGURE 13.8
The real difference between textures is the way light reacts to their surfaces.

FIGURE 13.9
Dimensional drops provide visual interest through the use of depth and texture.
Image courtesy of Atomic Design, Inc. (www.atomicdesign.tv)

FIGURE 13.10
A visually dynamic backdrop by Atomic Design, Inc; the Burrito Wall.
Image courtesy of Atomic Design, Inc. (www.atomicdesign.tv)

The way materials and textures react to light and appear through a camera's lens as well as the naked eye should become a lifelong study for event and scenic designers. Texture adds depth and visual interest to the surfaces within a design. Compare the surface of a smooth sheet of plastic to a wall of aged brick and crumbling stucco; the latter is more visually intriguing. The difference in the two is texture. Be careful, however, of adding too much texture in only one area of your design because the imbalance created will distract from the overall composition.

Add Something Unique

Admittedly, adding *something unique* is the vaguest of design additions. In practical terms, these are the pieces of a design that stand out and give the audience something they haven't seen before. Put simply, adding something unique to a design leaves attendees saying to themselves, "Now, that was a cool design."

Perhaps this something unique is a wall of shredded and knotted fabric that looks a mess under standard overhead lighting but, when hung as a backdrop and dramatically uplit, suddenly becomes grotesquely beautiful. It could be wire screen crumbled and hung for interesting texture, or cascading panels of rice paper to add depth to a design. When ordinary items are used in unusual ways, or unusual materials are used in new applications, a design becomes unique and visually interesting.

Exaggerating the ordinary can also become a unique design solution. Giant rotating gears with the ticking hands of a clock could become a unique design solution, as could colossal inflatable spheres of varying sizes simply scattered across the stage. These oversized scenic elements, however, border on the cartoonish if not used cleverly or for reason within a design.

Finally, creating a focal point such as a custom sculpture or art piece within a design can leave attendees talking. Perhaps hanging a life-size biplane or hot air balloon above the stage is the right solution for the event. When creating these focal points, however, ensure they are rigid during presentations so as not to distract from presentations onstage.

DESIGN APPROACHES

Due to the nature of corporate event design, that nature's focus being to inform rather than to entertain, there are reoccurring approaches to scenic design in the field, and this is due in large part to the technology used. Much of the visual space of a corporate scenic design is composed of projection surfaces, the key tool to relaying information during presentations. However, there will be times when a client simply wants an exciting design that will dazzle audiences. Thus, scenic designs in the field can be placed in two categories of approach: aesthetic and technology-based designs. Understanding the differences between these two categories will aid designers in selecting the appropriate approach for a particular design.

Aesthetic Designs

Aesthetic designs begin with the look and feel of the performance space and then work in or find room for technology such as projection screens and video monitors. When clients explain they want to "really put on a show" or "create a really *cool* environment," then an aesthetically based design is what they are seeking. Such opportunities allow designers to flex their design muscles and recharge their creativity. Design palettes are especially helpful when developing aesthetic concepts leading to innovative designs that uniquely support a client's message.

Be wary of comparisons to sets used for television shows such as *American Idol* or the *Academy Awards*, both common comparisons made by clients, because these productions work with budgets and timelines unavailable to most corporate events. Work with your clients to determine what specific elements of these examples they desire and find appropriate solutions that are realistic within the event parameters.

Even when approaching a design aesthetically, a designer must not shed all responsibility of keeping a design functional and supporting a message. Avoid designs that make use of the space difficult. As an example, a monolithic replica of an award center stage may provide a dramatic setting but could pose a major traffic problem when award recipients and presenters are gathered onstage. Remember that most of the time, those using the stage are not trained performers and will not respond well to difficult layouts. Furthermore, avoid losing sight of the design's purpose: to provide an environment that supports the client's message.

Aesthetically based designs tend to be costly to produce because they often include several custom scenic elements. Work closely with the scene shop producing these custom elements to find ways to save on costs. In addition, ensure that each custom element must be constructed and that a similar item is not readily available for rental.

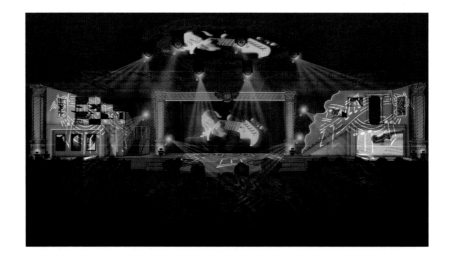

FIGURE 13.11
An aesthetic design focuses first on the design and then works in technology.
Designers: Troy Halsey and Guillermo Becerra

FIGURE 13.12
A technology design first applies video screens and projection and then incorporates a scenic design.
Designer: Troy Halsey

Technology-Based Designs

When technology such as projection screens is the focus of the performance space, the design can be referred to as being technology-based. Technology designs are more prevalent for internal audiences than aesthetic designs in the corporate event world and for good reason. Companies and organizations do not invest millions into an event and bring a large portion of their workforce, essentially bringing productivity to a halt, to merely impress them with a cool experience. The goal is to inform, and in the corporate world, that often translates to videos and PowerPoint presentations; thus, the true star of the meeting is the projection screen.

This is not to say that aesthetic design is inappropriate for these events, merely that scenic design comes second to technology and function. Technology-based designs can be approached pragmatically, first determining how and where technology will be used and then designing scenic elements around projection screen configurations, entrances, and podium placements. These voids of space between technologies can be referred to as *design regions*. Design regions are visual containers in which scenery and backdrops can be added to complement the event's theme or support the intended message. While "thinking outside the box" is a common battle cry for creative designers, designing outside a design region would obscure projection screens or reduce the functionality of a performance space.

Classically trained scenic designers may find working within technology restraints and design regions challenging. Furthermore, years of designing for only technology-based environments can hinder creativity, a result of using variations of the same solution repeatedly. In an effort to prevent this design pitfall, make a conscious effort to try new things within design regions. Consider how projection screens can be used in unique ways without reducing their effectiveness for delivering content. Take your designs beyond the performance space and into the audience and around the venue – spaces that do not have specific regions for design. Learn through experimentation how to blur the line between aesthetic and technology-based designs.

Low-budget technology-based designs can be produced using stock scenery that is modular and adaptable to various screen sizes and configurations.

FIGURE 13.13
A design region is the space available for design after technology has been put in place.

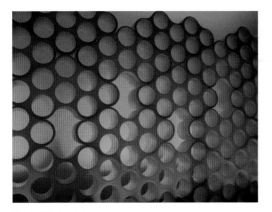

FIGURE 13.14
Modular scenic elements like these clouds from Atomic Design, Inc., can adapt to nearly any staging layout.
Image courtesy of Atomic Design, Inc. (www.atomicdesign.tv)

Cycloramas and backdrops are common choices as well. Custom scenic elements are still a viable option, but the funding for such will be significantly less than that available to aesthetically based productions. As is the case with traditional theater, scenic and environment designers who learn to stretch every dollar within their budgets will be rewarded with successful and lasting careers. Keep a journal of scenic rental sources available throughout the country and internationally. Develop a library of modular designs that can be customized with limited adjustments.

COMMON SCENIC STYLES FOR THE CORPORATE EVENT WORLD

There is a lack of formal scenic styles in the corporate event world when compared to traditional theater, but a few common configurations that can be referred to as styles do exist. Designers should not feel restricted to any specific configuration but will undoubtedly find many of their designs naturally gravitating toward these common characteristics. The following descriptions of styles are an attempt to categorize common staging and scenic configurations.

Soft Good Scenery

Soft good sets are composed primarily of backdrops, cycloramas, and scrims. These elements are very affordable and generally available for rental. In addition, soft goods are flexible for use with various staging configurations, ceiling heights, and projection screen aspect ratios and sizes. Transporting soft good sets is also more manageable because materials can be rolled and compacted and are relatively lightweight. Tension stretch fabric shapes fall into this category because they can be stored compactly and are dependent only on lighting to be incorporated into a design seamlessly.

These sets are versatile in application, providing a blank canvas for lighting designers. These canvases can be painted with light using intense colors and dramatic gobo projections for an edgier feel or softened using a general color wash with subtle uplighting for a more subdued environment. Introducing voluminous fabrics such as chiffon or satin is great for creating elegant designs for awards presentations and galas. The versatility of soft goods makes this configuration popular for a variety of events and budgets.

Bookend Sets

A design that consists of two scenic elements on either side of a central focus can be referred to as a *bookend set*. As you can imagine, this configuration is named for its visual similarity to using bookends to keep a collection of books upright.

FIGURE 13.15
A design constructed entirely of soft goods.
Image courtesy of Freeman (www.freemanco.com)

FIGURE 13.16
A bookend design has one focal point center, with mirrored bookends; the award statues are the book-ends in this design.
Designer: Troy Halsey

A common interpretation of a bookend set is to frame a center projection screen or logo with columns or clusters of tall scenic pieces.

Bookend sets are often symmetrical, meaning the elements on stage right mirror those on stage left. This symmetry requires that the flanking scenic elements be visually interesting; otherwise, the design risks being dull. When the bookend elements on either side of the stage are not identical, this is referred to as an irregular or asymmetrical bookend.

FIGURE 13.17
An example of a reality abstract – using various backdrops to simulate a forest setting.
Designer: Troy Halsey

Reality Abstracts

A reality abstract refers to a set design that brings real-life elements into the environment of the stage. A few examples include a stage design that resembles a cruise ship, an abandoned gas station, the interior of an office building, or any location based in detail on physical locations outside the venue. Reality abstracts are very theatrical and can be a lot of fun for both designers and presenters when executed well. Careful attention must be paid, however, to maintaining safety and functionality within the design. The downside to reality abstract designs is their cost to produce, typically requiring many custom elements and prop rentals.

Minimalistic

Minimalistic designs provide mostly an open stage with only a few key scenic elements added to the environment. This is not a traditional definition of minimalism as it applies to art; rather, it uses only the most necessary scenic elements to create an environment. This approach is ideal for events with smaller budgets that want to make a powerful statement. A large stage with only one unique scenic element center, dramatically uplit, and a bright white cyc upstage would be an example of a minimalistic scenic design. The designer must make clear choices, however, when utilizing this configuration; otherwise, the design may appear incomplete to the casual observer. Like soft good sets, this style relies heavily on lighting to be successful.

Truss-Based Designs

Trusses are not limited in usefulness to rigging stage lighting and scenery. They can actually serve as a scenic element when used in an interesting way. Exposed trusses have been used onstage, both for corporate events and music concerts, for quite some time. With the addition of uplighting, trussing can appear high-tech or futuristic.

This being said, internally lit and uplit trusses have become so prevalent in the past decade that this design is beginning to border on the ordinary. To breathe life into this overused material, consider updating the lighting instruments used to color-changing LED fixtures. This upgrade allows lighting designers to incorporate lit trusses into the general scheme of the stage, allowing for multiple lighting looks within one meeting.

In addition to uplighting or internally lighting trusses, you can use stretch fabric to cover trussing, enhancing the impact of lighting and giving the approach a modern touch. However, if trusses are covered with stretch fabric, ensure that the material has been properly treated with fire-retardant chemicals and use low-heat LED lighting fixtures for internal lighting.

FIGURE 13.18
An example of a mini-
malistic design – clean
lines and 90-degree
angles. A very contem-
porary look.
Designer: Troy Halsey

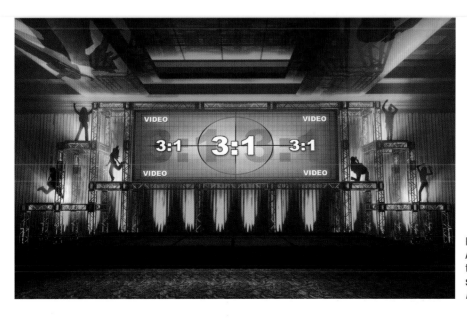

FIGURE 13.19
A fun design using
trussing and silhouette
standees.
Designer: Todd Ethridge

An alternative to internally lighting trusses is to simply use the material in a creative way, such as designing with irregular curves and angles or using trussing as columns of varying height to give your design depth and texture.

FINAL THOUGHTS ON SCENIC DESIGN

As a designer for the corporate event industry, you will be faced with several challenges ranging from tight deadlines, less-than-ideal venues, and hard-to-please clients. In addition, working with the same inventory of scenic options can be creatively draining. Make a strong effort to try new things and tackle challenges with confidence and positive thinking. Many great designs are born by overcoming challenges that seem insurmountable.

Challenge yourself to find something new to add to each design. Review your design notebooks and clippings often and try out different approaches. Truly become a student of every form of design and watch these studies guide and transform your own work. Most importantly, have fun. As corny or cliché as that may sound, having fun and creating designs that you are proud of are imperative to survive in this industry. Focus on the message, use your design palette, have fun, and remember that the show ultimately belongs to your clients and their audiences. Stick with this mantra, and your clients will keep coming back to you year after year.

CHAPTER 14
Environment Design

INTRODUCTION TO ENVIRONMENT DESIGN

Environment design is the art of transforming a generic venue into an event locale. Furthermore, it is about designing and creating the *ideal atmosphere* in which the event takes place. The choices that make up this design directly impact the attendees' experience. As a result, the environment design can be seen as the physical representation of the experience design.

Carpeting, lighting, branding decor, and lounge designs are just a few examples that contribute to the atmosphere and vibe of an event. Furthermore, environment design aids in improving a venue's functionality through directional signs, information monitors and kiosks, and well-designed registration areas. Environment design is a craft that requires a good sense of design as well as a strategic mind and is composed of two main areas of focus: providing direction and providing atmosphere.

PROVIDING DIRECTION

Regardless of whether an attendee paid or was required to attend an event, nothing is more frustrating than getting disoriented or lost during the event. Providing clear directions and information is a necessity that should be addressed during event planning and design. Directional signage, although important, is not the only component that aids in an attendee's ability to navigate an event. Entrance elements, registration areas, and information kiosks are also key resources that provide direction and information. Not every solution will be needed during an event, but as an event planner or designer, you should fully understand the function of each.

Entrance Elements

Entrance elements establish an event's presence at a venue; they are a way of saying, "Yes, this is the right venue." They also establish the theme and announce the quality of the event design as a whole. Entrance elements subconsciously begin the event experience for attendees and act as imaginary starting lines. The design palette created during preproduction should be used to develop design-coherent entrance elements regardless of the form they take. There are two types of entrance elements: grand entrances and room entrances.

GRAND ENTRANCE ELEMENTS

Grand entrances can begin before attendees even step foot into the venue. Banners, signs, or even commissioned artworks created just for the event can guide attendees to the venue from blocks away. Occasionally, even airport terminals may be branded to welcome attendees as they exit their planes.

Obviously, these examples stretch the definition of an *entrance* element, but they do fall into the same realm and function: to welcome attendees and begin the event experience. Physical entrance structures, whether placed in front of or just inside venue entryways, act as a figurative portal, transporting attendees from the outside world and into the event experience.

FIGURE 14.1
A sample entry design that could be placed outside an exhibit floor or general session.
Designer: Pia Saxena

Such structures can be constructed from various materials, including trusses, extruded metal systems, or wood. To take the concept a step further, consider adding video monitors or projections displaying theme-related footage or a custom segment welcoming attendees. Again, entrance elements do not need to be literal structures. Stretching beyond the venue doors and conventional design can yield unique solutions for grand entrance elements.

ROOM ENTRANCE ELEMENTS

Naturally, room entrance elements are restricted to the specific space for which they are intended. They do not, however, have to follow any predetermined formula. Although a banner hung above a doorway does count as a room entrance element, it isn't a very creative one. Many other available options are only a few dollars more, such as incorporating LED lighting, fabric shapes, or custom scenic elements. For example, a simple entrance archway can be constructed from trusses, covered in white stretch fabric and internally lit with color-changing LED lights – all rented for nearly the same price as a custom-printed banner.

Although a truss archway is a bit more creative than a lone banner, creating an entire entry tunnel just inside the room takes the idea of entrance elements to a new level. Entry tunnels are temporary structures, typically two parallel walls or fabric shapes that serve as surfaces for branding, video, or lighting. As attendees walk into the meeting space, they continue through the tunnel before being seated. Based on an event's budget, entry tunnel designs can range from simple but dramatically lit hallways of fabric to elaborate visual experiences with floor-to-ceiling video projection.

FIGURE 14.2
An experience tunnel
concept that uses
warped projection.
Designer: Troy Halsey

Registration Areas

Registration areas serve an obvious function: to register attendees. Because these areas are used only the first few days of an event, not a lot of money is typically invested in these structures. This is, however, the first area attendees will experience when arriving at an event. Some believe registration areas are the most important design regions of an event; this opinion, of course, stems from the importance of first impressions.

However, from an attendee's point of view, function greatly outweighs form. Clear directions and friendly greetings will begin an attendee's experience on the right foot. Cool designs that do nothing to help the registration process can simply be a waste of money. A healthy balance of design and functionality is the best solution and leaves the first impressions of the event design for entrance elements.

A common practice for large events is for sign-in tables or kiosks to be positioned in the lobby space of a registration area. Sign-in kiosks allow attendees to fill out any necessary forms needed for registration without delaying the process for others. After attendees fill out their forms, signage directs them to specific registration counters, generally sorted by last name or a unique registration number. The registration counters are then marked accordingly with overhead graphic panels or signs. Here again, the focus is function over form. If registration counters are not clearly marked or attendees are confused regarding where to go next, then the environment design for registration has failed. Always keep the attendees' experience as your focus during preproduction planning and design.

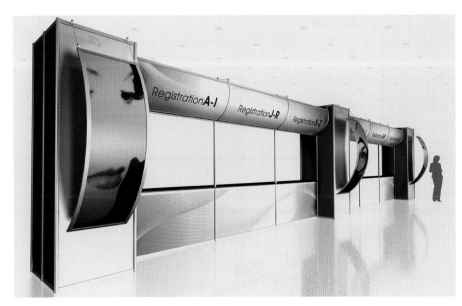

FIGURE 14.3
A sample registration design.
Designer:
Scott Williams

Directional Signage

Most people, even those who have never attended an event, are familiar with directional signs and their purpose. However, there is a limit to how many signs are needed before they become confusing. Overuse of directional signage is common and can be very frustrating for event attendees.

Directional signs should be concise and used logically, and should be understood with little more than a glance. Avoid having several individual signs side by side sending attendees on various vague routes. Conversely, do not rely solely on the venue's own directional plaques because they may not be visible during times of high foot traffic.

Using breakout sessions as an example, one sign should be used at the beginning of each hallway listing the rooms the hall contains. Outside each room, an additional sign should give the name of the room in bold print while listing below all meetings to be held in the room. Simple and clean are key. There is little need for much art direction other than perhaps the event's logo at the top or bottom of the sign.

Digital directional signage is becoming more common and is much more flexible than printed material. Digital signs can not only direct traffic but, for units placed outside meeting spaces, can also display meeting synopses unique to each session. The same rules still apply to digital directional signs, however: keep the content simple. Avoid creating directional content that more closely resembles airport terminal arrival screens than helpful directions.

FIGURE 14.4
Digital signage can be updated in real time and even display up-to-the-minute presenter schedules.

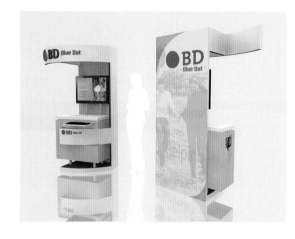

FIGURE 14.5
An example of a kiosk design.
Designer: Scott Williams

Information Monitors and Kiosks

Unlike directional signs, information monitors and kiosks are intended to provide more in-depth information such as event schedules, meeting agendas, and speaker biographies. Kiosks generally consist of computer systems that allow attendees to navigate to specific topics through a keyboard and mouse or touch screen. Kiosk content should be designed for quick navigation. Even with the added information available from these units, users should not spend more than a few moments locating the information they are seeking, such as where a breakout session is located or what time the general session begins.

When possible, the design of the kiosk structure should incorporate elements of the event design palette. If rental units are used, apply custom branding to make clear that the kiosks are for attendees to use during the event and not unrelated venue features.

Information monitors display only preprogrammed content. This content, however, can be updated from a central location and distributed to networked monitors. This technology is especially helpful to inform attendees of last-minute room changes or session cancellations. Graphic overlay boards can be temporarily adhered to monitors, providing a branded finish to the units during an event.

FIGURE 14.6
Overlay boards can be applied to monitors to add branding and signage.

PROVIDING ATMOSPHERE

Environment design takes much of its creative direction from the experience designer. If an experience designer is not part of your production team, then the task falls on you as the event designer, scenic designer, or event planner to define and develop the experience of the event. Should this event be bright and clean, or oversized and colorful? Should the event feel high tech or natural and down to earth? How can your design palette be applied to the entire event rather than just a scenic design or entrance unit?

Using the research you collected at the beginning of the design process, you should have determined what materials, textures, and color schemes are most appropriate for the event. Now it is time to translate those decisions into accent elements that, when combined, create the atmosphere of the event.

Drapery

Run-off drape, sometimes referred to as *pipe and drape*, describes the use of drapery panels to mask off unsightly areas in the venue space. The phrase *pipe and drape* specifically implies that the material is floor-supported. Drapery panels are available in any number of materials and colors, but the most common is black fire-retardant velour. However, vinyl drapery is quickly becoming a close second to velour because the material is cheap, can be cut to any size, is recyclable, and takes light well. A new trend in the field is to use white vinyl drapery at 200 percent fullness pulled tight at the top and bottom, acting as a cyclorama but with much more texture.

Even if a venue is beautiful, your design may call for a dramatic bright red wall down the side of a main corridor or require an oversized white canvas for special lighting;

drapery can accommodate both requests. Designs using drapery are not limited to what is available from rental sources. Rolls of chiffon, silk, or even netting can be quickly fashioned into drapery, adding texture to an environment design.

Although it technically falls into the category of providing direction, drapery can also be used to declare event staff offices or storage areas. It can block hallways or a section of the venue not used during the event. With the addition of dramatic lighting, however, even *directional* drapery can create atmosphere.

Cycloramas

If a more clean and stylish feel is preferred, cycloramas, or cycs, may be a better choice. Cycs are available in a variety of colors and sizes and can be used to quickly create clean surfaces for lighting effects. Cycs can also provide the illusion of temporary walls, remodeling an entire venue space into a more desirable shape. For example, a 20-foot high cyc can be hung from a curved pipe to fashion a sleek round meeting space or registration area in what was before a rectangular lobby. Perhaps several cycs may be hung around the perimeter of a meeting space and uplit with color-changing LED lighting, creating a very dramatic environment without breaking your budget.

There is a downside to cycs, however, and that is they tear and stain easily. These imperfections may not be as visible when used behind a scenic design, but are quite obvious from only a few feet away and will detract from a cyclorama's effect. When ordering cycs from rental sources, be sure to ask for bleached, seamless cycloramas that are in like-new condition.

Scrims

Scrims are essentially mesh or screen-like cycs. They have the unique capability to appear opaque when lit from the front and transparent when something is lit only from behind them. When both the scrim and objects or walls behind the scrim are lit, a ghosted or hazy effect is created. This effect is great for transforming hallways into stylish experiences. When interesting light patterns are introduced with robotic lighting fixtures and gobos, a scrim can be transformed into a living artist's canvas. Although the same can be said for cycloramas, they do not provide the depth that scrims offer. Scrims are also more durable than cycs because they do not show imperfections as clearly. They too are available in several sizes and typically come in black, gray, or white.

Carpeting

Carpeting may seem straightforward, and for the most part it is, but when used strategically, it can become a design element. Exhibit floors and stage surfaces tend to use the most carpeting during an event, but these are not the only areas carpeting can be used. A venue's decor may be in stark contrast to an event design. Rental carpeting can be brought in to cover undesirable venue carpeting to align more closely with an event's design palette. Event and decorating

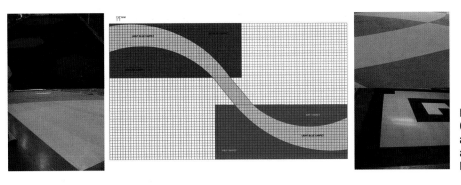

FIGURE 14.7
Custom carpet inlays are surprisingly afford-able and excellent for branding an event.

companies offer a vast assortment of rental carpeting that can be rolled out and cut to size for quick installation.

Custom carpet inlays are also becoming more affordable and can add strength to an event's branding. Inlays are merely cut shapes of carpeting sewn into larger pieces, and with modern technology, these shapes can be quite intricate. Because carpet can be cleaned and resewn after an event, custom inlays are even available for rental carpeting. Oversized logos and directional lines are just a few examples of how carpet inlays can be used during an event.

Event decorators offer a range of colors and quality in their rental carpet catalogs. And the quality of carpet used during an event does have an impact on the attendee experience. If carpeting is thin, worn, or stained, it will cheapen an environment design. In contrast, there is something relaxing about walking on thick new carpet, especially during a long day of shuffling through crowds. If your budget can afford it, splurge for the high-end carpeting with custom inlays. Doing so will add an air of quality to the event as a whole.

Audio Ambiance

Ambient music is great for setting an event tone and vibe. However, it is important to keep in mind that events are very noisy places. Even the low murmur of side conversations mixed with drones of footsteps can become overwhelmingly loud when multiplied by the thousands. Hence, ambient music will not be audible during times of heavy foot traffic, such as between sessions and breakout meetings.

This does not mean ambient music should be scratched altogether. Instead, choosing the right locations, such as attendee lounges or dining areas, is a better use of this element. Be aware, however, copyright laws still apply to music used during events. Ensure that ambient music libraries are purchased as royalty-free or are licensed appropriately before piping any selection into an event space.

Scents

Adding scent into an environment design may seem a bit over the top, but it does have an impact. Large concentrations of people in compact spaces can produce strong undesirable odors that can only be compared to the smell of a locker room. A good way to combat these odors is to place air fresheners throughout an event space.

Scent can also add to thematic designs. If the intent of a design is to give the sense of a clean and fresh tomorrow, air fresheners like Glade *Outdoor Fresh* or *Suddenly Spring* may be appropriate choices. A winter wonderland would be complemented by the scent of fresh cinnamon.

Scents and air fresheners should be kept to a mild hint, however, because many people are sensitive to various smells. As mentioned in Chapter 4, "Seating," regarding centerpieces, avoid floral arrangements with strong odors. As with ambient music, the placement of this element adds to an event experience. Stick with areas of high traffic or the perimeter of meeting and registration spaces to incorporate scent into your design successfully.

Accent Lighting

Lighting is a very powerful tool of event design. It can transform a boring scenic design of plain white flats into dramatic awe-inspiring artwork or dazzle audiences with exciting gobos projected through moving lights. This same versatile technology can be adapted quite well into environment designs in a number of ways.

FIGURE 14.8
A little uplighting can go a long way in transforming a less-than-ideal locale.

A simple application of lighting in environment design is *uplighting*. Uplighting is the practice of placing lights at the base of an object, wall, or fabric panel and casting light in a vertical direction onto an element. This approach can be quite dramatic when venue lights are dimmed, intensifying the effect of the uplighting. Uplighting is ideal for environment design in main corridors or the perimeter of rooms. When either gels or LED instruments are used, the color of these lights can be coordinated with the event's design palette or room decor. Cycs, scrims, and vinyl drapery take uplighting very well. The effect can still be seen on black velour drapery, but the light source must be intense.

When you want to draw attention to specific objects, such as a logo inlay in carpet or printed theme artwork, spotlights and pin lights may be the right solution. These small but powerful lights can be focused on areas of interest and are popular in museums and art galleries. When possible, opt for LED instruments because they produce less heat and are safe for use near fabrics and sprinkler systems.

Moving and robotic light instruments allow for lighting effects and schemes to change with the click of a button or can be preprogrammed to run atomically during an event. Moving lights are common in stage designs but often overlooked for enhancing environments. Registration areas, lobbies, welcome receptions, and lounges are ideal candidates for moving lights. This technology becomes creatively limitless when combined with gobos.

Gobos, as explained in Chapter 6, "Lighting," are small circular lighting inserts that are made of metal or glass. Patterns can be printed or cut into these inserts to create projected shapes when light passes through them. Gobos can be created for most lighting fixtures and provide an affordable way to address large areas of an environment. For example, a lobby or meeting space can be transformed into a dense forest through the clever use of gobos, or a beautiful blue sky with drifting clouds can be projected onto venue ceilings. Patterns used for gobos, however, are not limited to obvious illusions of reality; abstract shapes can be used to simply add visual texture to walls or drapery. Custom gobos can also be made to brand environments with logos or taglines.

Specialty light instruments and attachments are also available to add motion to gobos, simulating fire or flames or abstract cascading patterns. With this technology, the image of a waterfall can be cast onto draped material, or walls can be uplit with flickering flames. It is safe to say various gobos and lighting fixtures are available to enhance any environment design. Rosco, a leading provider of theatrical and lighting equipment, even offers a gobo selection application for the iPhone, a handy tool during creative meetings.

Truly any design can be enhanced by lighting, and incorporating lighting into a design requires little effort. Although robotic lighting systems are a bit more costly, affordable solutions are available through a vast assortment of traditional lighting instruments. Ensure the venue's electrician is aware of the intended

FIGURE 14.9
Cloud gobos projected on a scrim masking an unsightly brick wall. (Simulated)

design, however, because both traditional and robotic lighting instruments consume large amounts of power and may require special electrical distribution. LED instruments, on the other hand, consume very little power and can be plugged directly into standard 20-amp wall outlets.

Backdrops and Banners

Backdrops are useful not only in stage designs, but also in environment designs and can be quite effective. Take, for example, the world's largest image printed on fabric, a mountain-top scene created by Big Image Systems. This custom-printed 37,000 square foot drop was created in commemoration of the 50-year anniversary of Sir Edmund Hillary's and Tenzing Norgay's climb to the top of Mount Everest. The panoramic image, together with sound and light effects, gave a dizzying feeling, as if viewers were really on top of the world's highest mountain – quite a literal translation of environment design.

Banners are common in event designs but are generally limited to branding. They can also be used creatively to enhance an environment design. The example in Figure 14.11 shows a welcome reception themed around world travel. The backdrop provides a generic landscape while custom banners resembling postcards bring the concept to life, providing variety and visual depth.

Oversized prints of any kind are just fun to look at and can make powerful statements. Placing a giant backdrop with the word *welcome* stretching across its width behind a registration area would certainly let attendees know they are indeed welcome! Like accent lighting, custom-printed banners and backdrops are useful in a number of ways and are becoming very affordable as printing technologies progress.

FIGURE 14.10
The world's largest digital print by Big Image Systems, Inc., giving a panoramic view of Mt. Everest.
Image courtesy of Big Image Systems, Inc. (www.bigimagesystems .com)

FIGURE 14.11
Large format prints can be used in any number of ways to transform an environment.
Image courtesy of Big Image Systems, Inc. (www.bigimagesystems .com)

Fabric Structures and Art Pieces

This last group of environment design elements may seem a bit scattered. It consists of unique structures and pieces that act as focal points of the environment design. They are elements that attendees might look at and say, "Now, that is cool." Although they may serve a practical function, such as defining a perimeter, these elements are essentially art pieces.

Fabric structures or tensioned fabric shapes, such as those offered by Transformit or Pink Inc., provide affordable solutions for creating visually interesting physical elements. These lightweight structures can be hung from above, requiring minimal rigging or floor support. They are perfect for addressing environments with cavernous ceilings, filling the void with unique fabric shapes colored by moving lights. Floor-supported structures are handy for creating quick entryways or defining the edges of a particular space. The fabrics used in both lines of products take light remarkably well, and custom-printed skins are available.

Stretch fabric without framing can also be used to address large vertical spaces as large ribbons of color extending from floor to ceiling. This approach works well for covering unsightly columns and transforming them into lighting canvases. Adding a small fan unit at the base of the material will give the fabric a bit of motion and excitement.

Commissioned sculptures, constructed of hard-coated foam, are another option for environment focal points. A giant fruit or vegetable arrangement would make a nice centerpiece for registration at a convention of whole food store owners. Perhaps another application would be a life-size sculpture of a humpback whale hanging overhead in an exhibit hall of marine sciences. Although commissioned

FIGURE 14.12
Tension fabric shapes
can be used in a
variety of ways to
transform an
environment.
*Image courtesy of
Atomic Design, Inc.
(www.atomicdesign.tv)*

artworks and sculptures can be very expensive, their impact is amazing and the completed piece often finds its way into corporate lobbies or future events.

Inflatable elements are also growing in popularity because they are easily transported, affordable to make, and can be used for several years. For classy events, it may be a good idea to avoid the inflatable characters you might see atop a car dealership. Instead, opt for simple shapes like oversized spheres, cubes, or columns clustered in groups of varying sizes. Giant inflatable globes are common choices for global events, and several rental products available can be internally lit or act as screens for video projection. Custom inflatable elements, however, are not limited to basic shapes. In fact, entire scenic designs have been created using inflatable pieces. Be wary of using nonsealed pieces in areas that require any semblance of silence because the compressors used to keep these elements inflated can be quite noisy.

Lounges and Cyber Cafes

Lounges are designated locations throughout an event space where attendees can mingle, relax, use laptops, or make phone calls. Cyber cafes are similar to lounges but include collections of computers, giving attendees access to email, up-to-date schedules, or any number of Web-related activities. Lounges and cyber cafes are centers of activity and as a result make great focal points for environment design.

Perhaps the vibe of the event is hightech and futuristic. To complement this atmosphere, consider renting internally lit acrylic tables or use rope lights as

FIGURE 14.13
A temporary custom sculpture
created from tension fabric
shapes.
*Image courtesy of Transformit
(www.transformitdesign.com).
Designer/Creative Producer: Adrian
Smith of DESIGNSTAGE. Laureus
World Sports Awards Welcome
Party, Barcelona, Spain, May 2006
(www.designstage.tv)*

FIGURE 14.14
A concept design of a
cyber cafe, providing
a place for attendees
to access the Internet
and mingle.
Designer: Troy Halsey

accents. For an eco-friendly feel, you could use bamboo furniture, a backdrop of a green field, and planter boxes of wheat grass in varying sizes. All the elements touched on in this chapter can be incorporated into attendee lounges and cyber cafes. Most importantly, like all design elements of the event, keep material and color choices within the design palette to ensure continuity.

ENVIRONMENT DESIGN CHECKLIST

Environment design encompasses a lot of pieces and at first glance can be a bit overwhelming. By breaking each piece into a logical checklist, however, and thinking strategically as to where funds should be spent for the most impact, planners and designers can keep focused on the big picture.

View the experience through the attendees' eyes. What do they see the moment they get off the plane? Are there any branding opportunities during their commute to the hotel or convention center? What should their experience be the moment they walk through the venue doors?

Pick apart each step of the attendees' day and consider how to extend the event's message or theme to that moment. Overloading attendees with branding is always a risk, so be careful of choosing subtle approaches rather than abrasive bombardments. As an extreme example, applying themed graphics to the perimeter of bathroom mirrors is clever, while waking attendees with loud theme music is obnoxious.

Focus on the objective of environment design: creating the ideal locale and experience for the event. Each element incorporated into the environment design should serve a function, even if that function is to serve as a visual focal point. Finally, determine what pieces of the design are most important and work backward. If it is an association event and the exhibit floor is the star, focus the design on drawing attendees toward the exhibit hall. If it is a networking event, spend more time developing lounges and lobby areas. Piece by piece, the environment design will come together and the event experience will be a success.

CHAPTER 15

Scenic Materials and Construction

INTRODUCTION TO SCENIC MATERIALS AND CONSTRUCTION

Scene shops and fabrication houses play one of the most important roles in making scenery and environment designs come to life. Regardless of how impressive the concept sketches or renderings look for an event, without skilled carpenters, the finished elements are doomed to be less than memorable. This chapter will attempt to inform designers and meeting planners of the most common scenic elements available, their uses, and a few basic construction methods.

During the design phase, it is the scenic or environment designer's responsibility to ensure that the concept he creates is "doable." In other words, can it be realistically executed? Can this concept be constructed of existing materials, and can it be structurally supported? Is it within budget, and can it be installed in the venue within a reasonable amount of time? Every fabrication house or scene shop will have different requirements for the designer to illustrate the construction details. Some houses require a detailed computer-aided drawing (CAD) showing every nut and bolt, whereas others simply ask for dimensions and material suggestions. If the fabricator prefers the latter approach, the details of construction fall to the head carpenter or engineer of the scene shop.

For larger and more complex productions, a technical director may be needed to ensure the design is executed safely. Technical directors, or TDs, specialize in the art of making designs work. They serve as master problem solvers. They keep current on the latest gadgets and devices from various industries and determine how to incorporate such technology into the event or entertainment industry when needed. Serving as both engineers and designers, TDs solve such dilemmas as how to attach a screen surround or safely construct and operate a motorized turntable.

When included in the production design team, technical directors act as the liaison between the scene shop or fabrication house and the designer, most often working in tandem with the designer to generate working drawings for the shop and finding materials, determining construction and installation budgets, and sourcing on-site scenic labor. Although in many cases the production manager will undertake such responsibilities, having a dedicated technical director is advisable when budgets allow or a production design exceeds the capabilities and expertise of the contracted production manager.

Regardless of which roles are available to the design team, designers should make a habit of keeping up with trade trends, researching materials and technology toys, and building a library of successful and unsuccessful designs. Carpentry and technical directing, on the other hand, are entirely different crafts and, like design, take years to master. Relying on a head carpenter to determine the best joints for your custom step unit or a technical director to determine the best approach in executing design elements is highly advised. In short, the designer focuses on what the clients and audience should see, and the scene shop and technical director make that vision into reality.

It is helpful to understand that designers, fabricators, and technical directors often see things from different viewpoints. Designers focus on design elements such as lines, textures, and visual balance, whereas the scene shop and TDs focus on tangible and practical elements, such as hardware, materials, and methods of execution. These differences are inherent and should be taken into consideration as teams prepare to work together. A strong collaboration is vital for the design and execution to be successful. Furthermore, the greater the understanding designers have of the construction process and scenic resources available, the more they will be able to ensure their designs are realistic and achievable.

SOFT GOODS

The phrase *soft goods* can apply to a variety of resources available within the industry, and many elements are borrowed from traditional theater. The primary advantage to using soft goods is their ease of transportation and versatility of use within designs. A defining feature of most soft goods is their requirement of being hung from either trussing or piping. Of course, exceptions do exist to this rule, such as fabric used to mask undesirable technology and production equipment. Furthermore, just because an element is hung does not mean it is a soft good.

Drapery, scrims, drops, and cycloramas are the predominant pieces described in this chapter and have been used in theater and meeting environments since the beginning of both industries. They are basic tools but can transform a stage and environment design so dramatically that they have stuck around for the long haul. Often they are used as backgrounds and trimming for stage designs; however, they are not limited to the furthest upstage point of a stage design and do not have to be used in isolation. Mixing theses pieces can create dynamic designs without breaking your budget. Although these elements are addressed in the scenic and environment design chapters, a more in-depth explanation is provided here.

Drapery

Drapery is a staple of the event industry and used in many ways, from masking unsightly areas of a venue, defining a performance space, and directing traffic to adding atmosphere within a meeting space. In addition to the many ways it can be used, drapery is available in a variety of materials, finishes, and colors. Knowing the options available and how to properly describe what is needed will ensure the desired product is ordered from drapery vendors and rental sources.

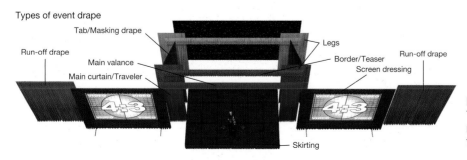

Types of event drape
Tab/Masking drape
Legs
Run-off drape
Border/Teaser
Run-off drape
Main valance
Screen dressing
Main curtain/Traveler
Skirting

FIGURE 15.1
The various uses and names of drapery in the event environment.

Drapery used in the event industry must be fire retardant. Fortunately, most products available from vendors like Rose Brand (www.rosebrand.com) and Dazian (dazian.com) meet this requirement, as well as rental products available through event production companies. Ensuring drapery is fire retardant is especially important when it is used near stage lighting fixtures, which emit intense heat.

Lightweight cotton velour is perhaps the most common drapery material used in both theater and event environments and is available in black and a variety of other colors and finishes. Vinyl drapery is also a popular choice but used more for creating atmosphere and not typically found on staging or used as masking.

Fullness is an important descriptor for drapery. A flat curtain, such as a cyclorama or drop, is said to have 0 percent fullness or no fullness, meaning there is no pleating or gathering of material. A curtain with 100 percent fullness, on the other hand, has been pleated to the point of reducing the original fabric panel width by half. So a 10-foot-wide flat curtain is only 5-foot wide when sewn for 100 percent fullness. Using the same 10-foot-wide flat curtain at 50 percent fullness would result in a 7.5-foot-wide finished panel. Adding fullness to drapery is great for giving the material a more elegant look, as well as improving sound and light absorption. Most rented drapery ranges between 50 and 100 percent in fullness.

In addition to fullness, the top and bottom finishes of drapery are important; this applies to cyclorama, drop, and scrim finishes as well. Because drapery can be hung either from trussing or floor-supported piping, referred to as *pipe and drape*, there is a need to clarify which top finish is desired. When pipe and drape is used, the top hem can be sewn as a *pipe hem*. This finish creates a sleeve in which pipe can slide through before being attached to upright supports. When drapery is hung from trussing or rigged piping, the preferred finish is known as *grommets and ties* or *lace and grommet*. This allows the drape to be tied to the truss or piping after a rigging system has been put in place.

The most common bottom finishes of drapery are flat hems, in-sewn chain, and pipe hems. Pipe hem bottom finishes are typically used for flat drapery panels, cycloramas, and drops, giving the material weight and a clean bottom line. In-sewn chain finishes add weight to pleated drapery without pulling the drape flat. Adding weight to drapery prevents the material from swaying when air currents are generated by backstage movement or air conditioning systems. If the drapery does not require added weight, such as masking and atmosphere draping, a standard flat hem should suffice.

FIGURE 15.2
Lace and grommet top finishes allow drops and drapery to be tied to batons and trussing.
Image courtesy of Rose Brand, Inc.
(www.rosebrand.com)

Cycloramas

In photography, a true cyclorama, or cyc, is used to create the illusion of an infinite background, such as when a model or actor appears to stand in front of a perfectly white void. This effect is achieved by curving the bottom of the cyc wall so that it meets seamlessly with the floor to allow for even lighting.

In event design, however, a cyc does not curve to the floor, nor is it a solid wall, but rather a flat curtain or panel of fabric hung from pipe or trussing. It is the scale and purity of color, typically white or off-white, that allows an audience to accept that it represents an infinite or neutral background. Cycs are also used as lighting canvases to create beautiful backgrounds that complement a stage design.

When ordering your first cyc from a vendor, you may be given a few options in addition to finishes, namely bleached or natural and seamless or seamed. Cycs that are not bleached have a natural cotton hue, which is an off-white tan color as opposed to the bright white of bleached cotton. *Seamless* means the cyc is constructed from one piece of material as opposed to *seamed*, which is composed of several pieces sewn together. More than likely, you will want a seamless bleached cyc for your design. However, there are size limitations to seamless materials, and bleached materials are a bit more expensive than natural cotton.

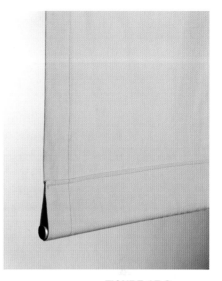

FIGURE 15.3
A pipe hem commonly used on backdrops, scrims, and cycs.
Image courtesy of Rose Brand, Inc.
(www.rosebrand.com)

FIGURE 15.4
Cycloramas, or cycs, provide a natural canvas behind stage designs.

Scrims

Scrims, more specifically Sharkstooth scrims, are usually made from cotton or synthetic materials and resemble medical gauze or drywall tape. This unique weave pattern allows light to be both reflected and transmitted through the fabric. A scrim appears almost entirely opaque or solid if lit from an angle and there is nothing lit behind it. If something is lit behind the scrim, but there is no front lighting on the scrim itself, then it will appear mostly transparent. If a gobo is shot directly at the scrim, it will appear on both the scrim and whatever is behind it. Scrims do not absorb light; therefore, backlighting them is not an option.

Scrims can also be painted with dye to create images visible only when the scrim is lit from an angle. An example of a scrim being used in a nontraditional way is a museum exhibit showing the Battle of the Alamo. The front of the framed exhibit was a beautifully hand-painted gray scrim depicting a scene from the Alamo the night before the battle. Then the lights dimmed on the scrim, and another beautiful mural of the same scene the next morning after the battle appeared on the exhibit wall behind the scrim. This very moving effect was created using timeless theatrical trickery.

A great use of scrims within the event industry is to place a fiber-optic curtain, which will be discussed momentarily, behind a scrim. When the scrim is lit from above with blue or purple lighting, while the fiber-optic curtain is turned

FIGURE 15.5
Scrims have the unique ability to appear opaque when front lit and transparent when an object or person is lit from behind.

on, you can achieve the illusion of evening or dusk sky. Slowly dim the lighting on the scrim until only the fiber-optic lights are visible, and you transition the design into a nighttime scene. Reverse the process using orange and violet lighting, and you can simulate a sunrise. Scrims are truly versatile solutions for a number of design effects and accents.

Take a note from personal experience: using multiple scrims that overlap is not advised because the end result is a moiré pattern, similar to that discussed in Chapter 7, "Video and Projection." Consider using wide netting or silhouette flats to create layers rather than multiple scrims.

Netting, Mesh, and Gauze

In addition to scrims, a few other material types allow for some form of transparency in a finished drop. Netting, for example, is primarily added to the back of intricately cut backdrops to add strength to smaller pieces such as the foliage and tree branches of a forest scene. Mesh and gauze have wider weaves than scrims, with meshes having the widest or most open weave, but can be lit similarly. Both are typically used as texture and can be gathered or pooled for an elegant touch.

Drops

Backdrops, often simply called *drops*, are flat curtains, typically made of muslin or finely woven cotton, that have been painted or printed to resemble a location or texture. Perhaps the scene is a mountainscape or an English garden. If a scenic view is not right for your design, a brick wall or oversized abstract painting may be a better fit. These expansive works of art provide a quick and easily installed general background for your design. Utilizing premade rentable backdrops is an affordable way to add something extra to low-budget events. For only a few dollars more, though, a custom-printed backdrop, designed specifically for your concept, can be fabricated and tailored for use during an event.

RENTED

Rented backdrops are a great solution for tight budgets. For only a few hundred dollars, premade rented backdrops can be incorporated into a design to re-create a plethora of environments. The average size of rented drops is 20' × 40' wide, and they may be hand-painted or printed. Some products available have cut-out entrances or are applied to netting to allow for transparency. Visit the Web sites of Grosh Backdrops and Drapery (www.grosh.com) or Backdrops Fantastic (backdropsfantastic.com) to view over a thousand available backdrop options.

CUSTOM-PRINTED DROPS

With oversized digital printing becoming more affordable, custom backdrops are now within reach of most budgets. Using a combination of 3D software, Adobe Photoshop or Illustrator, and oversized printing, you can simulate virtually any environment. In one example, a client wanted to appear to step off a plane and walk down rolling stairs like on an airport tarmac for his grand

FIGURE 15.6
Rental backdrops are affordable on most event budgets and handy for creating a variety of staging environments.
Backdrop samples courtesy of Grosh Scenic Rentals (www.grosh.com)

entrance. The client's budget didn't allow a fake plane to be constructed, so a plane was modeled in 3D and rendered using 3ds Max in extreme high resolution. It was then printed onto cotton, and the doorway was cut out to allow for the entrance. Rollaway stairs were rented, and the effect was achieved.

One consideration to keep in mind when designing custom backdrops is the color scheme used. Intense colors can compete with lighting looks or limit color schemes that can be used within the design. Consider creating images that are high in contrast but have low color saturation to allow color washes to transform the appearance of your designed artwork. A grayscale photo of a cloudy sky, for example, allows the lighting designer to create the appearance of a sunrise, high noon, or even dusk with a single backdrop.

Most printed drops created for the event industry can be purchased for under $15 per square foot and are finished with either pipe hems or lace and grommet. Visit Big Image Systems (bigimagesystems.com) to get an estimate for your custom backdrops as well as discover the variety of unique and eco-friendly materials that can be printed on.

Dimensional Drops

Dimensional drops take the concept of a backdrop to a new level and instantly add depth to a stage design. Dimensional drops are similar to bead curtains, but rather than beads, large abstract objects, gold spheres, or oversized diamonds – to name a few examples – are used to create walls of texture. Some dimensional drops fall slightly outside the realm of soft goods and are instead constructed of modular elements that either bolt or snap together. Atomic Design (www.atomicdesign.tv) has a vast collection of innovative dimensional backdrops that are affordable for most budgets. Consider adding a cyc behind dimensional drops to maximize on the illusion of depth they create.

Fabric Pulls and Shapes

Fabric pulls are little more than large shapes of stretch fabric that can be used to add depth to a design as well as provide lighting surfaces. Even large rectangles of white stretch fabric prove interesting when dramatically uplit or textured with gobos. What makes a fabric pull more than just a large bed sheet is the material used, the edge finishing, and corner tabs. Stretch fabric used for pulls is very similar in nature to Spandex and has a reinforced edge finish to prevent fraying.

FIGURE 15.7
With digital printing, any image can become a custom backdrop. This image was used to simulate an airplane landing with the presenter entering through the cutout doorway and onto rolling stairs.

FIGURE 15.8
Dimensional drops provide visual interest through the use of depth and texture. *Image courtesy of Atomic Design, Inc. (www.atomicdesign.tv)*

FIGURE 15.9
Fabric pulls are a simple solution for providing lighting canvases.
Image courtesy of Freeman (www.freemanco .com)

The further-reinforced corner tabs or loops allow the material to be anchored to trussing, base plates, or even sand bags.

Technology-Infused Drops

Lighting and video technology has come a long way in recent years and naturally has been infused with traditional theater and live event staples such as drops and modified scrims. As technology continues to advance, these hybrid products will begin to become commonplace and may even replace printed backdrops and video screens altogether. The most frequently utilized examples of technology-infused drops in use today are fiber-optic and LED curtains.

Fiber-optic curtains, sometimes referred to as *star curtains*, are infused with an impressive network of end-glowing fiber-optic strands that poke through the front of heavy black material with designed randomness. These strands are illuminated by light fixtures controlled by the lighting board, allowing control of the color of twinkle of individual nodes. The resulting effect is a glittering field of starlight.

LED curtains are sophisticated works of technology utilizing several thousand LED diodes precisely sewn into fabric or attached to a thin grid substrate. Simpler forms of LED curtains are little more than elaborate nets of Christmas lights, whereas more advanced systems serve as low-resolution video displays. The resolution is determined by how close individual LED diodes are positioned to one another. Even the highest-resolution products, however, should not be used

FIGURE 15.10
Fiber-optic drapery is excellent at creating the illusion of a night sky filled with stars.
Image courtesy of Freeman (www.freemanco .com)

FIGURE 15.11
LED curtains, like Mainlight's Soft-LED, allow for complete backdrops and accents to become video sources and are available in a variety of resolutions and sizes.
Image courtesy of Mainlight (www.mainlight .com)

as video displays for content, meaning PowerPoint presentations or important video segments. However, they are ideal for using abstract video footage and animations to create dynamic backdrops that add a modern touch to even the simplest of environment designs.

Inflatable Scenic Elements

Inflatable scenery is a great solution for budgets of all sizes. Need a full-size airplane or giant globe for your design? Not a problem with inflatable scenery. Even custom elements can be created and typically at less cost and effort than constructing the same element out of hard goods. Inflatable scenery is often the only option for oversized scenic elements, especially when the venue has only a 36-inch-wide door or load-in time is limited. And we are not talking about shiny bounce houses or giant guerrillas, although they are certainly possible and readily available. Many inflatable scenic pieces look like solid structures and can easily fool an audience from only a few feet away.

There are two basic types of inflatables: cold air balloons, which are inflated on-site and require a continuous fan to remain inflated; and sealed inflatables, which are inflated on-site and sealed, similar to pool furniture. The only downside to inflatables is the fans or compressors needed to keep cold air balloons inflated, which can be quite noisy at times. When a compressor is used, consider placing it in a service hallway behind the stage or surround it with thick draping to suppress the sound of the compressor refilling. When only fans are used, they are not typically loud enough to disrupt a stage production but will be noticeable when used in an environment design. SceneryFirst.com and Landmark Creations International (www.landmarkcreations.com) are two great sources for rented and custom inflatable elements.

FIGURE 15.12
Inflatable scenic pieces, like this ship, allow for easy transportation and storage.
Image courtesy of SceneryFirst.com

HARD GOODS

The phrase *hard goods* covers any solid scenic element within a design, including flats, columns, sculptures, and even screen surrounds. If it cannot be folded or compacted, it is a hard good. Like soft goods, hard goods give a design depth and visual interest. Playing on their name, hard goods can be tricky elements to design and construct. You must consider how they will be stored, transported, and ultimately brought into the event space early in the design phase. For example, a 6-foot diameter sphere will not work in a venue with standard 36-inch-wide doors, unless a creative construction method is derived. The following categories describe some of the more common hard goods used in the modern event industry.

Flats

Scenic or stage flats have been an integral piece of stage design since the time of Ancient Greece, and were traditionally used by scenic painters to give the illusion of solid walls or building structures, or as canvases for scenic paintings. Flats are vertical surfaces within a design, providing depth and lighting and texture canvases. They are typically constructed as 4' × 8' or 4' × 10' units, due in part to the sizes of materials available and to allow for easy storage and transportation. Furthermore, they are engineered to allow for several units to be joined side to side, making one continuous wall, or adjoined at 90-degree angles. Flats today can be placed in four categories: soft, hard, Broadway, and studio.

SOFT/HARD FLATS

Soft flats consist of wood frames, typically constructed from 1" × 4" boards, and covered with cotton or muslin, making them lightweight and ideal canvases for

Basic scenic flat construction

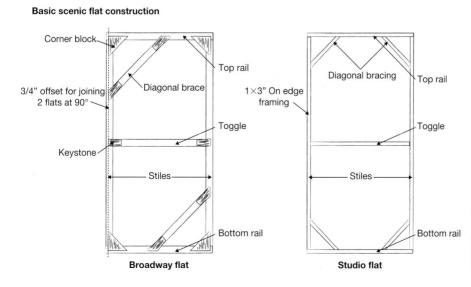

Broadway flat

Studio flat

FIGURE 15.13
The basic parts of a stage flat. On the left, a Broadway flat; on the right, a studio flat.

scenic painting. Being made of fabric, soft flats damage easily and cannot support much weight, such as picture frames or wall accessories. These limitations make soft flats less popular for use in the event industry, which requires durability for scenic elements.

An alternative to a soft flat is the hard flat, which is covered with a solid material, such as thin plywood or laminate. Hard flats are much more durable and can be painted or wallpapered like an actual interior wall. In addition, they can support the weight of small accessories, such as picture frames or drapery, and lend themselves much better to built-in windows and door frames. However, heavier-mounted elements like video monitors and plasma screens require a more elaborate framing structure to support the additional weight. Although hard flats are a bit heavier, their durability and potential for repeated use make them a popular choice for the event industry.

BROADWAY/STUDIO FLATS

The terms *Broadway flats* and *studio flats* refer to how a flat is constructed. Broadway flats are built with the face of a 1" × 4" lying flush against the flat covering, whereas studio flats are built using the edge of a 1" × 4". The finished result is a Broadway flat that is less than 1-inch thick, allowing for compact storage and transportation. Studio flats have an approximate 4-inch thickness, depending on the surface material used. Although these flats are heavier and require additional storage space, their thickness requires less support to remain upright, so several units can be clamped or screwed together to create solid walls. All flats require some form of vertical support commonly known as *jacks*. Jacks are 90-degree supports, typically constructed of wood, that are

FIGURE 15.14
A simple design using stage flats.
Designer: Travis Malinowsky

attached to the back of stage flats to keep them upright. The jacks themselves are then secured to the stage floor using screws or sandbags. If a scenic design requires the use of functioning doors, studio flats are preferable because their design can handle the shock of a slamming door, whereas Broadway flats tend to wobble.

SILHOUETTE FLATS

Not all stage flats have to be rectangular in shape or even geometric in nature. Silhouette flats are used when the outline of logo or object is needed within a design. Think of the cardboard cutout trees used in grade school productions. Although more sophisticated tree solutions are available, the principle is the same. Cityscapes are common in corporate event stage designs and a great example of silhouette flats, occasionally even including cutouts for backlit windows. Such an elaborate and intricate shape is possible because of computer numerical controlled (CNC) cutting machines. These awesome pieces of machinery can transform a sheet of metal, plywood, laminate, or foam into precision cut shapes in a matter of minutes. These cut shapes are then applied to a modified flat frame and either painted or covered with printed graphics. A common practice, giving rise to the name, is to paint these custom flats black or gray and place them in front of a cyclorama to create silhouettes rather than detailed works of art.

FIGURE 15.15
Silhouette or profile flats are built to resemble various structures such as mountains or buildings.
Designer: Troy Halsey

GROUND ROWS

Ground rows are short flats, generally not more than a foot high, used to hide technical equipment or undesirable staging features. A common example would be a ground row used to mask cyc lights placed at the bottom of an upstage cyclorama or backdrop. These flats are generally constructed quickly and painted black or white. They serve a function rather than contribute to the aesthetics of a design. With a bit of clever thinking, however, they can be seamlessly incorporated into a design resembling bushes in a forest scene or a brick retaining wall for more urban designs. Work with the lighting designer to determine if a ground row will be needed and how it can be incorporated into your design.

Screen Surrounds

Some large projection screens require that box trussing be used as a frame. The screen itself is then tied to the truss on all four sides. As a result, a designer is left with four options: leave the truss exposed, hide it with drape, internally light the truss and make it a design element, or fashion a covering of some form. When a designed solution is developed, it is referred to as a *screen surround*.

SOFT SURROUNDS

One option when covering truss is to use fabric because it can be sewn, pinned, or taped for custom fits. This option is referred to as a *soft surround*. Block-out material such as black felt or Duvateen works very well for creating affordable

FIGURE 15.16
A ground row is used to hide lighting instruments placed on the stage surface and provides a clean base line for designs.

methods of truss covering. This approach, however, is not the most visually interesting. Another fabric option is to have custom socks made from white stretch fabric for the truss. The term *sock* can be misleading because the fabric actually covers only three sides of the truss and attaches using hook-and-loop tape (or Velcro), which is sewn into the material. This gives access to the truss, allowing the screen to be attached as usual.

HARD SURROUNDS

The second option for creating a screen surround is the *hard surround*. Hard surrounds can be made from a number of materials, but the most common are plywood, metal, or laminate. And a hard surround is not limited to a square or rectangular shape. When a frame that will attach the truss surrounding a screen is built, any number of shapes can be incorporated into a screen surround design.

TECHNOLOGY SURROUNDS

Technology can also be incorporated into a screen surround. LED color-changing rope light can trim a surround, creating the feel of a neon sign. LED video panels can also be connected to the truss supporting the screen, creating a digital frame capable of displaying abstract shapes to support the overall design.

NO TRUSS?

Screen surrounds are not limited to hiding truss framing. Often a design may call for a screen surround when it is not technically needed, merely aesthetically. Both hard surrounds and technology surrounds can be used in such cases and hung from rigging systems rather than attached to trussing. If a design calls for internally lit trussing, but the screen does not require it, the trussing can still be used and the self-framed screen can be attached to the back of the trussing using zip ties or tie lines.

FIGURE 15.17
When screen surrounds that attach using Velcro are fabricated, trussing can be transformed into an internally lit scenic element.

FIGURE 15.18
Screen surrounds are not limited to rectangular shapes, as shown by these three examples.
Designer: Zhiyong Li

Columns and Curved Surfaces

Curved flats are constructed in much the same way as standard flats, in that both consist of a wood or metal frame to which a skin is applied. The obvious challenge is how to construct a curved frame. For simplicity, let's assume you are designing a curved wall that consists of one convex bend. When we are describing curved surfaces, the curve is either *convex*, meaning it bows outward, or *concave*, meaning it bows inward. Convex curves are easier to skin because the material is essentially wrapped around the frame, whereas the skin of a concave curve is pushed into the curve.

So, for our example, we have a convex bend, or curve that bends outward. First, the ribs, also called sweeps, are cut from a sheet of plywood. Ribs, or sweeps, are the horizontal pieces at the top, middle, and bottom of the frame that give the curve its shape. Depending on the size and depth of curve, additional ribs may be needed. Then using dado joints or notches in the rib pieces and uprights, the vertical supports are added, creating a curved wooden grid of sorts. After the frame is constructed, a skin of thin plywood is applied to the frame using adhesive and fasteners. Of course, this is only one very simple approach, and the actual technique used will vary from shop to shop. As a designer, you must understand the general process to ensure the elements you design can be constructed in reality.

There are many types of columns in architecture, such as the Greek columns of Doric, Ionic, and Corinthian styles. In addition, there are fluted columns, which have vertical grooves, and columns with ornate capitals (the tops of columns)

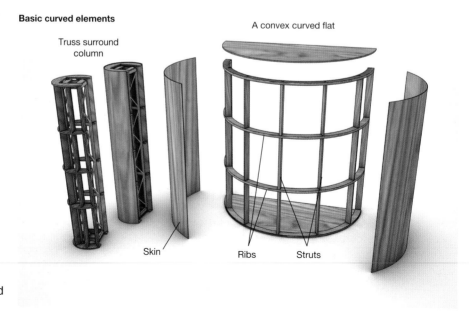

Basic curved elements

Truss surround column

A convex curved flat

Skin

Ribs

Struts

FIGURE 15.19
One possible construction method for a curved wall and column using ribs and struts.

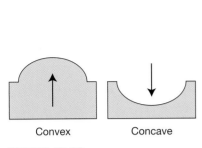

FIGURE 15.20
Convex and concave curves, convex being the easier of the two to construct.

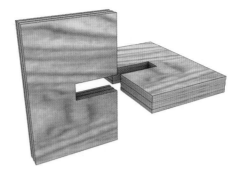

FIGURE 15.21
A dado joint is a common wood joint used in scenery construction.

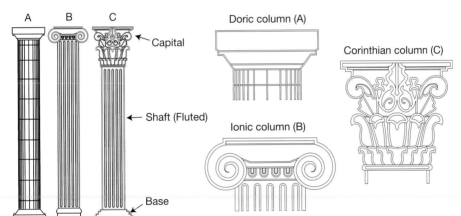

Doric column (A)

Ionic column (B)

Corinthian column (C)

Capital

Shaft (Fluted)

Base

FIGURE 15.22
Classic columns and their parts.

and bases. It is not the objective here to give a history of columns, because it is a surprisingly broad topic, but to provide an understanding of how basic columns are constructed for stage and scenic designs. However, if your design calls for a more classic column, visit Rotonics.com or Outwater Plastics (outwatercatalogs.com) for a variety of affordable column replicas.

Basic straight columns are made in much the same manner as curved surfaces. Depending on their height and diameter, they may require a stronger support structure such as aluminum trussing. When trussing is used, the column does not make a full circle. Instead, the ribbing is cut to fit snuggly around the truss piece. When the construction is completed, vertical uprights inside the column are clamped or bolted to the cross-bracing of the truss. Often columns are constructed as only half-rounds, allowing them to be placed against scenic flats or screens. When this approach is used, the columns can be clamped or bolted to the scenic flat for added stability.

After the wood skin has been applied to columns or curved walls, they can then be primed and painted. Additionally, sheets of laminate or metal can be adhered to the wood skin for a more polished finish. For more complex curved surfaces and columns or when the elements are merely used for adding depth or as lighting canvases, consider using custom or rentable tension fabric shapes that can be contorted into shapes not possible with wood structures.

Tension Fabric Shapes

Tension fabric shapes are extremely common in the event design industry – and for good reason, considering their ease of installation and capacity to hold lighting. Their frames are typically constructed of bent and shaped aluminum piping, and a skin of white stretch material is then either pulled over the framing or zipped along hidden seams. Depending on the shape and design of the structure, tension fabric shapes can be free-standing, hung, or both. An added bonus of tension fabric shapes is they ship in very compact containers, reducing transportation costs and conserving precious truck cargo space.

When front lit, tension fabric shapes serve as clean lighting surfaces that create interesting shadow patterns due to their organic shapes. When backlit or internally

FIGURE 15.23
Stretch fabric shapes allow for affordable works of art to be incorporated into a design and can easily be transported and stored.
Image courtesy of Rose Brand, Inc. (www.rosebrand.com)

lit, these structures resemble Chinese lanterns, adding a dramatic flair to staging and environment designs. Although back or internal lighting makes these pieces visually dynamic, the internal ribbing or cross-supports of the structures will be shown in shadow. Therefore, when designing or renting tension fabric shapes, incorporate the internal ribbing or spacers into your design. The companies Transformit (www.transformitdesign.com), Pink Inc. (pinkincdesign.com), Moss Inc. (mossinc.com), and Rose Brand, Inc. (www.rosebrand.com) have great selections of rental shapes available, and these companies can create custom pieces based on your own designs.

Foam Sculptures and Organic Shapes

Foam is a very versatile scenic building material and, when sculpted by a skilled artist, can be formed to nearly any shape. Organic shapes found in nature, such as rocks, tree trunks, and rough terrain, can easily be reproduced using foam. In addition, custom statues, reliefs, and sculptures are potential elements to be crafted from foam. Literally any shape that can be imagined can be sculpted from foam and painted to look as good as the original at a fraction of the weight.

Styrofoam is the most affordable of foam materials and is available in many shapes and sizes, including 4' × 4' × 8' blocks. However, Styrofoam does not respond well to solvents, the kind found in spray paints or oil- and enamel-based paints, and requires a hard coating before these finishes can be applied. A

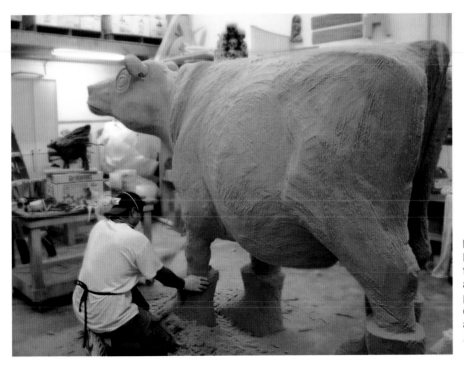

FIGURE 15.24
Foam sculptures, after they are hard-coated and painted, can provide the illusion of expensive custom artwork.
Image courtesy of Guillermo Becerra

hard coating protects the original foam shape sculpted and gives the completed element durability. The most basic hard coating is affectionately known as *Stage Goop*. Stage Goop is a mixture of clay powder and white glue, two materials available at most sculpture supply stores. This concoction is then applied to the foam using a brush or hopper and dries to a hard finish. The element can then be painted with the artist's choice of materials. Stage Goop cannot be sanded, however, because painting typically results in a lumpy and uneven texture. If a smooth finish is preferred, so as to simulate a marble statue, a polyurethane resin that can be sanded and primed should be used for hard coating.

For more detailed sculptures, consider using urethane foam as opposed to Styrofoam. Urethane foam has a much finer grit and resembles the green foam used by florists. Hard-coat urethane foam the same way described previously before painting. As you do with all hard goods, consider how large your venue doors are and determine how your finished product will be broken into smaller pieces and reassembled on-site.

Extruded Metal Structures

Metal extrusion was developed in the late 1700s and has several applications in our daily lives. The process is very similar to pushing Play-Doh through plastic shapes; the difference is that instead of Play-Doh, various metals are forced or extruded through hardened steel dies. This process allows for the production of complex continuous construction pieces. Aluminum is one common material that is used in this process because it produces strong but lightweight extrusions. When aluminum pieces are extruded with channels, interlocking systems can be created for quick construction and installations ideal for the event and trade show industry. These systems can be broken down into four basic hardware categories: posts, cross bars, connectors, and inserts or substrates.

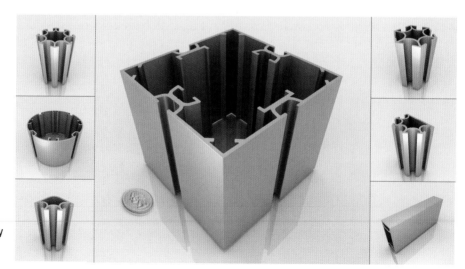

FIGURE 15.25
Examples of extruded metal posts commonly used to construct exhibits and scenery.

Posts are the vertical pieces that give the structure height, similar to the vertical members of a curved flat. These channeled pieces can be cut to any size and come in various thicknesses. Cross bars or members, which are also channeled, are then slid into the vertical channels and secured using any number of connectors. Substrates or material inserts, such as sheets of thick plastic, acrylic, laminate, or even wood, are then slid in between the vertical and horizontal extrusions. Although this is admittedly a poor description of the system, it is very easy to design for and use within your event environments. It is essentially an oversized Erector Set. Many tradeshow vendors use such systems as their primary construction material for exhibit booths and entryways. Do-it-yourself kits and products are available from AGAM (agam.com) and Octanorm USA (octanormusa.com).

SPECIALTY ITEMS

Specialty items are those that fall just outside the realm of typical scenic and environment design. These are the elements that tend to be unique to the event industry when used onstage. Podiums, furniture, light boxes, and dimensional logos are the primary elements that may come into play during event designs. Following are a few notes to keep in mind when addressing such specialty items.

Podiums/Lecterns

Podiums, unfortunately, are a necessary evil, and as a designer, you may find it easy to ignore that the client asked for a podium and just focus on developing a stellar staging environment. Although there are rare occasions when podiums are not used, most corporate and amateur speakers like the security a podium provides. For this reason, if a podium isn't worked into the design in some form, your beautiful stage design will end up with an unsightly generic hotel podium center stage.

Designing custom podiums can be a daunting task because they are more sophisticated pieces of furniture than apparent at first glance. Many podiums

FIGURE 15.26
A few sample podium styles.

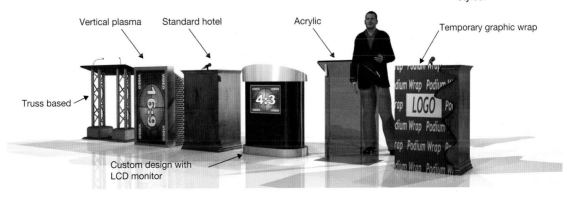

Vertical plasma   Standard hotel   Acrylic   Temporary graphic wrap

Truss based

Custom design with LCD monitor

have built-in microphone connections, reading lights, and even LCD monitors for viewing slides or scripts. Plasma screens have also found their way into podiums, providing a digital canvas on the front of the podium. Fortunately, as the designer, you can concern yourself with the shape and look of the podium and work with fabrication and video specialists to determine the best approach to incorporating technology into the design. Just keep the basics in mind: a working surface for notes should be around 38" to 42" high and wide enough for at least two sheets of paper. Most working surfaces are inclined slightly and require a lip to prevent papers from sliding off the podium. In addition, consider adding a shelf within the podium for water bottles, backup wireless microphones, and documents. Finally, leave the bottom inside of the podium hollow to store apple boxes. *Apple boxes* are single black steps or risers that height-challenged presenters can stand on when presenting behind a podium. These are especially important when teleprompters and confidence monitors are used because they are positioned to be seen from an average height.

A much more affordable option is to purchase or rent manufactured podiums. Manufactured podiums come in a variety of shapes, sizes, and materials. Acrylic, truss, wood veneer, and tension fabrics are the more common materials of choice. Be cautious of acrylic podiums, however, because many presenters prefer their shaky legs not be seen. Height-adjustable podiums are available that can be remotely or manually raised and lowered for specific presenter heights. There are a number of podium vendors online, including Podiums.us.com (www.podiums .us.com) and PodiumandLecternStore.com (www.podiumandlecternstore.com). Whatever choice is made, be sure it works within the environment and is not left to the venue to provide.

Furniture Elements

Although furniture was addressed in Chapters 13 and 14 on scenic and environment design, designers and event planners should be aware that custom furniture pieces are always an option for stage designs, but stick with tables and desks only and rent or purchase seating. Designing tables and desks, while requiring skilled carpenters to construct, is similar to designing podiums. Consider how technology will be worked into these pieces, such as microphone connections and video monitors. Be considerate of women wearing skirts and avoid leaving legs exposed. Finally, determine how these elements will be broken into pieces that can fit through a standard doorway. For quick and easy solutions, visit the Cort Web site (www.cort.com) and browse its vast furniture collections.

Light Boxes

Light boxes are great for adding eye candy to a stage design. They can be constructed from wood, plastic, or metal frames and are limited only by a designer's imagination. At their core, they are little more than internally lit boxes faced with a backlit graphic. Fast-food menu boards and movie poster marquees are light boxes, as are channel letters used for storefront signs. The key is to evenly distribute the light source and properly produce the backlit graphic.

FIGURE 15.27
Rental furniture is available in a variety of styles and colors.
Image courtesy of Cort Event Furnishings (www.cort.com)

For rich color saturation, most backlit graphics are printed onto thin film with a reverse image on the back of the material. Although the film diffuses the light to some degree, choosing the right light source is important. Fluorescent bulbs and neon tubes have been the preferred method for years, but neither one is dimmable and both flicker when powered on. A better alternative is to use LED light sources, which consume low amounts of energy, emit very little heat, and are dimmable. LED rope light, which can flex and bend for curved shapes, and LED strips work well for this application. Visit TheLEDLight.com for a variety of LED strips or Rose Brand (www.rosebrand.com) to purchase a versatile LED rope light product called NeoFlex Flexible LED.

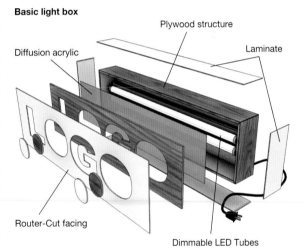

Basic light box
Plywood structure
Laminate
Diffusion acrylic
Router-Cut facing
Dimmable LED Tubes

FIGURE 15.28
A simple light box.

Dimensional Logos and Text

Simple dimensional logos and text combine CNC machining and laminate appliqués to add thickness and depth to otherwise flat artwork. When logos are applied to a scenic flat, the process is relatively straightforward. The challenge arises when a logo or text needs to be hung. If printed as a single sign and backed with foam, with only the perimeter cut to shape, the piece can be hung as usual. If each letter or element of the logo is cut individually, however, they must be connected in some manner to be hung. Either wood or plastic dowels or acrylic rods can be used for connecting individual pieces, or even a solid sheet of acrylic can be cut to the silhouette of the shape with the pieces then being applied as they would on a scenic flat.

Two problems arise with both approaches. First, although monofilament materials have come a long way, the wires used to hang the piece will be visible

FIGURE 15.29
Three examples of dimensional logos.

regardless of color. Even black wire against black drape will be visible when the wire is highlighted by stage lights. Unfortunately, there is no clever work-around for this problem, so it is simply an issue that must be accepted. Second, rods, even acrylic rods, will be visible under stage lighting, and solid sheets of acrylic used as backing may reflect stage lights directly at the audience.

So what is a designer to do when dimensional logos and text need to be hung? An honest answer is find an alternative way to elevate the pieces or accept the fact that wires and rods will be visible, especially in certain camera angles. Although they will still be visible, selecting a wire or filament color that closely matches the background will reduce how noticeable the wires appear. The scale of the logo or text will also reduce the visibility of the wires by comparison.

An alternative to hanging dimensional text is fabricating oversized pieces that rest on the stage floor. These pieces are built from several layers of thick foam, which are then hard-coated and supported by jacks or slid onto rods welded to heavy metal bases.

SCENIC PAINTING

Similar to lighting designs that paint a stage with color, scenic painting can make or break a staging or environment design – so much so that a mere spattering of gray or even off-white paint may be preferred over using intense colors, allowing the staging environment to be colored and transformed by lighting alone. Some effects, however, cannot be achieved solely by lighting, and for this reason, paint or laminates are needed to bring a design to life. Furthermore, for scenic elements to react properly to lighting, they need to be textured in some manner to enhance the visual appeal of their surfaces within the staging environment.

The art of stage or scenic painting – and it is indeed an art form in every sense – pulls from all styles and techniques of painting. To achieve desired and repeatable results takes years of practice and, as cheesy as it may sound, a lifetime to master. The reason is that there are so many different ways to apply paint to a surface that libraries of works have been created discussing the topic. As a designer, you need to understand the core techniques and methods of scenic painting to ensure the realized design matches the conceptual vision. Although most corporate scenic designers do not physically paint their own set pieces, knowing the right terminology is necessary for clearly communicating your design intent to scenic artists and fabricators.

Paint Finishes

An often-overlooked feature of paint used for stage designs is the paint's finish. Paint finish describes how shiny or reflective it is after it dries. There are four grades of finish for most paints: flat, eggshell, satin, and glossy. Some paint suppliers add a fifth finish: semi-gloss, which is naturally between satin and glossy. There are different schools of thinking in regards to paint finishes for a scenic environment, but we suggest using eggshell finishes for most applications because it provides a vibrant appearance while reducing the visibility of scuffs and scratches. Glossy and satin finishes should be avoided for covering large surfaces because their highlights will be too intense under stage lighting. Glossy finishes do work well on trim pieces and accents, however, and their shine can give the set a fancy touch without becoming distracting.

Adding Texture

Adding texture to a scenic element adds visual interest and contrast within its surface. There will be times when texture is not desired. High-tech and futuristic sets, for example, may need smooth finishes with a medium gloss finish over traditionally textured finishes. Such examples aside, it is advisable to texture all scenic elements to slightly diffuse stage lighting and add depth to surfaces. Although texture can be achieved in a number of ways with paint and every artist has his own approach, here are some techniques commonly used for adding texture to surfaces with paint. All the approaches begin with a neutral base coating with texturing then being applied over the dried base unless otherwise noted. Colors used for texturing should include a highlight and shadow, or lighter and darker shades of the base color:

- *Spattering* creates a speckled effect. To create it, you thin the paint to a fine consistency, lightly load the brush, and flick the paint onto the surface with

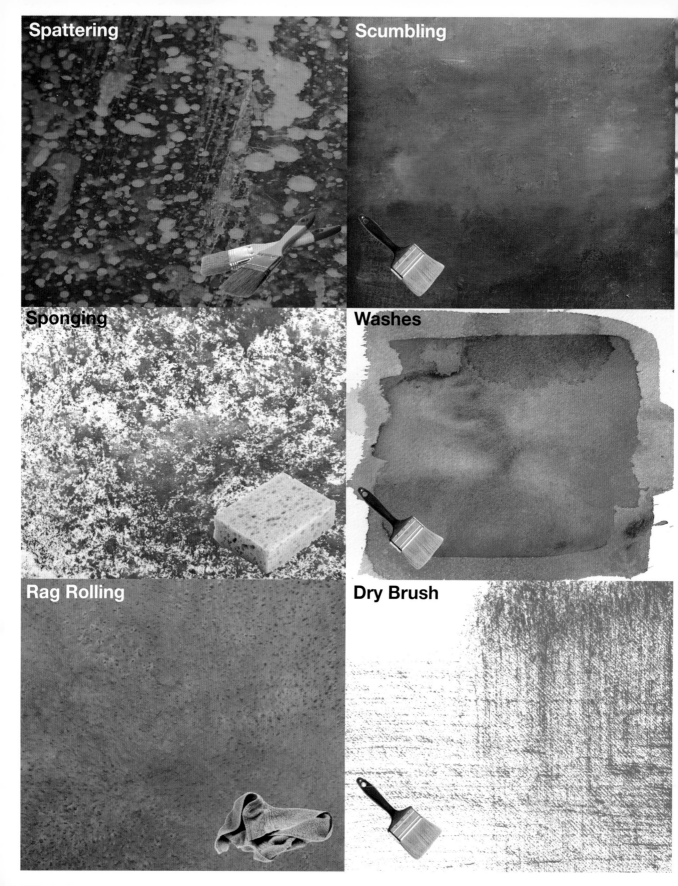

Spattering

Scumbling

Sponging

Washes

Rag Rolling

Dry Brush

quick and gentle movements of the wrist. Like all techniques, this approach takes a bit of practice to get even distribution.

■ *Scumbling* uses three or more shades of the base color and blends them with random strokes of the brush while the paints are still wet. The finished pattern can then be used as a base for additional textures or as a neutral lighting canvas.

■ *Sponging* is so named because a sponge, either a natural sea sponge or synthetic, is used to lift paint from a still-wet base in random dabs or apply paint in a similar manner. This approach is best used on vertical flat surfaces and can be applied to large areas quickly.

■ *Washes and glazes* are thin top coats of color or gloss rolled or brushed over a basecoat. Several coats of washes create a layered effect that adds depth to a surface. Combining sponging and washes can quickly lead to visually interesting surfaces.

■ *Rag rolling* uses various materials such as terrycloth rags, plastic bags, or even crumbled paper to roll across a surface, lifting or applying paint, producing an effect similar to sponging. Like spattering, this technique takes a bit of practice and is easiest when applied to a vertical surface in a down stroke.

■ *Dry brushing* is great for dulling down a surface or creating the illusion of age. After the basecoat has dried, select a color a few shades darker than the basecoat and barely touch the surface of the paint with the end of the brush. Use a piece of cardboard and quickly swipe the brush back and forth, using almost all the paint loaded. Now, using the hint of paint left in the bristles, either pull across the top of the basecoat in one motion, for a hint of wood grain, or apply with a criss-crossed motion to dull a surface or add age.

Faux Finishes

Faux finishes attempt to replicate real-world textures with paint. However, because the audience is several feet from the stage, the effects have to be exaggerated to be seen at a distance. For corporate events, which are typically documented on video, and where speakers and performers are I-Mag'ed to projection screens, a happy medium must be found when exaggerating textures for the live audience and the camera lens. Overly exaggerated textures will make sets appear cartoonish on camera, whereas textures scaled realistically may be washed out under stage lighting when viewed from a distance.

■ *Combing* is similar to scumbling, but instead of random strokes, a grain is created as the brush or comb is pulled in one direction. Simulating wood grain is the most common use of this technique. Several unique tools can help to simulate wood grain, such as grain combs, rollers, and rubber graining rockers. This technique should be practiced for some time before being attempted on a scenic element. Remember to slightly exaggerate the scale of graining so as to be readable from the audience.

FIGURE 15.31
Stencils, whether
bought or made,
are useful for quick
and repeated paint
detailing.

- *Stencils and stamping* are pretty straightforward and have been used by most people at some point in their lives. Oversized stencils are available from most scenic material providers and can be useful for mimicking wallpaper trim or ornate paint accents. Stamping is the same as rubber stamping, except that paint is used, instead of ink, and almost any object can be used as the stamp. Even the yellow sponges used at car washes can be cut to shapes and used as stamps. More elaborate custom stamps might be cut from 3/4-inch plywood, which is covered with muslin, and a handle is attached to the back of the plywood. Building a library of these custom stamps can come in handy for quick turnaround projects down the road.

- *Forced perspective*, also known by its fancy name *trompe l'oeil* (French for *trick the eye*), is a method of scenic painting that creates the optical illusion of depth and perspective through the use of highlights and shadows. Painting raised rivets along flat seams is one example, while creating the illusion of a dark alley with paint is another. Forced perspective requires a keen ability of observation when using photographs for reference and determining where highlights and shadows should fall. In the case of rivets along the edge of a vertical flat, the shadow should fall under the rivet with the highlight being just along the top inside edge to simulate the shadows caused by overhead stage lights. For larger flat canvases, such as backdrops, the desired effect may be more easily achieved by simply designing custom-printed artwork created in either Adobe Photoshop or Illustrator. For smaller or more complex scenic pieces, however, hand painting is still the quickest and most cost-effective way to go. When the opportunity arrives, take time to observe experienced scenic artists using this technique because it is quite impressive to watch. When you do not have access to a scenic artist, consider using laminates and appliqués to achieve your desired effect.

Laminates and Appliqués

Laminates and appliqués are useful when a hint of realism is needed within a design. Perhaps if the design calls for a wood veneer or brick finish, laminates might be a better way to go over paint. Laminates are constructed from several layers of various materials pressed and glued together, a process known as *laminating*. Plywood is one example of lamination, but the laminates that are typically used for scenic finishes are known as High Pressure Decorative Laminate (HPDL) sheets. These sheets can be adhered to plywood for making floor coverings, adding texture and detail to stage flats, and finishing furniture surfaces. The nicest part about laminates is the detail they can provide. Laminates are printed with a pattern of any number of building materials such as tile, metal, and wood. These patterns so closely resemble the actual texture referenced that an observer may never know it isn't the real thing. Like paint, laminates are available with various grades and finishes, and the same rules should be used when selecting a finish that will work well under stage lighting. There are literally dozens of laminate providers, so a quick Google search will get you started. Nevamar (www.nevamar.com) and Formica (formica.com) are among the more established providers of decorative laminate products.

Appliqués work much the same way as laminates except that they may be applied in pieces rather than sheets and tend to be thicker than sheet laminate. Foam bricks and stone are common appliqués, as are moldings and trim. Technically, though, moldings and trim tend to be in their own category. Another great appliqué source is vacuform panels. These thin sheets of plastic are molded to various textures, providing immense detail. Bamboo, wood shingles, siding, and cobblestone are just a few sample textures that can be purchased as vacuform panels. Although some products come prefinished and painted, a better option is a clean white panel that can then be primed and painted to your own desired finish. Tulnoylumber.com and Rose Brand (www.rosebrand.com) are both great sources for vacuform panels.

FIGURE 15.32
Sidewalk and chalk murals are great examples of forced perspective.
Image courtesy of Kurt Wenner (www .kurtwenner.com)

FIGURE 15.33
Vacuform is an affordable option for finishing textured surfaces, along with a lot of paint and practice. *Image courtesy of Rose Brand, Inc. (www.rosebrand.com)*

Tree bark   Old brick   Cobblestone

ADDING THE FINISHING TOUCHES

Every environment and scenic design, when constructed, will have a few rough edges that need to be addressed before the installation can be considered complete. Whether it is masking technology, adding trim, or rolling on carpeting, these small additions and adjustments can separate professionally produced productions from the run of the mill.

Floor Coverings

Floor coverings have been addressed a few times in the book but are worth describing one more time. Although carpeting is the most affordable of options, it is far from the only option. A number of vinyl and urethane flooring options can be applied just like carpeting. These products allow for realistic textures, such as stone, tile, and wood, to be applied to a stage or environment floor quickly and affordably. Flexitec urethane flooring is one such product line available from www.vinylflooring.com. For a high-gloss finish to the stage floor, one that will annoy lighting designers, consider vinyl and PVC flooring products from Rosco (rosco.com).

The most important point to remember when it comes to floor coverings is to ensure they are safe for use by professional and amateur presenters alike and for various forms of footwear, including high heels and dress shoes. Consider highlighting the edges of a stage surface with glow tape or bright white gaffer's tape. Just remember to keep it safe – and that goes for all elements within an event environment.

Props, Set Dressings, and Technology Toys

The theatrical meaning of a prop is not often used during a corporate event. There are, of course, exceptions, such as props used during skits or as sight gags during a presentation. Traditional props are not generally used during event meetings because they are not needed to help tell a story or deliver a message the way

FIGURE 15.34
Laminates are just one option for floor coverings, and a versatile finish for most surfaces.

FIGURE 15.35
This cruise liner design, a reality abstract, relies heavily on props to complete the design.
Designer: Todd Ethridge

they are for theatrical productions. Most props used within the event industry lean more toward technology toys and set dressings.

Technology toys include faux fire apparatuses, fog and rain curtains, and with a slight stretch, kabuki drops and unique video displays. These elements are added to an environment design to enhance excitement and provide a dramatic flair. They are also elements that can be added after an environment has been fully developed. For this reason, they are viewed as a type of prop used for a time and then removed from the staging environment.

Set dressings, on the other hand, are meticulously placed within an environment and left for the entire event. Like all things, there are exceptions to this statement as well because a stage design may be set dressed for a tropical theme one day and stripped for a more neutral look the next. Generally speaking, though, set dressings are associated with a particular scenic look. Whiskey barrels and tumbleweeds might be included as set dressings for a Wild West theme, while beach balls and lifeboats might be used to enhance a design inspired by tropical resorts. Such properties can be rented from various prop houses and may even be borrowed from local theaters. Always opt for real items over replicas when possible because the age and unique details of a real whiskey barrel or lifeboat are much more visually intriguing than manufactured plastic replications. Plastic replicas are ideal, however, for crown moldings, banisters, and ornate accents, which are next in the topic of finishing touches.

Trim, Molding, and Railings

Trim is very handy for finishing scenic elements and giving flats and stages nice edges. Flats that incorporate crown molding into their design give the observers'

The Green Movement

What It Means to Be Green
As companies become more aware of their role in the Earth's sustainability, they are willing to take the extra steps needed to ensure their events have the smallest waste footprint possible. From recycled and biodegradable building materials to providing alternative electricity sources, companies today are making great strides toward an environmentally cleaner event industry. The three pillars of the Green movement are: Reduce, Reuse, and Recycle.

Being Green with Plastics
Plastic isn't always a dirty word when it comes to the environment. For example, plastic table covers, vinyl drape, and carpet coverings are all made from up to 40% recycled materials. In addition, items that are laminated in plastic such as event signs are able to be used on multiple occasions instead of being trashed and reprinted after each use.

Carpeting
Between exhibit floors and general sessions, miles of carpet are used every day in the event industry. Fortunately, it is very reusable. Even custom cut pieces can be collected, cleaned, and sewn together to be reused. Freeman, a leader in the event industry, has recycled over 44 million square feet of carpet to date. Even carpet padding is made from 98% recycled urethane foam.

SWAG and Gift Bags
SWAG (Stuff We All Get) encompasses any form of free gifts attendees receive when they are at a conference or event. One green product available is a book bag that uses old billboard canvases as decorative accents. Another product is a set of award cuff links made from antique typewriter keys! A quick web search for "Eco-Friendly Corporate Gifts" or "Recycled SWAG" will provide a plethora of options for your next event.

Green Scenic Design
Many stage sets and other event structures are fabricated with full sheets of lumber, laminate, or various construction materials. When the event is struck, reusable elements are returned to production facilities, but several pieces are deemed unusable because of paint finish, scuffs, or other minor imperfections. These slightly subpar materials are ideal for donating to local Habitat for Humanity organizations to aid in the construction of basic shelter for the homeless. In addition, several third-world support organizations will accept building materials regardless of their condition. ProjectMexico.org is one such group that uses donated construction materials to build and repair homes and shelters in low to no income areas of Mexico.

Recycling and reusing materials are a great step towards a greener Earth, but it is only the first step. The ultimate goal of the green movement is not only to preserve the planet's precious resources but to build towards a better world. Taking the time to find clever ways to be green will leave a lasting impression on attendees and more importantly, your clients.

eyes a stopping point. Stages covered in carpeting or vinyl flooring can benefit from 90-degree molding to keep the covering from looking unfinished along the edges of the stage. Decorative railings or banisters might be added to raised platforms not only to glitz up a design, but also to give those standing on the platforms a visual cue they are approaching an edge. Just like in the interior finish of a home, these accent pieces give an environment a clean and tailored finish.

Wood and plaster molding and accent pieces can be quite costly, and considering the distance the audience is from the stage and the short amount of time scenery is used, cheaper materials can be used for finishing touches. Many companies offer plastic alternatives that are easier to install, more cost effective, and lighter in weight than their architectural counterparts. Outwater Plastics (outwatercatalogs.com) is one such vendor that offers every trim and molding piece imaginable replicated in lightweight wood, foam, or plastic.

Keep in mind that some trim and molding pieces, such as 90-degree corner molding, must be applied on-site and the initial paint coating touched up after it has been installed. Molding attached to flats and scenic elements can typically be added before the installation, provided the set can be constructed in the scene shop to ensure tight seams.

Masking Material

Masking materials are used to hide unsightly elements within a staging environment, such as cabling, the back of audio speakers and confidence monitors, and even trussing. Typically, black cloth is used because the color tends to draw the least amount of attention. This is, of course, unless you have an all-white stage, in which case white cloth would be advised. Duvetyn is the predominant material used for masking because it is a thick and tightly woven cotton that masks light well and can withstand greater heats than felt or other cotton materials. Masking drapery, or run-off drapery, is also used for masking the edges of a performance space, giving the area clean edges. Rose Brand (www.rosebrand.com) and Dazian Fabrics (dazian.com) both offer a variety of masking materials and products.

PREPPING SCENERY FOR TRANSPORTATION

As mentioned a number of times throughout this book, scenic elements often have to be broken down into pieces to be packed into trucks and fit through venue doors. Even columns, when constructed as solid pieces, can be difficult to maneuver around the tight corners notoriously found in service corridors of venues. In addition to engineering how large scenic pieces will be dismantled and reassembled on-site, designers and fabricators must know how to safely package scenic elements for transportation.

Custom podiums and desks can be very expensive to have fabricated, and there is nothing worse than unpacking a crushed product that cost several thousand dollars to have made. Likewise, foam sculptures, even when hard coated, are susceptible to being destroyed in shipment. To prevent such a result, road cases and shipment crates must be fashioned to ensure scenic elements are delivered intact. Such crates often require as much engineering as the element it is protecting and can be just as costly to fabricate. Smaller elements can be packed tightly using bubble wrap and packing peanuts, but heavier pieces like desks and podiums require more elaborate enclosures. Crates that include padded ribs and cross supports should be constructed to keep elements from shifting in their casings. Furthermore, clear directions should be labeled on the road case or shipping crate, indicating how the packaging should be opened and which side should face up at all times. Although such precautions may seem like overkill, the bouncy cargo containers of an 18-wheeler traveling cross-country can destroy the work of skilled craftsmen and designers when not properly packed and crated. Work with the fabricator to ensure measures are taken to ensure safe transport of all scenic elements.

FIGURE 15.36
Custom-built road cases are just as important as the scenic pieces they protect.

CHAPTER 16

Presenting Your Design

INTRODUCTION TO DESIGN PRESENTATION

Aside from creating the design itself, presenting your concept is the most important moment of the job for a designer. No matter how great your design skills are, if you cannot explain your rationale or sell your coworkers and clients on your overall vision, your design pitch will likely not succeed. What you have to remember is that you are a visual artist and you see your work in a very different light than the client, account manager, or show producer acting on behalf of the client.

When you are presenting, it is important to remember your audience, which is often composed of corporate executives who do not come from a graphic design background and may or may not understand the intentions of your design. Therefore, it is necessary to keep your ego on the side and realize that, in the end, this is your clients' show. If clients are determined to do something you feel very strongly against, you can always present your concerns, but know that you will need to show rationale beyond personal opinion to justify negating any of your clients' wants.

When it comes to presenting, keep it professional, keep it visual, and keep an open mind when it comes to feedback and revisions.

HOW SCENIC CONCEPTS ARE PRESENTED

Corporate clients are busy people, and although your presentation may be a nice distraction from their hectic schedule, it is respectful of their time to prepare a well-thought-out presentation that gets to the *point*. Microsoft's PowerPoint is a staple in the corporate jungle and is a presentation tool that clients understand. By supporting your design pitch with a fluid PowerPoint presentation, you are providing a bridge between corporate and artistic mentalities.

In addition, product and material samples may be necessary to aid in explaining how your design will work. Although you can explain how a scrim works until you are blue in the face, some clients will not understand the product until they see it for themselves. Similarly, texture finishes are difficult to explain with words. Providing a sample board with various scenic textures used in your design helps translate your intent.

And, of course, you need to provide some form of illustration visualizing your design concept. It is up to you and your design team to determine which type of illustration style suits the job best. Some clients or show producers prefer pencil sketches, whereas others may require photorealistic 3D renderings of the scenic design. Keep in mind that what works for some does not always work for others. Experienced clients may be able to view a 3D rendering and fully understand that it is merely a detailed concept visualization. Less savvy clients, however, may mistake it for an actual photograph or incorrectly take it as a finalized concept and expect the end product to reflect the rendering exactly – and that is not generally possible.

FIGURE 16.1
Concept boards are a common staple during client presentations.

Most of the time, when presenting, you need to have with you a few concept boards. Concept boards are typically 12" × 18" prints mounted to either black foam or matte board. These boards will be passed around the presentation table as you speak on each topic. On occasion, you may have several sets of boards, one for each person attending the meeting, but if you go this route, be sure not to share the boards until you are ready for the clients to view them. Having boards, even face down, in front of each seat as the clients walk into the meeting room may seem like great customer service, but in reality you are providing the clients with a distraction during your presentation. Furthermore, they may (rather, they will) sneak a peek before you intend for them to do so, allowing them to make judgments about the design prior to your explanation of the concept's rationale.

Now that you understand what is needed during a concept presentation, we can define a few of the most common styles of illustration used in these scenarios. Again, work with your design team to determine which style will best suit the client for whom you will be making the presentation.

ILLUSTRATION STYLES

Illustration styles for presenting scenic concepts can be grouped into three primary categories: hand illustrations, three-dimensional computer renderings, and physical models. Although you may not use each style for every project, they will undoubtedly be referenced or requested during your career as a designer.

Hand Illustrations

Hand illustrations are the oldest and most basic method of presenting concepts and are truly works of art that masterfully mix style with precision. Even with the

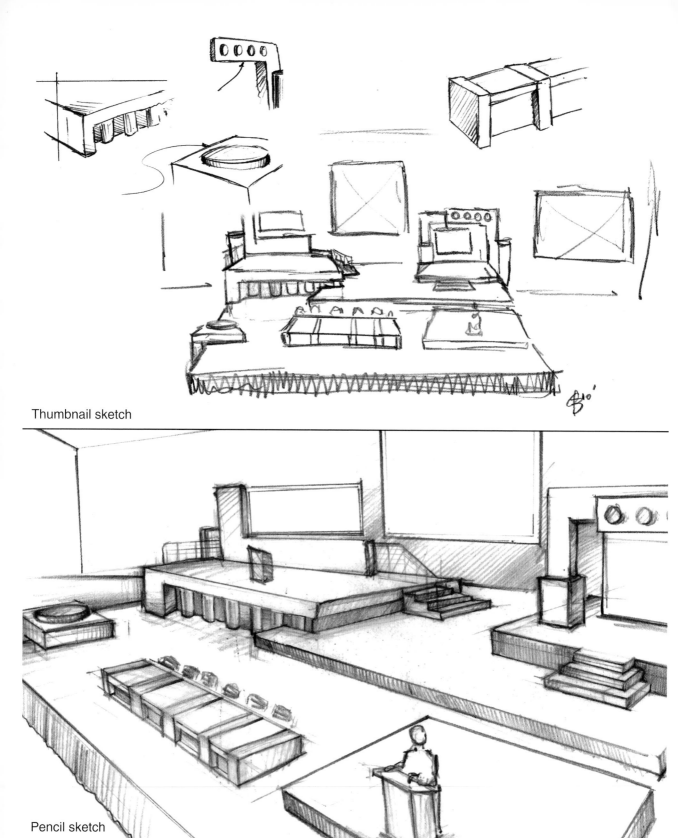

Thumbnail sketch

Pencil sketch

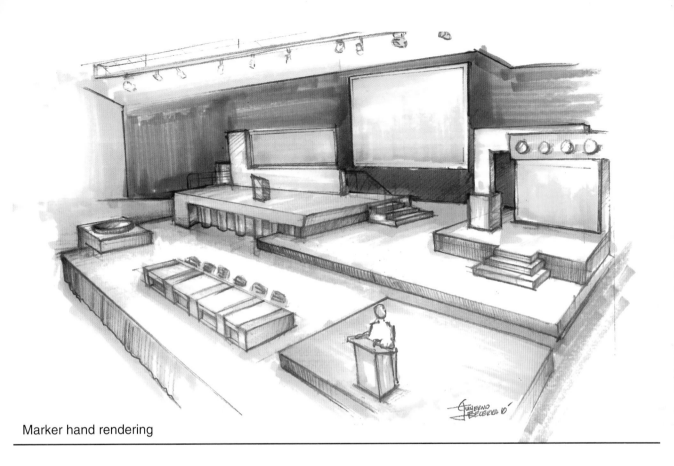

Marker hand rendering

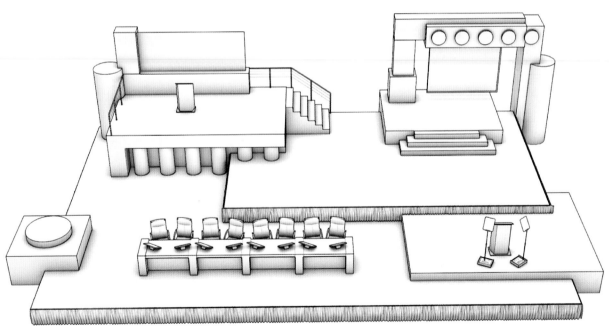

Line drawing

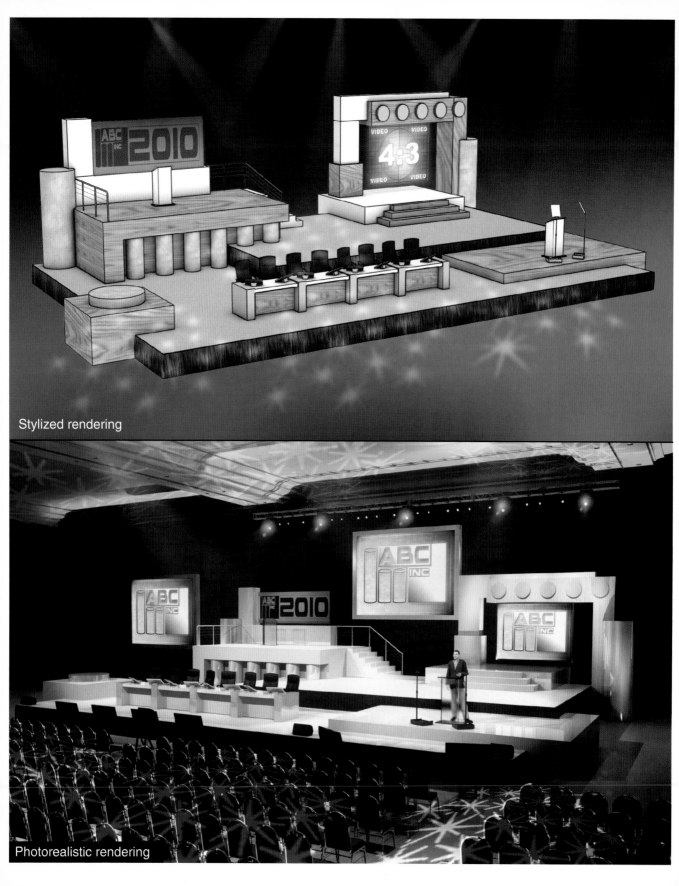

Stylized rendering

Photorealistic rendering

FIGURE 16.2
Drafting stations are quickly – and sadly – becoming a lost tool for designers.

advent of 3D rendering software, many designers still prefer hand illustrations because they can better convey an emotional state than sometimes stagnant computer renderings.

Another advantage to hand-drawn illustrations is they keep the concept slightly vague and fluid, a feature that detailed 3D renderings can lack, thwarting creative feedback. In addition, thumbnail and pencil sketches can typically be produced more quickly than computer illustrations and are useful for sharing basic design concepts when deadlines are tight. Following are four styles of hand illustrations.

THUMBNAIL SKETCHES

Thumbnail sketches are quick sketches that have very little detail or scale. They are simply meant to illustrate a broad concept. They can also serve as visual notes to remind the designer of a concept discussed during a brainstorming session.

PENCIL SKETCHES

Pencil sketches are more thorough hand drawings that bring the concept into focus. These semi-scaled illustrations put flesh to barebones thumbnail sketches. Pencil sketching is quick and effective, providing a clear sense of mood and style to a design while keeping the concept malleable.

LINE DRAWINGS

Line drawings focus on scale, ensuring that all the elements in the design are drawn in proportion to one another. Whether created by hand or computer, line drawings are useful for ensuring that the concept serves all the functional needs of the client.

MARKER/WATERCOLOR BOARDS

Marker boards are a bit of a hybrid between pencil sketches and line drawings, addressing both scale and mood. In addition, as the name implies, markers are used to add color and shading to the concept. However, with a lack of diverse color choices in marker sets, the colors used represent broad hues rather than specific shades. Watercolor paint is also used for adding color to concept boards and can offer a wider selection of color choices with the ability to mix pigments.

3D Renderings

The term *rendering* previously applied solely to hand drawings, but today primarily refers to computer-aided drawings. Computer-aided drawings or renderings are composed of three-dimensional models created in a digital environment, allowing designers to analyze the concept in real time. Three-dimensional rendering and modeling are becoming required skills for scenic designers in the modern age. While hand-drawing skills will always prove useful, the speed and accuracy in which a 3D rendering can be created are constantly increasing. Autodesk software packages such as 3ds Max and Maya are great tools for creating stunning images of scenic concepts.

The most impressive feature of using 3D software is just that ... it's 3D! The ability to quickly create basic shapes in a 3D environment allows designers to play with several options before committing to a specific direction. When the concept is complete, the designer can then rotate the virtual camera and view the design from any angle. This virtual camera feature is great for checking audience sight lines and truly understanding how well the design fits in the space.

Three-dimensional design software packages can also increase a designer's productivity by allowing him to build libraries of colors, textures, and objects used on a regular basis. For example, objects such as stage risers, drapery, trussing, and audio/video equipment can be created, saved, and recalled with the click of a button, preventing the need to create such elements from scratch with each new project. Most of the illustrations in this book were created using 3ds Max.

CONCEPT RENDERINGS

Concept renderings are basic models that accurately show scale and shape. These illustrations allow designers to ensure the concept is balanced visually and allow for comfortable movement by performers and speakers. How the set and scenery will be constructed is also examined and determined at this stage and will be refined further by the scenic fabricator.

PHOTOREALISTIC RENDERINGS

As computer hardware and technology advance, so do the capabilities of photorealistic renderings. Lighting, materials, and textures can be shown in incredible detail. As the name implies, this style of illustration can so closely resemble an actual photograph that often the untrained eye cannot tell the difference. The downside to this style is providing too much detail at an early stage. If clients do not respond to a specific lighting look illustrated or a particular texture shown, they may be turned off by the concept as a whole. It is important to inform those viewing photorealistic renderings for the first time that they are not finalized designs and are still merely concept works of art. It is also important to explain that although this is the intended design, there will always be changes made as the job progresses and elements are constructed due to a variety of factors, including venue regulations, audio and video requirements, and last-minute alterations from both sides.

STYLIZED RENDERINGS

Not all computer renderings need to be photorealistic. Sometimes, photorealistic renderings can distract clients with unimportant details. As a solution, a stylized rendering might be preferred. Although this style still shows the concept in accurate scale and dimension, it gives a bit of artistic liberty to skew the rendering in some way. The virtual camera lens used may be very fish-eyed, creating a more warped view of the set, or there may be no shadows generated by the lighting, or perhaps it is not a single rendering but a ghosted collage of multiple images overlapping like a page found in Leonardo da Vinci's sketch pads. Stylized renderings are useful for conveying a feeling or emotion that is sometimes absent from photorealistic renderings.

FLY-THROUGH ANIMATIONS

Fly-through animations, sometimes referred to as *walk-throughs*, are the next step in 3D illustrations. These animations take viewers on a virtual tour of the scenic concept. By animating a virtual camera within the 3D design software, the designer can focus on areas of interest, show different lighting looks, and even simulate the view of an attendee walking into the space. If a picture is worth a thousand words, then a fly-through would surely be worth a million more.

Due to the rapidly increasing speed of computer technology, fly-through animations will likely replace still illustrations as presentation tools within the next 10 years. Even a consumer-grade computer will soon be able to quickly generate amazing moving images.

As a freelance scenic designer, you can expect clients will be requesting these animations in the near future, if not already. Although it may seem like an entirely new skill set to learn, it will benefit your bank account greatly in the long run if you invest the time to learn how to animate your designs.

There are a few things to keep in mind when producing fly-through animations. First, avoid long continuous shots because such animations can feel tedious to viewers. Instead, opt for several short clips that flow naturally together. Think of your animation as a mini-movie telling a story … and the story is your design. If you watched a two-hour movie that was one long continuous shot, you would be clawing at the walls to get out of the theater.

Animations composed of several small clips edited seamlessly together also have advantages technically. One of the worst sensations after waiting over 30 hours for a two-minute animation to finish rendering is to notice something wrong with the clip, requiring an additional 30 hours or more to correct the mistake. With a series of smaller clips, only the shots with errors have to be rerendered, saving production time.

Second, try editing your animation to a music track. A good soundtrack can make a mundane animation seem exciting. Choosing a soundtrack that fits the feel of the design and editing your clips to the beat of the music will give the animation a professional touch. But make sure your edits are truly on the beat of the soundtrack; otherwise, something will feel off to viewers and may distract from the design being presented.

Finally, avoid using too many secondary video images in your animation. Secondary video is moving video within the animation, such as video playing on plasma monitors or projection screens within the design. Well-chosen and comfortably paced secondary video can add a lot to your animation. In contrast, an abundance of frivolous and flashy secondary video along with spastic camera movements can create a Japanimation effect.

For those who don't remember the news stories from the 1990s, the Japanimation effect, named for Japanese children's cartoon animation style, consisting of quick edits, bright flashing text and images, and extreme color saturation, allegedly caused epileptic seizures in young children.

The Japanimation effect can also lead to discomfort when viewing large projection screens showing quickly paced and overly bright videos. This is especially true with middle-aged to senior audiences whose eyes have difficulty adjusting to quick flashes of bright color and, due to the size of the projection screen, have no visual escape.

THE FUTURE OF FLY-THROUGH ANIMATIONS

In the not-so-distant future, the idea of produced animations may also become antiquated by interactive experiences that are controlled by the end user. By designing a 3D scenic concept using a gaming engine, the same software and hardware used to create video games, clients will be able to open the design in a stand-alone viewer, navigate the 3D environment at their own pace, and focus on areas of their own interest. In fact, samples of this technology have already been exhibited in national gaming conferences. Some demos of the technology take the concept to its fullest extreme, developing a fully interactive experience using popular video game consoles that allow clients to use a remote control or game controller to navigate an environment. It isn't a huge stretch to imagine this same technology allowing clients to adjust stage lighting and screen images to complete their own creative vision.

Physical Models

Physical models are miniature tangible replications of design concepts. Like hand drawings or pencil sketches, physical models are becoming a lost art form. The skill sets required for accurate model making are diverse, ranging from having a steady hand to a creative use of existing materials. Although hobby stores may have a vast collection of miniature construction materials, their products will not serve every need. For such situations, a clever eye and imagination may be needed. For example, painted pennies work great for banquet table tops while toothpicks, glue, tweezers, and a lot of patience can lead to great scaled truss structures. For complex designs that require precision, an automated cutting machine or laser cutter may be necessary for shaping unique elements.

Unfortunately, in the fast-paced industry of corporate scenic design, there is usually not enough time to construct physical models for proposals or presentations. This being said, from a designer's standpoint, when there is time, it is a great feeling to see clients' eyes light up as they look down upon a miniature version of their future scenic environment.

WHITE BOARD MODELS

White board models are the physical equivalent to line drawings; their function is to show scale and balance without the distraction of color or material selections. These models can be constructed from wood or foam boards and, when constructed well, are works of art themselves.

FIGURE 16.3
White board models are helpful for explaining an event's flow and a design's scale within an event locale.

MAQUETTE MODELS

Whereas white board models are used to show scale and balance, maquette models incorporate color, textures, graphics, and sometimes even lighting, using miniature lighting kits to better represent a design concept. This model style is typically reserved for more theatrical and architectural professions that dedicate several months to designs and are supported by significant budgets.

EFFECTIVE PRESENTATION METHODS

It cannot be stressed enough the importance of working with clients or the show producer and being attentive to the end goals of your project as you prepare to present your initial designs. Without this type of foresight and research, all the best design pitches in the world would inevitably fail because no matter how wonderful, it wasn't what the clients needed. If you are working with a show producer or account director, it is generally his job to "get a feel for the clients" and to provoke from them their true goals and desires. If you do not have an account director or show producer, then it will be your responsibility to acquire this information.

Preparation is always key for pitch meetings. At a minimum, you should have prepared notes that include your understanding of the clients' needs, venue research, your design goals and rationale, and concept boards and/or digital presentation.

If you are presenting to clients at their location, you should find out what type of environment you will be walking into and dress and comport yourself accordingly. Although some "creative types" prefer to dress and act in a way that reflects their originality, corporate clients may not give you the respect you deserve if you have not presented yourself in the most professional light possible. These days, you are just as likely to walk into a meeting full of executives in jeans, but there are still many organizations that require full professional dress and your best bet is to err on the side of conservative.

When talking, speak clearly and slowly, look clients in the eye, and steer clear of using design-centric jargon that might lead to confusion. It is your job to know design, not your clients', so try to speak their language when presenting to them. Whether you simply have boards or an entire prepared PowerPoint or digital presentation, be respectful and keep it short and to the point. Always bring a pen and pad and take plenty of notes as you receive feedback so you can more clearly address the clients' concerns in your revisions.

The most important thing to understand in any type of corporate meeting and pitch is that people want to work with people they like. Be that person and work hard to address their needs, and you will earn their business and respect.

A SAMPLE PRESENTATION

So the big day has come, and after three weeks of late nights, you have a solid concept and a great presentation ready for the client. The account manager or show producer has had an emergency elsewhere and left you on your own for the pitch. You arrive at the client's office 30 minutes early and ask the receptionist if you can set up and test your presentation equipment before the meeting. The receptionist agrees and shows you to the meeting room.

You immediately begin setting up your compact projector, projection screen (or you can project on a white wall if a screen is not available), and speakers, and then connecting your laptop to the equipment. You turn on everything and ensure it is all functioning properly. You play any embedded video in your PowerPoint presentation to confirm it shows on the screen because there always seems to be an issue with video in PowerPoint. You have your sample materials organized and within reach but not visible. Your concept boards are face down beside you in the order that you will present them. Before the client's team walk into the room, you turn on some soft music that you will recommend for the show to set the mood.

As the client's team enter the room, you rise, shake hands, and introduce yourself to each person, making friendly eye contact as you do so. Everyone takes a seat, and one person jokingly asks, "So what are we doing here?" And you respond with a smile, "My hope is that you won't have to listen to any more pitches after this one." Everyone gives a slight chuckle. After a little more small talk, the time feels right for you to rise from your seat and begin your presentation.

THE ORDER OF YOUR PRESENTATION

After a few rounds of presentations, you will determine what works best for you. In the meantime, here is a suggested flow for your presentation. Although it may seem a bit formal, it is a common progression that your clients will understand and follow easily. Even clients with whom you have a long relationship will appreciate a little song and dance occasionally as a reminder you appreciate their business.

The Cover Slide

Your first slide should clearly say the client's name, the name of the project, the names of the presenters, and the date of the presentation. Including all this information sounds boring and formal, but it makes a professional statement and clearly addresses the purpose of your meeting.

Introductions

Next, you should introduce those presenting. On a related note, it is best to bring no more than three people to a presentation in fear of greatly outnumbering the client side of the table. In my own experience, I have found a two- to three-person presentation team ideal, with one of those three being the main presenter. Although it is important that clients know your background and understand you have some form of credentials, they do not want to hear your life story or feel as though the presentation is really a pat on your own back. Keep the introduction of your team, and especially yourself, short and to the point.

Review Objectives and Issues

Following your introductions, review what you understood to be the client's expectations as described in the design request and any discussions you have had with the client prior to the pitch. If this is a pre-existing client, this is a good time to review what has been agreed upon as successful and "improvable" elements from previous shows. Think of this section as being titled "This is what I understand your design needs to be...."

Share Research

After you review the client's expectations, goals, and design history, transition to your research. Showing research will greatly interest some, whereas others will be waiting eagerly to see what designs you have come up with. A safe option is to briefly cover the highlights of your research, and if the client's team appear interested, you can elaborate. Also included in this section are your creative inspirations for the project.

Don't be afraid to share your design palette or cube with the clients, as discussed in Chapter 12, "Developing a Design Palette." Often, walking clients through the design process permits them to feel more involved, and when they see the finished concepts, they will interpret the design as a logical next step. Again, some couldn't care less about the process and just want to see the pretty concept boards; this gets back to knowing your clients before you present, or learning to read people well enough to determine if they are interested in a topic or wish to move on.

An additional topic that must be covered in this section, even briefly, is venue research. Venue research shows clients that your designs will work in the space and that your team members are aware of any obstacles that may need to be overcome. Nothing will shut down a pitch quicker than clients pointing out that your design will not fit in the venue.

Concept Reveals and Discussions

Finally, the part that everyone has been waiting for: the reveal of the design concept(s). Confidently turn to the screen and dissolve into the first concept. I prefer to first show still frames saying very little as the slides dissolve between different lighting looks and camera angles. Then to cap off the concept, I end the reveal with a slow fly-through. As mentioned earlier, keep this video element at a comfortable duration. Avoid staring at the clients as they watch the clip; they *will* notice, and doing so will make you seem too eager and novice. After the animation has completed, dissolve back into the still frame that best captures the concept. Return your attention to the client's team and pass out your boards for the first concept. After they have had a moment to let the concept sink in, begin discussing how the design addresses any obstacles or objectives you listed in the review section. As mentioned previously, avoid using design-centric verbiage and explain the concept in language the client will understand.

Now it is the clients' time to ask questions about the concept and to discuss. Don't be thrown off by side conversations between clients because such discussions could be sparked by something they liked as well as disliked – or have nothing to do with your presentation either way! If multiple concepts are to be presented, wait for the discussion of the first design to come to a natural close before repeating this section for the subsequent concepts.

And while we're on the subject of clients' questions, always strive for a positive response. Many times clients will join in the fun of design and suggest unrealistic ideas, such as describing a design that would cost several million dollars to produce. Avoid telling clients "no" at all cost. Instead, start with "yes, we can do that, but ... it will cost a million dollars," or "we will need a larger venue," or "we will need to budget for more resources," etc. This trick prevents you from sounding negative, which is a primary objective during client presentations. Just keep in mind, nothing is impossible in this business as long as the funds are available.

Presentation Recap and Wrap-Up

After presenting all concepts, begin wrapping up your presentation by recapping what was presented. This technique taps into the time-tested speaking approach: summarize what you're going to say, say it, and recap what you just said. Quickly recap the objectives and obstacles, your research, and how you achieved the objectives and overcame any obstacles. The goal is to give a quick summary of the presentation but not repeat the entire thing.

FIGURE 16.4
Smiling faces and applause;
the reward for a successful
presentation.

Finally, dissolve to a closing slide that says, "Thank you for your time today," and ask if anyone has any further questions. The client's team members smile, shake their heads no, and begin to rise from their seats. Thank everyone again and shake each person's hand as he exits the room. The last client team member to exit the room steps back for a moment as you begin to pack up your materials and says, "Great job. I really think you hit the mark." You reply, "Thank you; I think it will be a great show."

A FEW FINAL THOUGHTS

If there are only a few things you take from this chapter, and this book as a whole, let the first be to make your design vision clearly understood while remembering that, in the end, it is not your show but the clients' show. Although corporate clients may not know all the current event design lingo and trends, they do know what they want to accomplish. Ensuring that their goals are met while maintaining a visually interesting and structurally safe environment should always be your primary objective.

Because event design is a visual craft, providing illustrations that can speak for themselves is critical, but you must have practical knowledge and creative insight to support your designs when they are questioned, and even the best designs will be questioned on occasion. This questioning may at times tug at your pride, but if you want to create designs that express your artistic vision of the world, you are in the wrong industry.

Respect your clients by being prepared and using their time wisely. Conduct yourself professionally and leave your favorite self-expressive t-shirt and torn jeans at home. Speak clearly and to the point, and remember to avoid design-centric jargon.

Finally, show clients that you are excited about their event and the design you have prepared for them. People feed off positivity and will more likely respond favorably to designs presented with confidence and eagerness as opposed to arrogance or disinterest.

Although some of these recommendations may seem harsh, they have been tried and tested and will give you an edge over your competitors. After all the work you have put into a design, the sleepless nights pouring over research, or the hours of sketching and modeling, you will want to see your design become a reality. To do so requires an understanding of your clients and their industry, a solid design concept, and an effective presentation.